D1492230

IRELAND

AND THE

MAKING OF BRITAIN

IRELAND

AND THE

MAKING OF BRITAIN

By

BENEDICT FITZPATRICK

With Map of Medieval Ireland and Britain
(Following page 300)

FUNK & WAGNALLS COMPANY

New York and London

1922

CONTENTS

Contents

Contents

Contents

PREFACE

THIS book grew into being as the earlier half of a work describing the efforts of medieval Irishmen to establish civilization in continental Europe as well as in Britain following the downfall of the Roman Empire. As the work neared completion it was seen that the activities of Irishmen in relation to the different peoples inhabiting Britain would find their best representation in a separate and independent volume. The relations prevailing between medieval Ireland on the one hand and medieval Wales and Scotland on the other were relations of a kind that did not subsist between Ireland and any other country. In both these countries of Britain there were Irish military conquests and political settlements as well as Irish cultural and missionary enterprises, and both Wales and Scotland endured for centuries as Irish provinces, colonies and political dependencies. Among the English the work of medieval Irishmen partook more exclusively of the character of Irish missionary and cultural work on the Continent. Nevertheless the relations between Ireland and England in that era were relations of a special and peculiar kind, and if England before the so-called Norman Conquest was not a political dependency of Ireland it was in a true sense a moral and intellectual dependency.

As long as England remained really England its people looked not to the Continent but to Ireland for that sustenance and support without which its uncertain civilization might never have come into being or might have died almost at birth. Ireland, the mainspring of English civilization, acted also as its foster-mother till the investiture of the land by Romance rule, learning, and speech, consequent on the invasion of the Norman French, made culture in England at last self-sustaining and self-perpetuating.

Between the era of the Roman and the era of the Norman the Irish race was the master race in Britain, evoking the spontaneous homage and emulation of Pict, Briton, Angle and Saxon by reason of its rounded national life and rich and stable civilization, on which these exterior peoples were permitted to draw freely as the main reservoir of their aspiration and development. Withdraw out of the picture Ireland and the influences that emanated from it and it is safe to say that the history of what are now called the British Isles between the departure of the Roman and the arrival of the Norman would be represented by a blank almost as complete as the vacuum registered between the arrival of the English in what is now England and the arrival of Augustine and Aidan.

The part played by successive dynasties of Irish spiritual proconsuls in Britain constituted, however, merely a series of stages in the vast apostolate which the Irish missionaries of civilization were carrying forward in almost every country of Europe. The account of the almost incredible work performed by them in lands other than Britain will be contained in a second book, now also nearly completed, to which the present volume is largely introductory. The two books will represent the first comprehensive attempt to describe the work of these medieval Irishmen. That work constitutes the crowning glory of Irish history, and as a service undertaken by the members of one nation for the benefit of members of other nations is almost without a parallel in history. Had it been possible to credit it to the dominant elements in any of what are called the great nations of modern Europe a whole library would already have been written upon it. But being the work of Irishmen it has shared in the general suppression under which Irish studies have had to labor. I do not flatter myself that my work is exhaustive or that my handling of it is worthy of the theme. But it is at least a contribution such as up to the present no other individual has attempted and will, I hope, serve as a belated monument to the memory of heroic precursors of our age, meet, many of them, assuredly to be ranged among the famous men, of whom, in the words of Pericles, the whole earth is the sepulcher.

The work of Irish missionaries in England was necessarily of an elementary and preparatory character. On the Continent, among more highly developed peoples, the Irish schoolmen had opportunities of bringing into play that many-sided learning and skill and speculative force and ability for which no contemporary parallel could be found even in the East. Not only did Irish monks and clerics cultivate classical and philosophical studies when heathen philosophy and literature were anathema to Christian governors elsewhere, and when monasticism on the Continent, as among the Benedictines, meant merely flight from an apparently doomed world, but Irish laymen also pursued learned studies and carried their learning abroad about a thousand years before an educated laity became the rule in other lands. The continuous destruction of ancient Irish manuscripts, which has been a concomitant of the English ravishment of the country from the sixteenth century onwards, has made continental Irish manuscripts the chief witnesses to the manifold character of Irish intellectual activity at home and abroad. Yet the numerous continental manuscripts can only have been a small fraction in comparison with the manuscript literature formerly in Ireland itself.

Till the sixteenth century Ireland had probably the most fortunate history of any country in Europe. She escaped the devastating grip of Roman power. When German savages carried destruction into Britain and the continental Roman provinces Ireland remained a haven of blissful repose. She conquered and absorbed the Danes who had won a province of France and turned England into a compound of slaves. The turbulent and victorious French, who soldered rings round the necks of Englishmen and made England a pendant to the Norman crown, she bound by ties of devotion surpassing the affection of her own children. In the tranquil opening of the sixteenth century, from which her nearest neighbors could look back in suicidal gloom only on a thousand years of degradation and slavery, Ireland had behind her a luminous track, outdistancing the Christian era, of unbroken independence and freedom. The sceptered race of Milesian Gaels, the only northern people with a history and literature, whose least considerable families owned authentic pedigrees older than the claims of foreign kings, still held sovereignty in the land which they had entered during the great Celtic migrations of 2,000 years before. The system of the clan, the exact equivalent of the Roman gens, had been transformed with the establishment of surnames in the tenth and eleventh centuries, and great aristocratic families, Milesian Irish and later Franco-Irish also, provided the land with its kings, its tanists, and its officers of state. No foreign conqueror had ever ridden rough shod over them. No domestic tyrant ever broke the law and tradition that guarded their dignity as free sons of the Gael. To the sixteenth century indeed the Irish people knew as little about slavery as their nearest neighbors knew of freedom.

Preoccupation in the tragedy of modern Irish history has blinded historians to the unexampled phenomenon of a nation that annihilated or absorbed every would-be conqueror during a period of 2,000 years. The French and Cambro-French warriors who entered Ireland from Britain in the twelfth century seemed to themselves to be entering a new world—"in some sort," they said, "to be distinguished as another world." They spoke better than they knew. From the Adriatic to the Irish Sea Europe was feudal and Romance. In Ireland they found a Europe that existed before Rome was, an original elemental world, illumined by Greco-Roman culture. It was the circumstance that Ireland was a world as well as a state, guarded by a broad and unquiet sea from foreign peril, that made supererogatory that central despotism which the hereditary slave-mind, adoring the emblems of ancient tyranny from which it has been physically freed, accounts essential to the fashioning of a nation. Ireland stands forth in the world of the West as the supreme example of a long-enduring nation. We can at this stage only speculate on what she might have done if left free to develop her distinctive genius. Part of our duty will be accomplished if we can throw light on the character of some of her performances during the days of her miraculous promise.

This work embodies no attempt to write a history of Ireland during the centuries indicated. Events and institutions in Ireland are referred to only in so far as they bear on the activities of Irishmen abroad. This has involved some small description of medieval Ireland, of the seats of learning in Ireland, and of noted men whose work was accomplished in Ireland itself; but such description has been brought in with strict reference to Irish work in other lands. Any further consideration of the cultural development in Ireland would have been far beyond the scope of this work, and would have involved the laying under large tribute of the extensive medieval literature of Ireland, both Gaelic and Hiberno-Latin. The evidence on the other hand relating to the activities of Irishmen beyond the Gaedhaltacht will be found to be based almost wholly on foreign testimony.

The references given in the foot-notes represent only some of the sources which have been explored. The volumes consulted might be numbered by the hundred, and I have habitually gone back to original and contemporary authorities where these were available. In connection with the general subject of Irish medieval work I have waded repeatedly through the great collections—Migne, the Rolls Series, the Monumenta Germaniae Historica, the various Acta, the proceedings of German and French societies and the like—and have followed every sort of clue through the borderlands and background of my subject in whatever direction the path might lead. This however while indispensable is only secondary work. To give life and unity to his narrative the historian ought to be able to write of persons and events with the familiarity and understanding almost of an eyewitness and contemporary, and this condition of illumination can be present only as a result of an unflagging interest in his subject and continuous meditation upon it. And tho this composition from its pioneer character falls short of being an historical narrative, it could never have come into being save as a labor of love and as the product of continuous thinking and research covering a number of years.

I have had no collaborators in this work and on disputed points germane to the subject have had to rely on my solitary judgment, but I have been the recipient of services for which acknowledgment ought to be made. And first of all I owe an expression of thanks to Mr. Richard Duffy, numerous suggestions from whom aided greatly in the final shaping of the work and who took on himself much labor of another kind. And thanks are due also to Mr. Liam R. MacEocagain, frequent discussion with whom enabled me to try out some historical reconstructions; to Mr. J. Dominick Hackett, who on frequent occasions put at my disposal his facilities in the mechanical part of the work; and to Mrs. Cecelia Walters Harrigan, who aided me in the work of revision. With this I submit the book to the public, hoping it will please some, resigned to the fact that it may displease others, knowing it to be imperfect as all things human are imperfect, but confident that in all essentials it is sound and true, and capable of withstanding every attack that may be made upon it.

BENEDICT FITZPATRICK.

Ireland and the Making of Britain

CHAPTER I

THE STREAM OF CIVILIZATION

1. Home of Western Learning. 2. Missionary Instinct of Irish Culture. 3. Restoration of Civilization. 4. Variety and Extent of Irish Medieval Work.

1. HOME OF WESTERN LEARNING

A UNIVERSITY professor brought out not long ago a history of the Middle Ages in which the name of Ireland did not once occur. The professor did not dwell in the land of Laputa, where the academicians carry their heads tilted at right angles to their bodies, with one eye turned inward and the other on the zenith; but he had recourse to methods in favor on that philosophical island. Obedient to a political tradition of obscurantism he turned a blind eye to facts lying broadly before his feet while intent on others far away. There are few facts in European history broader or more distinct than the rôle played by Ireland in the early Middle Ages. In that period indeed the history of Ireland was almost the history of Europe.

Elsewhere in Europe, it is true, men were born and lived and died, and generation succeeded generation amid the monuments of a once glorious civilization. But the human generation came and went much as the quadruped generation came and went. There was no growth, no development, little heritage received from the past, no increment transmitted to the future. Men lived as if in a sleep, and if they partly awoke it was as though to play rôles in grizzly nightmares, in which thundered the crash of falling empires and the brute passions of man disported themselves in a drama of hell let loose. Intellectual activity, stability and progress found their theater almost in Ireland alone. The stream of civilization, which had gathered its waters from tributaries having their rise in India, Egypt, Persia, Assyria and other ancient centers, and which had run its broadest and deepest course in a channel carved by an alliance of Greek and Roman culture, had, following the inrush of barbarians and the fall of Rome, once again become divided and deflected so as henceforth to run partly in the East and partly in Ireland. At the threshold of the Middle Ages the regions that recognized the sway of Constantinople became the heirs to Greek culture and the Greek language. But the immediate heir to Roman culture, and such Greek culture as went with it, was not continental Europe but a land that had never bent to Roman authority. With the close of the period of antiquity Ireland became the home of western civilization and remained almost its sole home for hundreds of years.

It is true that there remained something of the old Greco-Roman culture in Spain; but the survival was feeble and showed neither health nor strength till renewed and cultivated by the Saracen invaders. It is true that in England also there appeared after its Christianization, an occasional exotic bloom of culture on the rank soil of a primitive barbarism. But English culture was only a pale reflex of Irish culture. It was a culture planted by Irish hands and that seldom blossomed except when Irish hands were there to tend it. The civilization of Anglo-Saxon England was not a self-perpetuating civilization. There were men among the early English here and there who raised themselves by prodigious effort above the mud and blood in which the mass of their countrymen dragged their lives. But they died in gloom and they had no heirs or successors. Schools of note also arose from time to time in England; but they were short lived. Canterbury died with Theodore and Adrian who established it. Jarrow died with Bede. York, the most noted of the English schools, of which the chief ornament was Alcuin, had a life of hardly fifty years. But of the great Irish schools few fell by the wayside. Armagh, Clonmacnois, Clonfert, Clonard, Iona, Bangor, Moville, Clonenagh, Glendalough, Lismore, and the others, great monastic cities and studia generali, centers of all the studies and all the arts and industries of their time, well over thirty in number, with a huge train of lesser lay and professional schools, maintained their magnificent course almost to the close of the Middle Ages. Founded in the fifth, sixth, and seventh centuries, most of them were in full vigor, despite Danes and despite conflagrations, when the first Norman and Angevin French, a century after they had taken England from the English, settled in Ireland toward the close of the twelfth century, and some of them endured till the beginning of the English devastations in the sixteenth century. Armagh, founded three centuries before Bagdad, was, in 1169, under the authority of the High King Ruadhri, of the Ua Concubhair dynasty, erected into a national university for all Ireland and all Scotland.

In that age there had been nothing comparable with

this sustained continuity in any land, save perhaps the wonderful succession of scholarchs in the groves of Academe from the time of Plato to the time of Justinian. The existence of these Irish schools, annually receiving crowds of foreign students, annually sending crowds of graduates and preceptors to other lands nurturing the entire western world through a thousand channels, visible and invisible, is almost the central phenomenon of the early Middle Ages. The literary output must have rivaled the fecundity of the Syrians under the Abassidae or of the schoolmen of the age of Aquinas and Duns Scotus, over a period more prolonged than was given to either. And Irish as well as Latin was the literary vehicle. The early medieval glosses extant in the Irish tongue, marvelously developed thus early to express the most delicate shades of feeling and thought, exceed the contemporary scholia in all the living languages west of Constantinople put together.[1]

2. Missionary Instinct of Irish Culture

It is only in the nature of things that an intellectual energy so abounding should in course of time overflow the confines of Ireland itself and extend its operations to other lands. The field open to the missionary instinct of Ireland's Christianized civilization was assuredly wide, for from Britain and Merovingian France almost to the confines of Asia a wilderness of barbarism presented an almost unbroken surface. In the year 529 the Emperor Justinian had closed the school of Athens. But the schools of Constantinople were still flourishing and the relics of the Brucheion and Serapeum of Alexandria had not yet been swept by Arab hordes. Between Constantinople

[1] They have been collected in *Thesaurus Palaeohibernicus*, 2 Vols., edited by Stokes and Strachan.

and Egypt the schools of Antioch, of Gandispora, of Nisibus and other centers formed a garland that bloomed with a luster almost comparable for a time with the splendor of the great establishments in Ireland. But their course, outside of Constantinople, was uncertain and the culture transmitted by them was communicable westward only over the area of Greek speech. In the lands, formerly included in the western Roman Empire, where Latin was the medium of Christianity and education, there hardly existed a school in the full meaning of the term, save such as had already been established, directly or indirectly, by Irish hands.

It was during this period of transition and under these conditions that the work of what has at times been called the "Irish Mission" got under way. The counterpart to Greek and Saracen culture in the East, Irish culture in the West showed a missionary instinct almost unknown to the Byzantine and known to the Saracen only in the lust of military conquest. Then began that dispersal, which, in its dimensions, its passion and its potency, has since stood forth as one of the great enigmas of history. Pelagius the Heresiarch and Sedulius the Poet have perhaps been rightly acclaimed as the first in point of time of that streaming Irish host that was to continue to flow for nearly a thousand years. Harbingers and precursors of the great army that was to follow Columbanus in the next century, both of them probably from the Irish colony in what is now Wales, they gave the first proofs in the Roman theater of the mettle of the Irish intellect then in process of being Christianized. Following immediately on Pelagius and Sedulius the stream is not readily discernible, but it is there, and it continues to increase in volume. In the sixth century it bears with it the founders of a host of monasteries in France, Switzerland, and Italy. In the eighth, ninth and tenth centuries it is at the high flood-tide. Irishmen arrive on the Continent "like bees from a hive,"[1] they pour over it "like an inundation";[2] they come in "troops of philosophers,"[3] medieval writers tell us. Then the stream grows thin again and finally disappears. Duns Scotus, in the thirteenth century, may be considered the brilliant ending, a splendid flash of the water in the sun, before the stream enters the ground again. But the stream had run for something like nine hundred years. What set it running? Whence and wherefore this noble procession of theologians and apostles, of monastic legislators and founders, of philosophers and schoolmen, of pioneers and martyrs, of monks and hermits, of architects and poets, of builders and statesmen, of men and women, who compassed the orbit of human possibility in passionate energy of word and deed? What manner of men were they? Whence did they derive their culture? What motives prompted them? What work did they actually accomplish? It is the purpose of this work to give a partial answer to these questions, in so far as it can be given by a general indication of their labor throughout Europe and a more detailed study of it in the lands within the immediate circle of Irish influence.

3. RESTORATION OF CIVILIZATION

While there is much about these Irishmen that is likely to remain something of a mystery, we can at least seek to estimate their work. Their work and their mission had as end and result nothing less than the restoration of civilization. A mission so sublime was not likely to

1 St. Bernard, Vita Malachiae.
2 St. Bernard, Ibid.
3 Eric of Auxerre, Vita S. Germani, Praef.

enter into the ambitions of men so contemptuous of earthly glory. There was nothing of military organization about them, though much of military discipline. They did not gather together a vast intellectual army, and, with Ireland behind them as a base of supply, advance on Europe with a view to its moral conquest. Their methods were much less grandiose. They descended on Europe as single individuals or in groups, sometimes as pilgrims or travelers, sometimes as ascetics seeking a voluntary exile, sometimes as spiritual athletes in voluntary immolation, sometimes also as conscious teachers and preachers and traders in wisdom. One group had little knowledge often of what another group was doing. Masters themselves of all the knowledge of their time they became the natural leaders and instructors of the peoples among whom they went to dwell. Men gathered round them and their homes became the kernels of cities that were to be. They passed also from one place to another as true apostles, the living similitudes of the missionaries of civilization from the beginning of time. Their work has lived after them and will endure forever. They were the true makers of Christendom and usherers-in of the modern world. "They were," says a German writer, "instructors of every known branch of the science and learning of the time, possessors and bearers of a higher culture than was at that period to be found anywhere on the Continent and can assuredly claim to have been the pioneers—to have laid the corner-stone of western civilization on the Continent, the rich results of which Germany shares and enjoys to-day in common with all other civilized nations."[1]

Christianity came to Ireland along a path already beaten by Greco-Roman learning in a period when the

[1] Zimmer, Preussiche Jahrbücher, 59, Jan. 1887, pp. 26-59; translated, "The Irish Element in Medieval Culture," by J. L. Edmonds (1891), p. 130.

isle of the Gael was in the full tide of military conquest. So in an inscrutable manner the military prowess that had carried the high-king Dathi on the heels of Roman rearguards to the foot of the Alps and almost secured to Ireland the enduring hegemony of what are now called the British Isles bent itself to the Christian yoke. The fierce intoxication of mortal combat on the field of battle ceased to allure the Irish heart, overtaken and surprized by the doctrines of the new religion. Instead, Christian temples and schools arose over the land and a new army of mental and moral champions succeeded to the warrior hosts of the Fianna. In their persons the Celt, the Gael[1] and the Gaul returned as spiritual knights-errant to the insular and continental fields over which in ultra-Roman days ancestral Keltoi and Galli had wielded empire from history's dawn. And the area over which the Irish Gaels carried the evangel of civilization was not inferior to the vast region that knew the Celt as lord when he parleyed with Alexander, sacked Delphi and Rome, lent his dying body to the Pergamene sculptor, and fought his last continental fight with the legions of Cæsar.

4. Variety and Extent of Irish Medieval Work

While there were very few countries in Europe where Irish missionaries and schoolmen did not dispense their services, their work differed in character, in degree and in result in each of them. Their chief work was in France, Germany, Switzerland, the Low Countries, England, Scotland, and north Italy. What is now called Scotland was the first theater of their operations and Irish missionaries Christianized and civilized it while Irish sol-

---

[1] Gaedhal or Gael is the word in the Irish tongue for "Irishman." *Scotus* is the Latin word for "Irishman." *Scotia* and *Hibernia* are the Latin words for "Ireland." *Scotland* means "land of the Irish." See Appendix B.

diers and colonists gradually reduced it, turning the old
Caledonia into the Irish province of Scotia Minor,[1] or
Lesser Ireland, which it has since in essentials remained.
Irishmen were also powerful in what is now called Wales,
parceling it out into princely estates "so that the Gael
dwelt not less on the east coast of the sea than in Erin."
The Irish ruled Wales as a military colony even in Roman
times and it continued an Irish-speaking province from
the second almost to the eighth century. The fact that
in Wales, differing from Scotland, the evidences of Irish
occupation have been in main obliterated, has made its
former condition an obscure chapter in history.

As the Romans left Britain there were repeated attempts by Irish military forces to conquer what is now
England, and the Irish campaign in England was carried
on almost simultaneously with the more successful campaign in what is now Scotland. The attempted conquest of
England failed, partly because Irishmen were at this time
being converted to Christianity and in their early fervoi
renounced their foreign enterprises. When the southern
part of Britain became England, however, it was devoted
Irishmen who rescued the English from their primeval
savagery and heathenism and first brought them into the
circle of Christianity and civilization. Augustine's mission to England was an almost complete failure and his
successors fled; while for the greater part of the Anglo-
Saxon period Irishmen taught and led the English.
Where the Romans signally failed Irishmen signally suc-

[1] The terms "Scotus" and "Scotia" when used by Roman and medieval
writers, refer to the Irishman and Ireland. The term "Scotia" only came to
be applied to what is now Scotland after the Irish had consolidated their conquest and colonization of that country, making it part of the Gaedhaltacht.
See Skene, Celtic Scotland, I. Intro. p. 1 seq.; Hill Burton, Hist. of Scotland,
I. 200 seq.; Ossianic Society, V.; Holder, Alt-Celtischer Sprachschatz, Bd. II
1902, col. 1406-18; Ussher, Britannicarum Ecclesiarum Antiquitates, Works, VI
266 seq.

ceeded. They built the first schools in England—Lindisfarne, Malmesbury, Whitby, Glastonbury, and the others. They ruled the English as bishops. They taught them to read, to write, to build, to work metals, and to illuminate books. They delivered them, as far as they were able, from the excesses of barbarism and taught them the truths of the Christian faith. They not only taught the English in England but they sent them by the shipload to Ireland, where they were received, and provided with food, shelter, and education and sometimes with colleges and farms without payment of any kind. Before the French or Norman conquest Irish influence in England was all pervading. The English knew almost no art but Irish art, almost no civilization but Irish civilization. So that of the relics of the Anglo-Saxon period that have come down to us, there is hardly an object, whether a manuscript or a jewel, whether a piece of sculpture or a piece of architecture, that is not either wholly Irish in character or with Irish characteristics.

Their work in other lands was equally noteworthy. The Irish were the first missionaries in Germany, and Germany had in the main been made a Christian land by them when Boniface, who has been called the Apostle of Germany, first arrived there. Near and along the Rhine they established the great monasteries which were to be the cradles of German civilization, St. Gall, Reichenau, Rheinau, Honau and the others. Columbanus and his disciples founded over a hundred monasteries in France and central Europe, many of them noble abbeys enduring to this day. But their field was wider still. Irish scholars, missionaries, pilgrims and travelers are found as far north as Iceland, which Irish mariners discovered, and as far south as Carthage and the Nile valley. They traded in the Dneiper valley and preached along the Elbe. They formed literary colonies in Liège, Toul, Cologne, Milan, Salzburg, Rheims, Tours, Aix-la-Chapelle, Verdun, Metz, Cambrai, Rome, Constantinople, and other centers. They sent out scientific expeditions to measure the Pyramids and to explore the Red Sea. They scoured the northern and southern seas for islands, and besides Iceland they discovered the Faroe Islands and seem to have known the Azores.

In the Carolingian era they were teachers in every cathedral and school. They initiated and conducted the Carolingian revival, a movement of far more import to Europe than that later renaissance which has appropriated the name. In the ninth century their intellectual prestige was so great that a minister of Charles the Bald hailed them as rivals of the Greeks and it became the fashion of the literati of Laon to study the Irish language[1] and Irish literature as at Rheims Greek was studied under Irish preceptors, who in that age were the sole possessors of Greek learning in the West. In their scriptoria the Roman classics were reproduced and preserved. Alone in Europe in that age they cultivated pagan literature side by side with Christian divinity. The oldest of several of the Roman classics are Irish manuscripts. Irish foundations proved the great treasure houses of the masterpieces of ancient Roman literature, and the list is long of those Roman authors for whose survival we are indebted to Irish scribes and Irish foundations. They were

[1] We can best judge of the development of the Irish language at this period by the extant eighth and ninth century Irish commentaries and glosses which stand on a high level by comparison, for example, with old High German glosses: "We find here a fully formed learned prose style which allows even the finest shades of thought to be easily and perfectly expressed, from which we must conclude that there must have been a long previous culture (of the language), going back at the very latest to the beginning of the sixth century." (Meyer, Kultur der Gegenwart, part I, sect. XI, p. 80.)

not merely the greatest scribes, but the greatest artists, miniature painters, metal-workers, stone-cutters and skilled craftsmen of their age. There is no more beautiful book in the world than the Book of Kells. The whole of antiquity, whether the Greek, Roman or Etruscan, has bequeathed to us no lovelier jewels than the Ardagh Chalice and the Tara Brooch. And altho these unique works of art were executed in Ireland itself, they supply ample evidence of the skill of the Irishmen who labored abroad for the intellectual and spiritual resurrection of the peoples among whom they dwelt through the teaching of Christian theology and the channels of all the sciences and all the arts.

Thus over a wide radius—in the regions now called Great Britain, France, Germany, Belgium, Holland, Austria and Upper Italy—Irishmen and their disciples planted or restored the root and stem of Christian culture, drilling and training for future work the raw tribes who were to make up the great nations of the modern world. So Ireland fulfilled her mission in life, which the beneficiaries were to forget, but which in the sight of heaven was to be her crowning glory. "Ireland can indeed lay claim to a great past," says the writer already quoted. "She can not only boast of having been the birthplace and abode of high culture in the fifth and sixth centuries, at a time when the Roman Empire was being undermined by the alliances and inroads of the German tribes which threatened to sink the whole Continent into barbarism, but also of having made strenuous efforts in the seventh and up to the tenth century to spread her learning among the German and Romance peoples, thus forming the actual foundations of our present continental civilization."[1]

[1] Zimmer, Preussiche Jahrbücher, Jan., 1887, translated into English as "The Irish Element in Medieval Culture," p. 3.

CHAPTER II

LINEAMENTS IN THE CONSPECTUS

1. Founders of Churches and Cities. 2. From Iceland to the Pyramids.
3. Incomparably Skilled in Human Learning. 4. The Carolingian
Renaissance.

1. FOUNDERS OF CHURCHES AND CITIES

THE men that Ireland sent forth therefore were more than intellectuals and devotees. Had they been merely such they could not have got very far. They were indefatigable all-round workers—engineers, architects, painters, penmen, woodcarvers and farmers, as well as the most accomplished schoolmen of their age. Deeply learned and highly bred, some of them the sons of kings, and, like Columcille, eligible to the high throne of Ireland itself, giving their wealth as well as their work, they regarded no form of labor as too lowly or arduous that helped in the compassing of the ends they had in view. A versatility in cases verging on the miraculous, a faith and enthusiasm that removed mountains, and a courage lionlike in its intrepidity, would seem to have been the elements necessary for the accomplishment of the deeds recorded of them. Here and there all over Europe, on high tablelands or by the side of rivers, or in the midst of a desert waste, there rise to-day fair cities boasting large populations and all the refinements of civilization. How came these cities there? Often because one of these Irish peregrini, trusting only God and his own arm and brain, struck out on a fateful and distant day into the trackless forest or across some wilder-

13

ness and there in the heart of it drove his staff into the ground and made it his home "for the love of the kingdom of the Lord."

First came the hermitage, and then the oratorio, then the monastery, and church, and school, a modified rath or lis or caiseal or caithir, after the Irish fashion, with people flocking from all parts to hear the wisdom-laden voice of the stranger. So a center of culture, of industry, and of commerce was set up, and roads were laid, and bridges built, and wells dug, and gardens planted, and clearances made in the woods, and herds of goats and cows and sheep and poultry were made to take the place of the wild animals that had greeted the stranger on his coming. And over all till death took him presided the stranger from far Scotia and a number of his countrymen who had in course of time come to him, dignified men with long flowing locks and painted eye-lids[1] and a serenity that nothing could ruffle, men who among themselves talked a strange tongue, not Latin though it resembled it, which the natives could not understand, but who talked to the natives in their own speech and seemed to them to be in possession of all knowledge and to be capable of accomplishing all things. And then at last when the stranger died and the people he had brought together began to credit their gain and count their loss, an unspeakable sorrow would fall upon them, and the lamentation would carry his fame to all parts. And a great cathedral would be built and his blessed bones placed therein, and crowds would come to venerate his memory. And so a new city would be born

[1] A striking peculiarity of the Irish peregrini was their painted eyelids, but they also colored or tattooed other parts of their bodies. They were tonsured in front from ear to ear and their garments were of white homespun. They carried staffs, leathern wallets, flasks and books. Pilgrims traveled usually on foot, but Irish travelers of rank, mingling pleasure with piety, traveled on horseback and with retinue, as in the case of Marcus and Moengal, described in the chronicle of St. Gall.

14

to the world and the seed planted by the stranger would fructify for ever more. Thus St. Gall, whose father and patron was Ceallach or Gallus, thus Lure, whose founder was Dicuil, thus Bobbio, whose founder was Columbanus, thus Perrone, whose father and patron was Fursa, grew into mountain villages or noble cities. Thus scores of cities and towns from the Irish Sea to the Adriatic— St. Bees, Malmesbury, St. Gibrian, St. Gobain, St. Die, St. Ursanne, Dissentis, San Columbano, San Cataldo, Altomunster, St. Desibod and Beatenberg, among them— came into being under the fostering arm of the missionary Gael.

A sacred fanaticism carried these tireless Irish pilgrims over the broad expanse of Europe, their tracks studded with hermit haunts and holy wells, round which rose up in the fulness of time noble monasteries and enduring cities. When the fiery Columbanus was expelled from Luxeuil, where on the buried heaps of a Roman city he had founded a lasting school and city, he wended his slow and tortuous way to northern Italy, and as he proceeded, parted one by one with compatriots who were disciples precious to him as life. Dicuil's failing limbs gave way as he accompanied the evicted superior to Besançon, and with his master's blessing he settled in a desert waste to lay the foundation of the noble monastery of Lure. Potentin was left behind at Soissons to become Abbot eventually of Coutances. Ursicinus[1] bade his superior a fond farewell at Basel and, penetrating into the passes of Jura, founded his great monastery at the foot of Mont

[1] The names of Irishmen abroad assumed a Latin form in the mouths of continental writers. Colum became Columbanus; Cathail, Cataldus; Siadhail, Sedulius; Ceallach, Gallus; Moengal, Marcellus; Muiredach, Marianus; Duncadh, Donatus; and so on. A new sobriquet was given in some cases. Thus Comgall, founder of Bangor, figures as Faustus in one of the directions of Columbanus. Other forms were arbitrary, Ailill becoming Elias. "Scotus" meaning *"Irishman,"* was a common appellation.

Terrible. Ceallach, or Gallus, stricken with fever, abandoned the fateful journey at Bregenz to found, soon after, the peerless monastery of St. Gall. Sigisbert turned aside at Coire to lay in a place of horror and vast wilderness the foundation of the Abbey of Dissentis. Fridoald, one of the last surviving companions of Columbanus, led a colony of monks into the wild Munsterthal and founded the monastery of Granfelden, united later with the hermitage at St. Ursanne and the monastery of Pfermund.

The disciples of Fursa and their contemporaries repeated the marvels achieved by Columbanus and his associates. Their toil and agony and martyr blood hallowed the soil that has resounded in these days to the thunders of the most brutal war in history. Wherever Fursa moved the people kissed his footsteps; at his death kings and princes vied for his remains. Treasure untold accumulated around his shrine at Peronne, where after his death a monastery for Irishmen was established, to be pillaged after the lapse of centuries by the marauding Northmen, as the centers founded by and named after St. Gobain, St. Gibrian, and many another Irish saint were overrun and plundered during the Calvinist wars of the sixteenth century. The monks who preceded Fursa labored along the Authie, Somme, Seine, Oise, Marne, Aisne, and Meuse—names all familiar to students of the great war; those who accompanied him cooperated in carrying the good work into Belgium and beyond it. Eata, Maelceadar, Amand, Bertuin and others preached the gospel in the Low Countries. Livinus labored at Ghent, throughout Flanders and Brabant indeed. Rumold became first bishop and apostle of historic Mechlin. Ultan governed monasteries at Mont St. Quentin and between the Meuse and Sambre in the region of Maestriche. Wiro founded

St. Peter's monastery, also in the territory of Liège. Fingen established the monastery of St. Vannes at Verdun; Abbot Maolcalain was the first bishop of St. Michael in Thierache. Others found their way much farther afield, notable among them Fridolin the Traveller, Killian, patron of Wurzburg, and Marianus Scotus, who labored at Paderborn, Fulda, Metz and elsewhere. In the tenth century learning flourished in the region of the Meuse and Moselle, at Toul and Verdun, which were occupied by colonies of monks from Greece and Ireland.

2. From Iceland to the Pyramids

Colman, patron of Lower Austria, had the experience of being seized as a Moravian spy during the war between the Moravians and the Austrians early in the eleventh century. Towards its close John, another Irish missionary, converted multitudes in Sclavonia, between the Elbe and the Vistula, and finally was beheaded at Rethre. St. Tressan and his companions announced the Gospel at Rheims and along the district of Châlons-sur-Marne. A host of others penetrating to the North made the mountains and forests of Germany and Scandinavia resound with the glad tidings of redemption. From Egypt in the East to Iceland in the North, hardly an acre can be found which has not been consecrated by the ceaseless strivings, the sweat and the blood of the men of Ireland. Little wonder that it seemed as tho in Green's words, "Celtic, and not Latin, Christianity was to mold the destinies of the Churches of the West."

Dicuil, early in the ninth century, tells of an Irishman, Fidelis, who measured the Pyramids and "went thence by the canal to the Red Sea." Far earlier another, Pellegrinus, penetrated to the Holy Land, fasted forty days in the desert, returned through Egypt, whence he sailed for Italy, landing at Ancona, to spend the rest of his life near the mountain called after him.   In 634 a deputation of scholarly Irishmen, sent by the Irish government, lodged in a hospice in Rome with a Greek and a Hebrew, an Egyptian and a Scythian, who told them the whole world celebrated the Roman and not the Irish Easter. In Constantinople in the ninth century Irish monks told the Greeks that every Irish monastery possest a Chrysostom. Cathaldus of Lismore, returning from the Holy Land, was shipwrecked at Taranto, of which, in recognition of his labors, he became bishop, patron and second apostle. Findan of Rheinau escaped from the Norse pirates of the Orkneys before settling in Switzerland.   Pilgrims settled in the Faroe Islands and in Iceland, where, in the year 860, the Norwegians found Irish books, bells and croziers, left there by men who profest the Christian religion.   In 659 the Irish Angus or Augustin wrote, apparently in Carthage, to the bishops of which he dedicated his work, perhaps the most original theological treatise of the early Middle Ages.

Note the practical industry of these Irish missionaries and their disciples. "To their untiring industry is it due that half of France and of ungrateful Europe has been restored to cultivation," is the testimony of Montalembert in respect to the monks in general, but it applies to the Irish monks and their disciples in particular. Ursicinus, expelled with Columbanus from Luxeuil, attached to his own monastery at St. Ursanne subsequently a hospital for the sick poor, with baggage cattle to help travelers over the Alps. Wandresgisel, disciple of Columbanus and founder of the monastery of Fontenelles, is reputed to have planted the first vineyard in Normandy. St.

Eata, patron saint of cowherds, is represented in art as surrounded by calves and oxen. St. Fiachra or Fiacre is the patron of the cab-drivers of Paris, to support the poor of which he is said to have turned the wilderness of Meaux into a garden. St. Eloi, disciple alike of Columbanus and Fursa, is patron of farriers and silver-smiths, as Dunstan, educated by Irish instructors and craftsmen, is the patron saint of goldsmiths. Frigidian, honored in Italy as San Frediano, engineered canals in the plains of Lucca. Rudpert, another Irishman whose figure is portrayed on the coins of Carinthia, started the salt mining that made Salzburg famous, and gave it its name. Magnoald, apostle of Suabia, is reputed to have discovered the mountain iron of Suilinic and taught the people how to work it.

Andrew of Fiesole, the brother of Donagh or Donatus of Fiesole, who had the reputation of working after the manner of a reasoning bee, helped with his own hands to build there a church of stone and mortar. As a result of pilgrimages to the shrine of Andrew's sister, Brigid, the surrounding wastes were reclaimed, the forests cleared, and the fields planted. Nor was Brigid herein peculiar. Gregory the Great has reference to Maura and Britta, two virgins, obviously Irish, who were buried at Tours, where they had come as pilgrims to the shrine of St. Martin. Remi, father of pilgrims, provided suitable retreats on the banks of the Marne for the three sisters of Gibrian, on pilgrimage too from Ireland, "for the love of Christ."

"They did not," says the biographer of Remi, "live only on the charity of those to whom pious Remi had commended them, but also on their own industry and the labor of their hands, in accordance with the custom of the religious bodies in Ireland. This life, united to wonderful holiness and constant prayer, won for them a great love among the natives of the country." Dymphna, as the reward of her industry, became the patron saint not only of the insane but also of Brabant. St. Begha or Bee, who first crossed from Ireland to St. Bee's Head, called after her, assisted with her own hands in erecting at Hartlepool the mother convent of England, as her countryman and spiritual director, Aidan, erected at Lindisfarne the mother church of Northumbria. At Lindisfarne the English were taught writing and the letters used among them till the Norman conquest. From Bangor and from among the Irish in Wales Alfred secured professors when he sought to set up schools in England.

3. INCOMPARABLY SKILLED IN HUMAN LEARNING

To the time of the Conqueror England existed simply as an intellectual dependency of Ireland. It was Irishmen like Aidan, Finan, Colman, Maeldubh, and Fursa who introduced the machinery of Christian civilization into the land which Roman missionaries had trod with fear and trembling. When the Danes destroyed the evidences of progress in England it was Irishmen again, themselves harassed by these same freebooters, who repaired the ravages. Almost every scholar of note in the Anglo-Saxon era was trained either in Ireland or by Irishmen in England. There was hardly a school in England, outside that at Canterbury—though here Irishmen were prominent also in Theodore's time—that was not established and conducted by Irishmen or by men who were Irish-taught. What is now called Scotland they simply made their own. The inauguration there by Columcille of Aidan is the earliest recorded instance of a

royal coronation in Great Britain, where the Irish cere-
monies came into universal use. "The Irish," says Col-
lins, "colonized Scotland, gave it a name, a literature and
a language, gave it a hundred kings, and gave it Christianity."

Aidan familiarized the English of the north with the
solemn melody of the Roman chant, and music and astronomy were among the subjects taught by the Irish
monks at Glastonbury. Foillan and Ultan, on crossing
from Bamborough to Flanders, were asked by Gertrude
of Nivelles to instruct her nuns in psalmody, while the
music school of St. Gall, under Moengal, was "the wonder and the delight of Europe." St. Gall itself became
known as "the intellectual center of the German world,"
as Bobbio, founded by Columbanus, was long "the light
of northern Italy." Baoithin, successor of Columcille
at Iona, "had no equal this side of the Alps in his knowledge of sacred scripture and the profundity of his science." Adamnan, abbot also of Iona, and "high scholar
of the western world," has left us in his exquisite life of
Columcille "one of the most important pieces of hagiology
in existence"—moreover "the most complete piece of
biography that all Europe can boast of, not only at so early
a period, but even through the whole Middle Ages," in
the opinion of Pinkerton.[1]

Fursa's marvelous visions, says **Ozanam**, inspired
Dante. Johannes Scotus Eriugena ranked with Dante,
Chrysostom and Albertus Magnus; no more puissant or
original thinker appeared in the long tract between Augustine and Aquinas. Clemens and "Albinus" were "incomparably skilled in human learning and in the
Scriptures." Tutilo or Tuthail of St. Gall was at once

[1] Enquiry, Pref. vol. 1, p. xlviii (Edinb., 1814).

musician, orator, poet, painter, sculptor, builder, gold-smith; Dungal, theologian, controversialist, poet, as-tronomer; Virgilius of Salzburg, prince of astronomers, "most learned among the learned." Nor was Dicuil the only great Irish geographer. Duncan or Dunchad, an Irish bishop, teaching in the monastery of Remi at Rheims, where he died about the close of the tenth cen-tury, wrote for the use of his students "Explanatory Obser-vations on the First Book of Pomponius Mela regarding the situation of the earth," as well as a "Commentary on the Nine Books of Martianus Capella on the Liberal Arts."[1] For these reasons "it was that Fingen and Duncan and other Irishmen had been so peculiarly patronized at Rheims, Metz, Verdun, and along the territories of France and Germany. Learning had been revived by Irish-men in the imperial city of Cologne; they taught the classics and the sciences in the extensive diocese of Toul; they established schools along the Rhine, in the Nether-lands, Switzerland, and the northern districts of Italy; in short, the Irish ecclesiastics of the tenth and preceding centuries were the persons by whose means the reign of literature had been established in many of the most dis-tinguished cities and provinces of Europe."[2] Every province in Germany proclaims the Irish as its benefac-tors, says a German author. "The Saxons and the tribes of northern Germany are indebted to them to an extent which may be judged from the fact that the first ten bishops who occupied the see of Verden belonged to that (Irish) race."

Noteworthy was the modesty of these Irish pioneers. Columbanus, friend of Agilulf, king of the Lombards,

---

[1] The MS. (Lat. 4854) is in the Bibliothèque Nationale, Paris. See Hist. Lit. de la France, I, 549-50.

[2] Brenan, Eccl. Hist. of Ireland, p. 199.

and of Chlothair, king of Neustria, declined late in life the recall to his well loved Luxeuil. Gallus similarly declined the preferred government of Luxeuil and the bishopric of Constance. Virgilius, tho appointed bishop of Salzburg by Pope Stephen II and King Pepin, deferred his consecration for two years. Donatus hesitated to accept the see of Fiesole. Dungal, high in the esteem of Charlemagne, specially desired that he might occupy no higher station in the church than simple deacon. Ultan is represented with a crown at his feet to signify his contempt for the things of the earth.

Not less striking were the mortifications they involuntarily endured. Columcille, a scion of the royal Hy Nial, lived on bread and water and vegetables, as often as not on common nettles; he slept on the bare sand with a stone for pillow, his pallet betimes the naked rock. Adamnan lived at Coludi on two meals a week and frequently passed the whole night in vigil. Columbanus, unwitting rival of St. Benedict, subsisted for three weeks on grass and bilberries and the bark of trees. His followers and successors, tho in many instances of princely birth and upbringing, were scarcely less given to frugal fare. Not St. Gall and Lure alone had princes for abbots: Waldebert, Count of Meaux and Ponthieu, ruled Luxeuil with unparalleled success for forty years. Despite their self-denial, the complaint was made at an early stage that the monks of Luxeuil by their clearances and cultivation were destroying the chase in the surrounding woods.[1]

[1] As the purpose here is to give a preliminary bird's-eye view numerous footnotes have been avoided. These where useful will come later.

4. THE CAROLINGIAN RENAISSANCE

The number of scholars which Ireland gave to the empire of Charlemagne amazed Eric of Auxerre.[1] From the beginning of the Carolingian renaissance they were the leaders in every intellectual activity. "Altho it was Italy that inspired Charles with the idea of founding schools throughout the empire, it was Ireland that sent him the masters who were to impart the new learning. . . . . Alcuin, altho an Englishman, is justly considered a representative of Irish learning; with him is associated Clement of Ireland, who assisted in the work of founding the Palace school. Unfortunately history has not preserved the names of Clement's fellow countrymen who, during the reign of Charles and throughout the ninth century, were found in every cathedral and monastery of the empire as well as at the court of the Frankish kings, and were so identified with the new intellectual movement that the teaching of the newly founded schools was characterized as Irish learning."[2]

There is nothing in the whole history of literature more extraordinary than Irish knowledge of Greek during this period when all knowledge of it had apparently died out among others in western Europe. The fact that the emperors in the West had to turn to Irishmen for the elucidation of manuscripts that no Greek knew Latin enough and no Latin knew Greek enough to interpret is a mystery as astonishing and difficult to solve in our day as it appeared to Anastasius,[3] the Roman librarian, in his day. From Pelagius and Columbanus through Johannes Scotus Eriugena to Michael the Irishman (Scotus) we are confronted by the evidences of this baffling Hellenic pre-

[1] Vita S. Germani, praef.
[2] Turner, History of Philosophy, pp. 241-2.
[3] Migne, Patrologia Latina, cxxii, 93.

eminence, an incommunicable illumination invisible as to its source and tributaries. In the fifth century Pelagius won an easy triumph over Orosius, the representative of St. Augustine, by his knowledge of Greek. Thomas Aquinas in the thirteenth century knew no Greek. Yet Eriugena in the ninth century not only translated from Greek into Latin and from Latin into Greek but wrote Greek poetry, and Michael Scotus, a contemporary of Aquinas, was among the first to acquaint Europe with the larger philosophy of Aristotle by translating his works from the Arabic. When in the same age Frederick II, who, like Charlemagne, loved to surround himself with Irishmen, decided on setting up the University of Naples, he invited Peter the Irishman to be its first rector, as another Irishman a little later became chancellor at Oxford. Among the students who listened to Peter was the Angelic Doctor himself.

I have fixed the telescope so as to bring into relief some of the lineaments in the conspectus. A summing-up and condensation is provided by an eager student of Irish medieval work abroad:

"By the armies of monastic missionaries and next by learned teachers first attracting pupils to Irish schools from all Christian Europe north of the Alps and the Pyrenees, and next by sending forth men to become the founders of schools or monasteries or churches abroad— the churches of St. Patrick and St. Columba stand out from the sixth century forward as the most energetic centers of religious life and knowledge in Europe; the main restorers of Christianity in paganized England and Roman Germany; the reformers and main founders of monastic life in northern France; the opponents of Arianism even in Italy itself; originators in the West of the well-meant, however mistaken, system of the Penitentials; the leading preservers in the eighth and ninth centuries of theological and classic culture, Greek as well as Latin; the scribes, both at home and abroad, of many a Bible text; the teachers of psalmody; the schoolmasters of the great monastic schools; the parents, in great part, as well as the forerunners of Anglo-Saxon learning and missionary zeal; the senders-forth of not the least bright stars among the galaxy of talent gathered by Charlemagne from all quarters to instruct his degenerate Franks—down to the very eleventh and twelfth centuries."[1]

We can measure the strength and richness of the old Irish civilization and the valor and energy of its depositaries by comparing the work performed by it and them with the contemporary work of other peoples similarly situated. The Church of Britain and Wales, for example, which is usually represented as a sister Celtic Church, the co-partner of the Church of Ireland in culture and zeal, did not produce a single missionary or schoolman who gained eminence abroad, and has not bequeathed to us even a single copy of the Scriptures. The dictum "The Roman sowed; the Irishman (Scotus) watered; the Briton did nothing" has a wider application than to the conversion of the English.

[1] Haddan, (Scots on the Continent), Remains 258-94 (Oxford, 1876).

CHAPTER III

BRIDGING THE OLD WORLD AND THE NEW

1. Ark of Safety for the Old Wisdom. 2. Ireland's Educational Proficiency. 3. Centers of Intellectual Activity. 4. Text-books and Learned Degrees.

1. ARK OF SAFETY FOR THE OLD WISDOM

OUR modern civilization has so clearly the imprints of Greece and Rome upon it that the student usually fails to realize the immense vicissitudes through which it has passed in its duration to our day. The fabric of the old world of antiquity to which Cæsar more than any other had given name and form was never more securely established than during the two centuries which followed his death. A long period of peace prevailed over the vast empire, and a knowledge of the liberal arts spread into the remotest provinces. From Rome as a center Christianity as well as letters went forth, the former spreading in the face of persecution till Constantine in 312 A. D. put the seal of legality upon it. But already the structure of Roman civilization, built up on foundations laid down by Assyrian, Persian, Greek and Celtic conquests, was shaking under the blows dealt upon it from the north. Till the termination of the reign of the Antonines, for a century and a half, the period of peace and prosperity continued. Then came a century that was full of menace and trouble but in which no vital injury was inflicted on the body politic. And then at last in the middle of the fourth century Rome began to crumble. Barbarians and pestilence were delivering

27

the annihilating blows. The Franks overran Gaul and descended into Spain, and the Goths poured into the east and into Asia Minor. Over the ruin which the Franks left behind them in Gaul and Spain the Vandals followed, nullifying the efforts at revival. In Asia the Huns poured over Cappadocia, Cilicia and Palestine, while Saracens passed through Egypt over north Africa into Spain. Britain was overrun by northern savages like the Saxons, Angles and Jutes, and Austria by Asiatic nomads like the Huns and Magyars. Then Goth followed Goth in Europe and German and Frank completed the work of destruction, in which earthquake, flood, fire and plague cooperated. In 407 A. D. a multitude of Franks and Vandals burst over Gaul. Roman rule practically ceased and the three kingdoms of the Visigoths, Burgundians and Franks began to form. In 476 Odoacer deposed the last Roman emperor in Italy and in 486 Clovis the Frank ended the last vestige of Roman rule in Gaul. Then as if some inscrutable design sought, by a huge phenomenon, to leave no doubt that the world of the Cæsars had gone forever, there followed the plague of 542. It raged for four months in Constantinople and for four years in the Roman Empire. "When the plague has ceased, we feel that we are moving in a completely other world than that of 540."[1]

At the fall of the Roman Empire Ireland did not share in the ruin of its civilization. That ruin was almost as complete as if the ocean had burst its banks and washed over the plains of Europe. Now Ireland had shared in the commerce, the learning and the traditions of Rome while Rome was still in its strength. The Roman Empire fell swallowed up by tide after tide of heathen savages,

[1] Bury's Later Roman Empire, I, 400.

eager for destruction and plunder. Outside the empire Russia and Germany, like the Scandinavian lands, were still barbarian and pagan. Thus all Europe almost became submerged under a deluge of savage heathendom. Ireland was the one exception, the ark of safety for the old beauty and wisdom of classical days. It was the bridge over what were truly the dark ages of Europe and as soon as the flood of heathen invasion ebbed, light and hope crossed the bridge and were first carried by Irish instructors to all the new-forming nations of Europe, the great heathen tribes destined to become the nations of the modern world.

While Europe, including Britain, was thus in tumult, peace and prosperity were brooding over favored Hibernia. Hundreds of years yet separated her from the Danish raids, and the English were scarcely yet known to civilization. The Romans had never succeeded in crossing, except for commerce, the waves that separated her from Britain. The Milesian Gaels, who had given organization to the country, had been so long settled in Ireland that the memory of that settlement had assumed a mythological character.[1] The assumption is that in the midst of the vast Celtic movements that are discernible over all Europe about 600 B. C. there was also a Celtic invasion of Ireland. One invasion probably followed another and an Irish historical tract, written about 721 A. D., and copied from older sources, gives the definite Gaelic monarchy as beginning contemporaneously with Alexander the Great in the fourth century B. C.[2] From that time onward one form of government, a limited elec-

[1] "The Irish are one of the most ancient nations that I know of at this end of the world"; and come of "as mighty a race as the world ever brought forth" (Edmund Spenser, "View of the State of Ireland," 1596, pp. 26 and 32).

[2] "Alexander had reigned five years when the sons of Mil came to Ireland, and the battle of Tailtu was fought in which fell the T. D. D. (Tuatha Da Danaan) with their queens." See MacNeill, Proc. Royal Ir. Acad., 1909-10, p. 132.

tive monarchy, and one dynasty, the Milesian, ruled over Ireland, through a many-branched patriarchal system, bound together by one language, one national literature, and one code of laws.

The century that saw the final disruption of imperial Rome saw Ireland growing greater and more splendid. At that period the martial might of the Irish was at its height; their fleets held the northern seas and their forces triumphed in the lands which are now called Scotland, England, Wales and France. Their foreign trade brought them captives from the Roman provinces, representative of a different culture, just as in former times the Greeks had been drawn to Rome.

Greek and Roman learning was freely imported from Marseilles, Narbonne and Bordeaux, where Ausonius and his uncle and their circle kept alive the ancient traditions, as well as from northern Gaul and Roman Britain. There were Christians in Ireland before the advent of St. Patrick, and the ease with which the country turned from paganism to Christianity is reasonably explained by its long previous preparation in cosmopolitan culture. A certain Ethicus in the third or fourth century tells us how he visited Ireland and what he thought of its books. Ussher says that in 360 A. D. a Christian priest was sent from Rome to teach the Christian faith in Ireland. The Glossary of Cormac, prince and bishop of Cashel, furnishes strong testimony to the cultivation of letters and learning before the arrival of St. Patrick. Cormac, who was a younger contemporary of Johannes Scotus Eriugena and wrote in the ninth century, quotes not only Christian writers but also many pagan Irish authors—poets, historians, grammarians and others—who must all have lived previous to or contemporaneously with St. Patrick.

In citing Ireland as the native land of the heresiarch Pelagius, St. Jerome gave expression to the foreign impression in respect to Ireland's educational proficiency at the end of the fourth century. St. Patrick in his Confession, composed in the middle of the fifth century, apologizes for the inferiority of his own to Irish culture, and his description of himself as a man of single speech from his birth is indicative of antagonists knowing more tongues than one. The works of the first Sedulius before 450 A. D., presuming that he was an Irishman, the poems of Sechnall, and the extant writings of Columbanus, Columcille and their contemporaries, add to the testimony before the end of the sixth century.

A year before the arrival of St. Patrick, Pope Celestine is recorded as sending Palladius to the "Scots of Ireland believing in Christ." But it would appear that up to the time in which St. Patrick began his great work the Christians of Ireland were in a great minority and practised their religion in secrecy.

2. Ireland's Educational Proficiency

Long before the advent of Christianity the numerous schools of the Druids and the bards carried on the tradition of pagan culture and taught history, poetry, and law, and there were also academies of a higher grade. There is in fact in the "Ogygia" an early instance of a species of university established at Tara in the third century by Cormac, the high-king, son of Airt: "Cormac exceeded all his predecessors in magnificence, munificence, wisdom, and learning, as also in military achievements. His palace was most superbly adorned and richly furnished, and his numerous family proclaim his majesty and munificence; the books he published and the schools he endowed at Tara bear unquestionable testimony to his learning; there were three schools instituted: In the first the most eminent professors of the art of war were engaged, in the second history was taught, and in the third jurisprudence was profest."[1] There is a long poem in the book of Ua Davegan on these colleges, the grandeur of Tara in the reign of Cormac, his encomiums and exploits.[2]

But the fame of Ireland as the "Island of Saints and Scholars" is based mainly on the chain of remarkable foundations that began to garland the land following the introduction of Christianity. The more important of these seats of learning, which in course of time made their influence felt over the whole civilized world, were in the true sense of the word universities. They made the whole circle of knowledge the subject of their inquiry and teaching; they drew their teachers and students from every part of Europe; and they were the original models on which in great measure modern universities have been formed. Measured even by the characteristic distinctions arbitrarily enumerated by Bulæus—ratione disciplinae, ratione loci, ratione fundatorum, ratione privilegiorum, ratione regimenis—they fulfilled the idea of universities.

Among them Armagh and Clonmacnois in particular possest a national, not to speak of an international, character. Leaving aside minor seats of learning with which Ireland was at that time honeycombed, there were in number thirty-six of these larger monastic establishments. Armagh, as the seat of the primal see of St. Patrick, was the greatest of them all, and it became and long

---

[1] Hely's Transl. Senchus na Relic (History of the Cemeteries) in Leabhar na h-Uidhre (Book of the Dun Cow), a MS. of the eleventh century founded on others much older.

[2] The poem begins: "Teamhair na riogh rath Cormaic"—(Tara of the kings is Cormac's seat"—).

remained the most renowned seat of learning in the world. Founded in the fifth century it retained its supremacy in the twelfth. Thus the synod of Clane in 1162 ordered that from that time forth only former students of Armagh were to obtain the position of "fer leiginn," or chief professor, in a school attached to any church in Ireland. This decree was really equivalent to a recognition of the school of Armagh as a national university for all Ireland. Seven years later the king of Ireland, Ruaidhri, established and endowed in Armagh a new professorship for the benefit of students from Ireland and Scotland.

After Armagh there followed Clonard in present Meath, ancient Bregia and Teffia, founded early in the sixth century by Finan or Finnian; Clonmacnois, on the banks of the Shannon in the present King's County, founded in the same century by Ciaran, called the "Carpenter's Son"; Bangor in Uladh, or Ulidia, amid the coastal ards of Ulster, "that glorious institution" as St. Bernard of Clairvaux calls it, founded by Comgall[1] in 558; Clonfert, founded by St. Brendan the Navigator; Lismore in Desies (now County Waterford), founded by Carthach, surnamed Mochuda, about the year 633; and Glendalough, in present Wicklow, part of the ancient territory of Hy-Kinsellagh.

Clonard (Cluain Erard, Erard's meadow), on the banks of the River Boyne, began as the cell of Finnian,[2]

1 Columbanus, founder of Luxeuil, Annegray, Fontaines and Bobbio, who was educated at Bangor, preserves in his second Instruction a fragment of the writings of Comgall (See Ulster Journal of Archæology, I, p. 174, Old Series, Reeves on Antiphonary of Bangor; Migne, LXXX, 229 seq.). Notker Balbulus, who flourished at the Irish foundation of St. Gall in 890, identifies the name of Faustus, which Columbanus gives to his old master, with the Irish name Comgall.

2 "Naimh (St.) Finnian of Clonard, the pious one.
And scholar, in whose school three thousand saints
Had studied wisdom, ere they wandered forth
To build their cells and churches throughout vast Erin." (Tain. Prol., Finding of the Tain, transl. by Hutton, p. 6.)

and later grew into a cluster of stone buildings, with some structures built of enduring woods. The fame of its learning brought to it multitudes of scholars, including laymen, clerics, abbots and bishops. From it went forth the group of remarkable men known as the "Twelve Apostles of Erin." In the office of St. Finnian, the founder, its students are said to have numbered three thousand. For centuries the school was renowned for scriptural learning. From it, says Ussher, "scholars came out in as great numbers as Greeks from the side of the horse of Troy."

Clonfert rivaled Clonard in fame and in the number of its students. It was an extremely wealthy foundation, endowed with large estates of fertile land, so that its later bishops on appointment paid into the papal treasury large sums of gold. We have an almost complete list of its bishops and abbots, one of whom was Cummian, whose celebrated letter on the Paschal controversy, addrest to Iona early in the seventh century, remarkable for its erudition, urbanity, and modesty, sheds a luminous ray on the liberal culture dispensed in these great seats of learning. The city of Brendan, once peopled by multitudes of eager students, noted as the training ground of the greatest of preceptors, is to-day a vast solitude.

The site of Clonmacnois is almost in the center of Ireland. This famous institution possest rich lands and Prince Diarmuid, one of the sons of Cerbaill, the highking, whom he succeeded as Diarmuid II, made it the particular object of his munificence, so that it became endowed as a seminary for the whole nation. Both Clonmacnois and Clonfert cultivated Irish learning with especial distinction, so that to the labor of their schools we are indebted for the leading authentic records of ancient Ireland, and for the preservation of important compositions of the bards and recensions of the old Irish laws, known as the Brehon codes. A forest of inscribed stones still stands amid the ruins of Clonmacnois—the ruined cathedral with seven oratories, round tower and decorated high crosses—some of the inscriptions in Latin, some even in Hebrew, but over two hundred of them in the medieval Irish tongue which the cultivation of Latin did not impede or supersede.[1] The fame of Bangor, which appears to have been the mother of Bangor in Wales, was known to St. Bernard in Gaul, who has described it as "the training ground of monks in many a thousand, the head of many a monastery, a truly holy place, fertile in saints, yielding the richest harvests for God."[2] Monasterboice, Moville, Glendalough, the Columbiad foundations, and the schools of Thomond and Desmond, nearly all founded in the sixth century, were educational institutions second only in celebrity. Arboreta of civilization, the medieval counterparts of Zeno's garden and Plato's Academe, the beneficiaries of modern learning might well take off their shoes in treading these now silent glades, for there are few more sacred spots over which the arts and refinements have bloomed.[3]

[1]   "At eve they came
To Ciaran's green, to holy Clonmacnois,
To Clonmacnois upon a flowery slope
Amid a rushry by the pure, bright Shannon,
Where all was blest and still.
And in that place
In after time a sacred school and city
Should rise—Naimh Ciaran's city—and should grow
Like a tall tree, where rule and truth and wisdom
Should spread through half the land."
          (Tain [Epil. Writing of the Tain], transl. Hutton, p. 448.)
[2] Vita Malach.
[3] The principal Irish schools were: Armagh, Kildare, Noendrum, Louth, Emly, St. Ibar, Cluainfois, St. Asicus, all founded in the fifth century; St. Enda of Aran, Clonard, Clonfert, Moville, Clonmacnois, Derry, Durrow, Kells, Iona, Bangor, Clonenagh, Glendalough, Tuam, founded in the sixth century; and Lismore, Cork, Ross, Inisfallen, Mungret, Iniscaltra, Birr, Roscrea, Inisboffin, Mayo of the Saxons, founded in the seventh century. These leave out of account the more numerous lay and professional schools, some of which were very celebrated, as that of Tuaim Drecain, where general literature, law and the arts were taught. (Vid. Healy. Ireland's Ancient Schools and Scholars; O'Curry, Lectures, II.)

3. CENTERS OF INTELLECTUAL ACTIVITY

The Irish monasteries were not places wholly attuned to mystic contemplation, but great centers of knowledge and intellectual activity. As the sixth century progressed they assumed more and more the character of great studia generali, reaching forth over the whole contemporary field of learning.[1]

The monastic buildings were mostly grouped round an oratorio or basilica, as Colgan calls it—with a rampart— as with caiseal, rath or lis—circularly or ovally surrounding the whole, tho sometimes rectangular also. This was after the fashion of the houses of the princely and well-to-do in Ireland and partook of the character of a dun. The plan, which was afterward followed in the Irish foundations which later garlanded Europe, included churches, storehouses, kilns, mills, sacristies or side houses, the abbot's house, the great house or refectory, the cuisine or kitchen, the hospice or guest house, the scriptorium and library, and a vast number of cells distributed in streets or squares. In course of time round towers rose over the assemblage of buildings with sculptured high crosses near by.

The monastic "family" included priests, deacons, minor clerks, and laymen, who all yielded obedience to the abbot, as an army to the commander-in-chief. It was a maxim that they had to support and clothe themselves, and their work included agriculture, dairying, the breeding of sheep and cattle, architecture, writing and ornamenting books, and cabinet-making. In all this labor they attained incomparable skill, and as smiths and braziers in various kinds of metals they outdistanced all rivalry in Europe.

[1] "One of the most striking features of the organization of the early monastic church in Ireland and Scotland was its provision for the cultivation of learning and for the training of its members in sacred and profane literature." (Skene, Celtic Scotland, II, p. 419.)

All the studies of the time were taught in the larger Irish schools mainly through the medium of the Gaelic language, not merely theology, but philosophy, mathematics, rhetoric, poetry, hagiography, natural science as then understood, grammar, chronology, astronomy, agriculture, Greek, Latin and even Hebrew. The references to "learned scribes," "professors of divinity," "wise doctors," "vessels full of wisdom," "moderators," "rectors," and "regents" in which the annals teem, bear witness to a full, rounded, unflagging intellectual life.

While Irish was the usual medium of instruction, Latin was also largely employed, and often a mixture of the two, as is immediately observable from a study of the Irish annals and the scholia, where the languages intermingle in a manner that show they were equally living tongues to the writers. The magister scholae or scholasticus held the text-book before him and expounded the author, and this was the method employed whether the subject was grammar, dialectics, Irish poetry or any other subject. Apart from the distinctively Irish studies and divinity the scope of learning in the Irish schools both at home and abroad was mainly comprised within the seven liberal arts and philosophy, to which something of medicine and law was added, although these professional studies had special schools of their own, as will be shown. The Trivium—grammar, dialectic and rhetoric—and the Quadrivium—geometry, arithmetic, music, astronomy—were, in their form at least, a legacy from old Roman education. They appear in the Disciplinarum libri novem of Varro in the first century B. C. and they were introduced into the educational system of the Middle Ages mainly through Augustine and Martianus Capella, both of whom were great favorites in the Irish schools.

It is clear that the scope of these arts could be made very much wider than the names suggest. There was nothing that was mechanical or traditional in the Irish use of them and from the beginning Irishmen showed little disposition to be content with what was handed down, but sought to explore new fields of their own. Under grammar became included the study of Irish, Latin and Greek literature. They carried the study of dialectic, which in their hands comprised the core of modern logic, to so high a pitch that in the Carolingian era they were the most bewilderingly skilled controversialists in Europe, and dialectic came to be looked upon and feared as a distinctively Irish branch of intellectual legerdemain. Rhetoric covered the study of law also, and a mere glance over the great volumes containing the old Irish laws, called the Brehon Laws, the most copious and authentic mass of material bearing on the history of Ireland, will give an idea of the labor such study entailed. Geometry included geography, natural history and the medicinal properties of plants. Though the Irish adopted the Gregorian chant, they were themselves the most advanced people in Europe in the field of music and their pursuit of that study was as a result almost exclusively Irish.

4. TEXT-BOOKS AND LEARNED DEGREES

We are not familiar with all the text-books in the hands of the Irish masters, for they were in possession of both Latin and Greek works that had become almost unknown on the Continent. We are pretty well informed, however, in regard to the text-books most in use in the Irish schools both in Ireland and abroad. They surpassed all the scholars of the time in their familiarity with such works of Aristotle as were available, and the trenchant employment they made of his De Interpretatione with Porphyry's Eisagoge made philosophy almost wholly occupied with logical problems in the earliest scholastic period. Of Plato's dialogs the Irish scholars appear to have known the Timæus in the original, tho on the Continent it was known only in the translation of Chalcidius, made in the fifth century. The commentaries of Chalcidius, the works of Augustine, the De Dogmate Platonis of Apuleius, and the commentary of Macrobius on Cicero's Dream of Scipio, gave them an acquaintance with the general philosophy of Plato. Translations and compilations of Marius Victorinus, Claudianus Mamertus and Donatus were read and expounded in the Irish schools, and later the works of the Neo-Platonists filtered through them. One of their current text-books in philosophy was the De Consolatione of Boethius and in the tenth century they became familiar also with his translation of the Categoriae of Aristotle. They used some of the rhetorical and dialectical treatises of Cicero, such as his Topica and De Offiiciis—indeed we have Irish scholars to thank for the preservation of parts of his Pro Fonteio and In Pisonem. They knew also the De Beneficiis of Seneca and the De Rerum Natura of Lucretius. Priscian and Donatus were their chief authorities on grammar, and other greatly used text-books in the Irish schools were the commentaries and original works of Martianus Capella, Charisius, Cassiodorus, Boethius and Isidore.

Jerome was their great authority on Scripture. The Moralia of Gregory the Great was the chief text-book in the field of moral theology, particularly at Armagh. Irish divinity students were also familiar with the works of Hilary, Ambrose, Athanasius, Orosius, Pope Leo, Chrysostom, Lactantius, Sedulius, Juvencus, Clement of Alexandria and Origen. Their favorite gospel was St. John. They made much use of the "Vetus Itala," an older biblical version than the Vulgate of Jerome, which displaced it. The Book of Psalms was their vade-mecum of praise and prayer, and many of them knew it by heart. With some the recital of the "Three Fifties" was a daily practise. Their wide acquaintance with the old classical writers is further shown by the reminiscences of them which occur in their works, and by the reproductions of them in the Irish script or in Irish foundations all over Europe.

In the great monastic universities, as well as in the lay schools, degrees were conferred just as they are conferred in the universities of to-day. There could be no clearer proof of the thoroughgoing character of Irish education, of the single-hearted pursuit of learning in the widest sense obtainable, and of the solid hard work of the scholars, than the elaborate system of graduation in learning and the professions which the Irish schools had developed in that early age. The "seven grades of wisdom" were carefully distinguished not merely in the schools but by the old national laws, and they are as numerous and distinctive as the academic titles and initials of modern times—Senators, Fellows, LL.D., M.A., A.B., and the like. In the old Irish system each degree represented a year of study, and there were degrees both for the students and the professors, in the case of the first covering seven years, and in the case of the second, covering fourteen. The degrees marking the student's career beginning from the lowest to the highest were: Felmac, Freimeidhed, Fursaindidh, Sruth do Aill, Sai, Anruth, and Rosai. In addition to these, the higher degrees for the professor were Caogdach, Foghlaintidhe, Desgibal, Staruidhe,

Foirceadlaidhe, Sair Canoine, and Drumcli. The High Professor was also called an Ollamh (Ollave), which represented the highest degree in every profession or branch of learning. There were degrees conferred in the professional and lay schools which will be mentioned later, and degrees which represented other distinctions, all of which are described in the Brehon law treatises; but these may be taken as representative.[1]

[1] Brehon Laws, Vol. IV, Sequel of the Crith Gablach; pp. 357-9; V, Small Primer; Cormac's Glossary, pp. 5, 6, 34, 53; Keating, History, pp. 446, 454. See also Healy, Ireland's Ancient Schools and Scholars, p. 596, seq.; Joyce, Social Hist. I, Chap. XI (Learning and Education) pp. 396-471; Richey, Short Hist., p. 83; Cambrensis Eversus, 277 seq.; O'Curry, Man. and Customs, I, 79-83.

CHAPTER IV

"HIGH SCHOLARS OF THE WESTERN WORLD"

1. Learned Classes of Laymen.   2. Great Colleges Simultaneously Active from Sixth Century Onwards.   3. "Philosophy" and "Wisdom."   4. Numbers of Students.

1. LEARNED CLASSES OF LAYMEN

THE advantages of the liberal education thus provided were widely distributed among the people of Ireland. "It has been sometimes asserted," says a modern writer, "that in early times in Ireland learning was confined within the walls of the monasteries; but this view is quite erroneous. Tho the majority of the men of learning in Christian times were ecclesiastics, secular learning was by no means confined to the clergy. We have seen that the monastic schools had many lay pupils and that there were numerous lay schools; so that a considerable body of the lay community must have been more or less educated—able to read and write. Nearly all the professional physicians, lawyers (or brehons), poets, builders and historians, were laymen; a large proportion of the men chronicled in our annals, during the whole period of Ireland's literary preeminence, as distinguished in art and general literature, were also laymen; lay tutors were often employed to teach princes; and, in fact, laymen played a very important part in the diffusion of knowledge and in building up that character for learning that rendered Ireland so famous in former times. One has only to glance through Ware's or O'Reilly's 'Irish Writers' or Dr. Hyde's 'Literary History of Ireland' to see the truth of this."[1]

[1] Joyce, Social History of Ireland, I, 417.

Laymen figured among the most illustrious of the Irish schoolmen. Johannes Scotus Eriugena[1] was, it would seem, a layman. So was Flann "most famous among the many writers, one of the most learned men in Europe in philosophy, literature, history, poetry and science," professor of the college of Monasterboice, several of whose poems as well as his Book of Annals are preserved. Then there was Mugeor Ua More, father of the celebrated St. Malachy, "chief lector of divinity of this school (Armagh) and of all the rest of Europe," as the Annals of the Four Masters call him. "It is not the least striking circumstance in those dreary times," notes Cardinal Newman, "that in an age when even kings and great men often could not read, professors in the Irish colleges were sometimes men of noble birth. St. Malachy's father, though a member of a family of distinction, as St. Bernard tells us, was a celebrated professor of Armagh. History records the names of others similarly eminent, both by their descent and by their learning. It is impossible not to admire and venerate a race which displayed such inextinguishable love of science and letters."[2] Apart from the monks, the average Irish layman was well educated. "The national tradition of monastic and lay schools preserved to Erin, what was lost in the rest of Europe, a learned class of laymen. Culture was as frequent and honorable in the Irish chief or warrior as in the cleric."[3]

To the monasteries and schools were attached teach scripta or scriptoria and libraries, furnished with waxen

[1] I use the form Eriugena because it is etymologically correct and because it was one of the forms used by Johannes himself. Its meaning is "born in Ireland"—"Eriu" being the most ancient form of the Gaelic name of Ireland known. John was known to his contemporaries chiefly as "John the Irishman" (Johannes Scotus). The form "Johannes Scotus Erigena" is not earlier than the seventeenth century.

[2] Historical Sketches, III, 279-80.

[3] Mrs. Alice Stopford Green, "Irish Nationality."

tablets, parchments, inks, styles, and quills, where manuscripts were edited and copied. To many of them were attached schools of art in illumination or ornamentation of books, in metal work, in painting, in sculpture, in carving, and in enamel work. Clonmacnois and Kells had art schools which produced work in metal and in the illumination of books which has remained unapproached to our day. But Irish preeminence and influence in metal work are evidenced above all in the striking fact that almost the entire extant ecclesiastical specimens of western Europe from the early medieval age are shown to be Irish or from Irish models. The vast colonnade of pillar towers that garlanded the island, the noble Rock of Cashel and the carved sea rocks of the Skelligs, furnish sufficient testimonials to Ireland's schools of architecture, during a period when architecture, in any true sense, was almost dead in Europe.

Irish architects appear to have been restrained by ancient traditions of apostolic measurements, tho they could fit and dovetail great stones from ten to seventeen feet in length. Architect and sculptor were often combined in the same person, as in the Italians of the Renaissance, for these Irishmen were nothing if not versatile.[1]

2. GREAT COLLEGES SIMULTANEOUSLY ACTIVE FROM SIXTH CENTURY ONWARD

The standards of learning were high. The schools themselves were "of unspeakable excellence," in the judgment of Aldhelm, who had himself Irish masters. "Ireland had become the heiress to the classical and theological learning of the western empire of the fourth and fifth centuries, and a period of humanism was thus ushered in

[1] See "Irish Archæological Remains," by Benedict Fitzpatrick, Encyclopedia Americana (1918) vol. 15.

which reached its culmination during the sixth and following centuries."[1] The graduates of the Irish academies wrote Latin, not to speak of Greek, better than it was written by any other people in western Europe.

They maintained the same method of education till the sixteenth century. In the year 1571, centuries after the golden age of Irish learning, amid the many misfortunes that had fallen on the country, Edmund Campion found Irish schools for law and medicine in operation, where Latin was still employed as a living tongue: "They speake Latine like a vulgar tongue, learned in their common schools of leach-craft and law, whereat they begin (as) children and hold on sixteene or twenty yeares, conning by roate the Aphorisms of Hypocrates and the Civill Institutions and a few other parings of these two faculties."[2] The long course of sixteen to twenty years indicates that Ireland in eclipse still held to her ideal of thoroughness in education.

Testimony as to the high and uniform level of education among the medieval Irish people is likewise afforded by the fact of the uniformity of the language. Old Irish differs considerably from the modern form of the language, but there were, as far as we can judge, no dialects in it. The same language was spoken and written in the Decies as in Tyrconnell, from the most southerly point of Ireland to the most northerly part of Scotland. A Gaelic book written in the sixth or ninth century would be understood from Cape Clear to the remotest parts of Scotland. The Irish in the "Book of Deir" is couched in the most ancient form of Gaelic known to have been written in Scotland and still existing. The Gaelic in this book was probably written in the Abbey of Deir in Aberdeenshire

1 Kuno Meyer, Ancient Irish Poetry, Pref.
2 "Account of Ireland," p. 18.

in or before the twelfth century. Its language, however, is pure Irish, exactly paralleling the speech used in Irish books of the same age. Complete national unity, a uniform literary speech, a like culture, prevailed through the broad Gaedhaltacht of Eire[1] and Alba.

We have the testimony of the Irish records that the great Irish colleges were in active existence not at different periods but all together from the sixth century onward. When we bear in mind that there were also, during the whole period, the secular or lay schools, to which I will refer later, and which tho smaller were far more numerous and scattered all over the country—we shall have some idea, as one writer remarks, of the universal love of learning that existed in Ireland in those days and of the general spread of education.[2]

3. "Philosophy" and "Wisdom"

Irish monasticism differed from continental monasticism in its intellectual outlook. Monachism in Egypt and on the European mainland simply represented flight from an apparently doomed and demoralized world. It was in response to the yearning and the need which men felt of getting away from worry and fear, and villainy and contention. It eschewed ambition and undue effort

---

[1] The Gaelic or Irish name for Ireland is Eire, genitive Eireann, whence Erin, also Ire-land. The Gaelic or Irish name for Scotland is Alba, which sometimes stood for the whole of Britain.

[2] The same schools in Ireland produced men of international fame in widely different periods. Thus Moville produced Finnian and Columcille in the sixth century and Marianus Scotus in the eleventh. Armagh sent forth Benignus in the fifth, Gildas in the sixth, and Imar in the twelfth century. Clonard produced the famous "Twelve Apostles" in the sixth and Aileran in the seventh. Clonard produced Fintan and Moinenn in the sixth, Fursey and Cummian in the seventh, and Cormac and others in the ninth. Clonmacnois founded by Ciaran on Saturday, January 23, 544, produced Alithir in the sixth, King Guaire in the seventh, MacConcumba in the eighth, and Colgu, Josephus Scotus, perhaps Sedulius Scotus and a host of others in the ninth. Columbanus went from Bangor in the sixth, Dungal in the eighth and ninth, and Malachy in the twelfth. And so with the other great seats of learning in Ireland.

or strain, intellectual or otherwise.[1] It sought simply for retirement, rest, peace, recollection, contentment, simplicity, the condition of communing with God and waiting for the end. The woes and iniquity of the fallen empire had indeed convinced men that there was nothing more to be done for it; it was simply a case of *sauve qui peut,* and earnest men as a result turned their back upon it and fixed their eyes on the world to come. This was the spirit of early continental monachism, and as the monasteries were henceforth the only places where there was any attempt at education at all, an age that was truly dark settled on Europe.[2]

While asceticism in Ireland was highly esteemed, asceticism did not inhibit intellectual culture. On the contrary wisdom, learning, mental development, were ardently sought after by these very ascetics. "They drew back from no inquiry; boldness was on a level with faith," says Montalembert. "Their strength lay in those exercises of pure reason which go by the name of philosophy or wisdom," remarks Newman. They were "proficient beyond all comparison in the world's wisdom," in the words of the ninth century "Monk of St. Gall." They were "celebrated for their philosophical knowledge" (sophia clari) remarks another ancient writer. In their own estimation given in the Irish Annals they were the "high scholars of the western world," philosophers "without equals this side of the Alps," and "vessels full of all the wisdom and knowledge of their time."

[1] Thus the rule of St. Benedict forbade a Benedictine to own a book or a pen, and provided only two hours a day for reading, and that pious reading.

[2] The general belief that the Benedictines, who were the only "rivals" of the Irish monks in the period under review, were learned men is totally erroneous. No branch of the Benedictines making learned studies their aim existed till the establishment of the Maurists in the seventeenth century. Men like Mabillon and Montfaucon have given the Benedictines their modern reputation for learning, but in the early medieval period the Benedictines were far from remarkable for culture. The work of the Irish monks has in large part been credited to them.

Their mental attitude is boldly enunciated by the incomparable Johannes Scotus Eriugena, himself in comparison with the age in which he lived as much a miracle as Plato or Augustine: "I am not so browbeaten by authority nor so fearful of the assault of less able minds as to be afraid to utter with fearless forehead what true reason clearly determines and indubitably demonstrates; especially as there must be question of such only among the wise, to whom nothing is more sweet to hear than true reason, nothing more delightful to investigate when it is found."[1]

"While on the mainland and in Britain budding Christianity and the germs of western culture, such as it was, were effectually trodden under foot by the various hordes of Vandals, Alemanni, Huns, Franks, Heruli, Langobards, Angles and Saxons, and the Merovingian kingdom sank lower and lower, when universal crudeness and depravity seemed to have gained the upper hand and the entire West threatened to sink hopelessly into barbarism, the Irish established several seminaries of learning in their own country," says a German authority. "The standard of learning (in Bangor, Armagh, Clonmacnois, Lismore) was much higher than with Gregory the Great and his followers. It was derived without interruption from the learning of the fourth century, from men such as Ambrose, Jerome, and Augustine. Here also were to be found such specimens of classical literature as Virgil's works among the ecclesiastical writings, and an acquaintance with Greek authors as well beside the opportunity of free access to the very sources of Christianity."[2]

1 De Divisione Naturae, V, I, p. 39.

2 Zimmer, Preuss, Jahrb, 1887, trs. "Irish Element in Med. Culture," p. 19.

4. NUMBERS OF STUDENTS

Judged by results the system of education in the Irish schools could hardly have been bettered in those days. The graduates it trained and disciplined assuredly left their impress on the epoch in which they lived. "From the schools of Ireland were to issue the men who were destined during the next two centuries not merely to leave their mark upon the church as theologians and founders of monasteries, but, further, to play an important part in molding the new civilization of the Frankish empire, to lay the foundations of modern philosophy, and to promote the study of natural science and literature."[1]

These Irish seats of learning had large numbers of students. Armagh had 3,000, many of them, as at other places, from the Continent. At Clonard there were over 3,000, all residing in and around the college, while Bangor and Clonfert had each as many. Other colleges had smaller numbers of students, ranging from 2,000 down to fifty.[2] At the head of each of these colleges was the "Fer leiginn" or "Man of Learning," who was sometimes a layman, generally a cleric, but always a scholar of great renown. The abbot presided over both institutions— monastery and school combined.

Calling to mind the deserted aspect of the sites of these early establishments at the present day there is nothing more remarkable in the early annals than the busy intercourse with the world which they disclose. Guests, illustrious by kingly descent or civil status or ecclesiastical rank, were ever coming and going. The abbots were wont to travel in chariots; in places like Iniscaltra, Clonfert, Clonmacnois, Iona, Bangor and Monasterboice, in

---

[1] C. S. Boswell, "An Irish Precursor of Dante."
[2] See Joyce, Social History, I, 408; Skene, Celtic Scotland, II, p. 419.

the vicinity of river, lake or sea they had also fleets of vessels at their disposal. Ships would come in laden with foreign merchandise and foreign visitors and students and they would bring with them the news of great events that were happening in foreign lands, of an earthquake in Italy, of happenings in the Orkneys or in the valley of the Loire, of the progress of Irish foundations abroad, and of the sacred places in Palestine. There were horses and sheep and cattle, and farming operations were conducted on a great scale. There were crowds of monks and students in the streets, carrying great books, waxen tablets, and leather satchels, and from the cells of the masters came the hum of animated discussion or the voice of one speaking with authority. New buildings of wood or stone were being erected, round towers were slowly arising or a sculptor worked on the panels of a high granite cross, with the eager students around him watching. Now and then the crowds would grow silent and make a passage as some "high scholar of the western world" or "apostle of Erin" passed through them, a noble ascetic with long hair falling on his shoulders and painted eyelids, a figure clad in white homespun, one perhaps that had turned his back on the throne of Ireland and had thrown down the sword to take up the cultivation of the Scriptures and classic letters. Or a gayer group might appear on the scene, luxurious in raiment, young, hilarious, care-free; these too the crowds would regard with interest and deference—they were the offspring of the great reigning families of Leinster, of Munster, of Connaught or Meath or Ulster, the tanist perhaps to the high-king amongst them, youths without a physical blemish and therefore of kingly potentiality, some the heirs of royal clans that had been honored in Eire before the

Christian era. University life in these great Irish centers was free from the excesses that were habitual in pagan Athens, but there was the same plenitude of high spirits, of eager ambition, of thirst after new knowledge, of reverence for great learning and lofty character, of fierce joy in intellectual conflict that marked generous youth in Athens and Rome as in the medieval universities that succeeded the establishment of those in Ireland.[1]

[1] See Healy, Ireland's Ancient Schools and Scholars; Burton, History of Scotland, I, 254 seq.; Joyce, Social History, I, Ch. XI, 417 seq.; Skene, Celtic Scotland, II, 75, 419-63; Reeves, Life of St. Columba, Adamnan, passim; Stokes, Anecdota Oxoniensia, Ser. 5, passim.

CHAPTER V

INSULA SANCTORUM ET DOCTORUM

1. Intellectual Leader of Christendom.   2. Anglo-Saxon Students in Ireland.   3. Special Colleges for Princes.   4. Going to Ireland for Education Long Continued.

1. INTELLECTUAL LEADER OF CHRISTENDOM

NOT only from the four corners of Ireland and Britain but also from every country in Europe students flocked into the Irish schools attracted by the fame of their professors and alumni, who with rare and sustained passion threw their souls into the exploration of the realm of knowledge with results that astonished civilized Europe. The celebrity of Ireland as the university of the West and the home of the most erudite and speculative of nations was thus bruited over the known world, which henceforth hailed the western isle as the intellectual leader of Christendom and the Island of Saints and Scholars. Of that enduring preeminence Darmesteter felicitously says: "The classic tradition to all appearances dead in Europe burst into full flower in the isle of Saints and the Renaissance began in Ireland seven hundred years before it was known in Italy. For three centuries Ireland was the asylum of the higher learning which took sanctuary there from the uncultivated states in Europe. At one time Armagh, the religious capital of Christian Ireland, was the metropolis of civilization."[1]

The evidence attesting the number of foreign students

[1] English Studies, pp. 202-3.

in the island has come from various sources in those days—

> "When Ireland flourished in fame
> Of Wealthe and goodnesse far above the rest
> Of all that bear the British Islands' name"

as Spenser puts it.

Hardly did Greece in the heyday of its magnetic power draw more powerfully to itself the adventurous intellects of foreign nations than Ireland during the centuries of its supremacy. We can appraise the surprising number of these foreigners from certain testimonies. Thus Ængus the Culdee, in his litany, written at the end of the eighth century, invokes the intercession of many hundreds of saints—Romans, Italians, Egyptians, Gauls, Germans, Britons, Picts, Saxons or English, and natives of other countries—who were buried and venerated in Ireland, and whom he divided into groups, chiefly according to the localities of Ireland in which they sojourned and died. The lives of St. Patrick, Ciaran, Declan, Albeus, Enda, Maidoc, Senan, Brendan and other famous Irishmen furnish testimonies likewise indicating the large numbers of foreigners who crossed the seas to obtain a liberal education in the great Irish academies.[1]

Thus as early as the year 536, in the time of Senan, there arrived in Desmond from the Continent a company of fifty students and seminarians, who were led thither to study in the great establishment at Lismore and for the purpose of perfecting themselves in the practices of an ascetic life under Irish directors. On another occasion Senan saw seven ships sailing up the Shannon in one day laden with continental scholars for the great school of Clonfert, situated on an island in the river.[2]

[1] Anecdota Oxoniensia, Med. and Mod., Ser. 5, passim.
[2] Anecdota Oxon., Ser. 5, Life of St. Senan.

An engraving of stone marks the grave of "Seven Romans" (VII Romani) near the church of St. Brecan in the great isle of Arran.[1] We are told that, among the multitudes of students who attended Armagh, many came from other countries besides Britain.

The office of Cathaldus states that Gauls, Angles, Scots, Teutons and very many people of neighboring nations went to hear the professor's lectures at Lismore, and Morini's life of him, published in Rome, expresses in poetic terms the tradition of Lismore's greatness as the educational resort of foreigners. "Crowds of Gaulish students," writes Haureau, "sought the Irish shores in order to win back again from their former pupils the learning they had lost themselves."[2]

Iona, the least accessible perhaps of the Irish seats of learning, had all sorts of visitors besides monks and students. Columcille talked with mariners sailing south from the Orkneys, and others coming north from the Loire with their tuns of wine told him the news from continental Europe and how a town in Istria had been wrecked by earthquake. From Arculf, a bishop of Gaul, who had traveled in Palestine, Syria, Constantinople, Alexandria and other parts of the East, Adamnan, the successor of Columcille as abbot, and his biographer, derived part of the information on which he based his work "De Locis Sanctis." Visitors from abroad, apart from students, were numerous in some of the other Irish establishments. Thus Paulinus, patriarch of Aquileia, who belonged to Charlemagne's court, has a poem addrest to one Zacharias,

[1] It is reproduced by Petrie, in Ecclesiastical Architecture.
[2] Singularités, C. I. The crowds of foreign students that went to Ireland appear more remarkable from the fact that there is apparently only one authenticated instance of a continental student going to a school in England, which was so much nearer, and which had usually to be crossed in the journey to Ireland. This was the case of Liudger, who studied at York in the time of Alcuin.

apparently a Greco-Italian, who went from the Continent to Britain and Ireland and there distinguished himself.[1]

2. ANGLO-SAXON STUDENTS IN IRELAND

After the year 635 the Anglo-Saxons in particular crossed over to Ireland to enjoy the liberal advantages offered by its schools which had admitted a filtering of Northumbrian natives for several decades previously. Armagh was one of the favorite resorts of British and English students and continued to be frequented by them down to the time of the Conqueror. Gildas, the first historian of the Britons, seems to have been first a student and then regent at Armagh. Anglo-Saxon missionaries who went abroad almost all received their training in Ireland, and were usually led by Irishmen. Alcuin is stated to have spent some years at Clonmacnois. Sulger, afterwards bishop of St. Davids, spent from ten to fifteen years in study in Ireland.

Bede provides striking testimony as to the numbers of English students in Ireland and the hospitality extended to them. He tells us that many of the English nation were living in Ireland, whither they had repaired either to cultivate the sacred studies or to lead a life of greater strictness. Some of them became monks; others were better pleased to apply to reading and study, going about from school to school through the cells of the masters; and all of them were most cheerfully received by the Irish, who supplied them gratis with books and instruction.[2]

Camden in his description of Ireland says: "At that

---

[1] Zacharias frater, domini venerande sacerdos,
Accola Brittaniae, Latii telluris alumne,
Hiberniaeque decus (Quellen u. Untersuchungen zur lateinischen Philologie des Mittelalters, vol. 3 (1908) p. 203). The poem is in MS. Oxford Bodl. Add. C 144, Sale XI.
[2] Hist. Eccles. III, XXVII.

age our Anglo-Saxons repaired on all sides to Ireland as to a general mart of learning. Whence we read in our writers of holy men that they went to study in Ireland (amandatus est ad disciplinam in Hiberniam)."[1]

Seven streets of a town called Kilbally, near Rahan, in what is now called King's County, were wholly occupied in the eighth century by Gauls or foreigners. "By crowds the readers resort thither carried over by ships" says Aldhelm. Round Aldhelm's period, Cadoc, Egbert, Willibrord,[2] the two Ewalds, Plechelm, were conspicuous among those who went from England to get their education in Ireland.

"But not by the Anglo-Saxons alone," says Zimmer, "was Ireland looked upon as the highest seminary of learning; the Franks were also at this time strongly attracted by her great fame. Bede mentions a Frank named Agilberct who spent several years in the study of theology in Ireland and on leaving that country was persuaded to remain for a time in England. On his return to his own country he was made bishop of Paris, where he died at an advanced age. But more striking than all these individual instances is the indisputable fact that the Irish were destined to become instructors of the Germans, Franks, and Alemanni in every department of knowledge of the time."[3]

An interesting visitor in Ireland was Haemgils, emiment for his good works, who was the friend of Drythelm, whose vision of the other world is told in detail by Bede. "He is still living a solitary life in the island of Ireland,

[1] Britannia.
[2] Alcuin wrote a life of Willibrord, a completely Hibernicized Angle, and in it he furnishes testimony to the flourishing state of the Irish schools. Willibrord left Northumbria, quia in Hibernia scholasticam eruditionem viguisse audivit.—(Vita Willib. c 4.)
[3] Preussiche Jahrb., 1887, Jan. trs. "The Irish Element in Med. Culture," pp. 42-3.

supporting his declining age with coarse bread and cold water," says Bede. It was from him that Bede heard the story of Drythelm's vision as told by Drythelm himself to King Aldfrid. Haemgils is commemorated among the hermits in the Liber Vitae.

3. SPECIAL COLLEGES FOR PRINCES

It is noteworthy too that the reigning families of Europe sent their heirs to Ireland to be educated. The French prince, Dagobert, son of Sigibert, king of Austrasia, spent eighteen years in Ireland. He was educated at the royal college of Slane, near Tara, where his fellow students included many Irish princes. On his return to France he succeeded his father as ruler and had many Irishmen at his court.

Dagobert, in some accounts, is said to have been banished to Ireland by the major-domo Grimold, who sought to usurp the kingly authority for his own family. Eddi's life of Wilfrid tells us that his friends and relatives, having learnt from travelers (a navigantibus) that he was living and in perfect health in Ireland, sent envoys to Wilfrid, then bishop in the north of England, asking him to send for him from Scotland and Ireland (de Scottia et Hibernia ad se invitasset).[1] Wilfrid consented to do this. Dagobert thereupon set out from Ireland and returned to his own country, where, enriched by the arms and forces of his companions, he occupied the throne. The king, remembering his obligation to Wilfrid, offered him when visiting on his way to Rome the largest bishopric in his realm, namely, that of Strassburg. Arbogast, an Irishman, and nineteenth bishop of Strassburg, is said to have died at this time, i. e., July 21, 679.

[1] This is apparently the first instance of the word Scottia being used in contrast to Hibernia. It may be a later corruption.

Oswald, king of Northumbria, and his brother Oswiu, received their education in Ireland and at Iona. The two young men became proficient in the Irish tongue, Bede tells us: "Oswiu . . . . illorum etiam lingua optime imbutus." Aldfrid, too, king of Northumbria, the son, according to some accounts, of an Irish mother, and the friend of Adamnan of Iona, was educated also in Ireland, and seems to have spent much time at Mayo of the Saxons, founded by Colman. He spoke Irish fluently, like his predecessor, and traveled around every principality in Ireland. Very interesting is the poem from his hand, which has survived both in Gaelic and Latin, in the light it throws on the Ireland of the period, and in which the note of worship, common to all the Anglo-Saxons where Ireland was concerned, is almost as well defined as in the pages of Bede. The first two verses follow in their English translation:

> I found in Inisfail the Fair
> In Ireland while in exile there
> Women of worth, both grave and gay men
> Learned clerics, heroic laymen.
>
> I travelled its fruitful provinces round
> And in every one of the five I found
> Alike in church and in palace hall
> Abundant apparel and food for all. [1]

Aldhelm, abbot of Malmesbury, dedicated to Aldfrid a poetic epistle in Latin meter in which he congratulated the king on his good fortune in having been educated in Ireland. Aldhelm's own master was the Irish Maeldubh or Maelduf, from whom the city of Malmesbury derives its name.

Clonard and Slane, near Tara, seem to have been schools

[1] See Dublin Review, XXI, 519.

favored by the sons of Irish monarchs and princes. Thus
we read in the Annals of the Four Masters under A. D. 645
that Cathal, second son of Ragallach, king of Connaught,
then a student at Clonard, with a party of twenty-seven
of his fellow students, all young laymen from Connaught,
sallied forth from the college and went to take vengeance
on the assassin of his royal father. In the case of families
of the highest rank, however, such as those of the high
monarch of Ireland, the young princes were generally
educated in the royal household, the tutors residing at the
court.

4. GOING TO IRELAND FOR EDUCATION LONG CONTINUED

The offspring of Irish families settled in Britain and
elsewhere likewise came to Ireland in great numbers to
seek an education in the liberal arts. From Scotland they
of course came in a continual stream, not for a few centuries but right up to the sixteenth century; but of course
Scotland was to all intents and purposes an Irish province
and large portions of it remain part of the Gaedhaltacht
to this day. But they came also from that part of Britain
now denominated Wales, which was also for some centuries an Irish colony, as will be later made plain, and
they came from Brittany in France. The perpetual *va et
vient* that went on between Ireland and Wales is mirrored in the lives of eminent Welshmen and Irishmen
of the early medieval age. A younger Gildas, born of
Irish parents in Wales and flourishing about the beginning
of the ninth century, who wrote a work which he dedicated to Rhabanus Maurus of Fulda, went to Ireland to
be educated. Marcus, born in Britain or Brittany, and
later bishop of Soissons, where he was preceptor to Eric
of Auxerre, likewise received his education in Ireland.

He may be identical with the Irish Marcus who, being on his way to Rome, in the year 822 wrote in Italy a history of Britain, but he seems to have been a younger man.

In the life of Fridolin, the son of an Irish reigning prince, who established the foundation of Seckingen on the Rhine, and other foundations at Helera on the Moselle, Hiliaricum near the Saar, in the Vosges Mountains and in other parts of France and Switzerland, Ireland is represented as enjoying an extraordinary abundance of material resources and of secular riches, while the wealthy gave with liberal hand to the poor and bestowed from their means what was necessary to maintain schools and all manner of useful learning. The education received by Fridolin, who later on established schools for young women and men in his Rhine and other foundations, is reported to have been of a nature suitable to the circumstances of his parents and to his own rank. He pursued with success the study of profane and sacred literature and while he learned, it is recorded, the speculations of Pythagoras and of Plato, he was most assiduous in poring over the pages of the sacred scriptures. Allusions such as these, found in profusion in the lives of medieval Irishmen, serve to present an exalted impression of the classic taste and acumen possest by the educated classes in Ireland.[1]

This going to school in Ireland was not a matter of one short generation. It became traditional and continuous. Thus a part of the university city of Armagh became known as "Saxon Armagh," and likewise part of Mayo

1 See Vita Fridolini, auctore Balthero monacho, Mon. Germ. Hist., Script. rer. Meroving. III, 351-65, ed. Krusch; Colgan, Acta S. Hib., Louv. 1645, I, 481, seq.; Mone, Quellensammlung der badischen Landesgeschichte, Karls. 1845, I; Acta SS. Mar., I, pp. 433-441.

became known as "Mayo of the Saxons." The Danish in-roads interrupted the stream but did not stop it. The rise of the numerous Irish foundations in Britain and on the Continent naturally served to make the long journey to Ireland superfluous and diminished the volume of those who resorted thither. But the attraction of Ireland as the university of the West long remained potent, and foreign students were found in Ireland in the eleventh and twelfth centuries as well as in the sixth and seventh. Aldhelm's petulant outburst in the seventh century over the students who neglected the English schools and flocked to Ireland is matched by parallel testimony in the eleventh century. "Why does Ireland," writes Aldhelm to three English students just returned from Ireland, "pride herself on a sort of priority in that such numbers of students flock there from England?" On the other hand we have the biographer of Sulger in the eleventh century telling us how he went to Ireland to study "after the fashion of his ancestors."

CHAPTER VI

LAY SCHOOLS AND SCHOOLS OF PHILOSOPHY

1. Professional and Lay Education in Ireland. 2. Synod of Drumceat, 575 A. D. 3. Original and Independent Culture. 4. Columbanus and Gregory—"Irish Ancients Who Were Philosophers."

1. Professional and Lay Education in Ireland

THE evidence that has been adduced will give an idea of the number of laymen attending the monastic universities in Ireland, and the facts are plain that Irishmen holding civil and military positions and having no clerical or monastic status were men of cultivated intellect and gained high distinction in studies that outside of Ireland were regarded as the special preserve of clerics. The idea of the nobleman or soldier or merchant or other person not an ecclesiastic cultivating letters was almost unknown to continental Europe in the Middle Ages even in the East. But it was an idea as familiar to the Irish as to the Athenians in the age of Pericles or to the Romans under the earliest Cæsars. It was an idea, not imported with Greco-Roman culture, but indigenously handed down from the pagan era, and an idea that continued to gain development following the Christianization of the island.

In addition therefore to the larger centers of learning on which the indestructible renown of Ireland is based as the medieval home of saints and scholars there were the more distinctively Irish schools, having fewer pupils, but multiplied all over the island. These schools were devoted to purely secular learning, and in them the pas-

sionate attachment of the Irish people to their language,
their literature, their laws, the preservation of their histories and genealogies, the development of their art and
the historic elements of their distinctive civilization, found
full expression. To read, write and speak in its fulness
and precision the Irish language, to learn Irish grammar
and the rules of poetical composition, to master geography
and history, especially the geography and history of
Ireland, and to acquire a knowledge of Irish poetry and of
the Irish epic tales—such was the curriculum of these lay
schools in so far as they aimed at a liberal or professional
education in the field of Irish studies. There were schools
of the brehons, the bards, and the seanchaidhe or historians, there were schools of medicine, and schools of the
military art, these last not dissimilar to the gymnasia of
Athens where Plato and Aristotle first taught. These
schools of the seanchaidhe, the poets and the bards had
a curriculum founded on the teaching transmitted from
the Druids, and that teaching was largely confined to the
Irish studies enumerated above. To these studies the
professional schools added the study of law, of medicine,
or of the military art as the case might be.

The ideal of secular schools, presided over by lay professors, and attended by lay students, devoted to purely
lay and professional studies, is an ideal so foreign to the
spirit of the Middle Ages, and particularly to the spirit
of the governors of the Christian church in the early
part of those ages, that considerable skepticism appears
quite natural in respect to their existence in Ireland. But
the truth is that the proofs bearing on the activity of
these schools are as copious and convincing as in the case
of those larger Irish establishments the intellectual leaders
of which were honored throughout Christendom and in

relation to the age in which they lived were to be counted amongst the greatest philosophers and preceptors the world has known.

Irish records—annals, tales, and treatises—contain numerous references to these Irish lay schools, but the old Irish law tracts, some of which have in recent years been edited and published,[1] furnish us with information in regard to them more precise than the evidence found in any other source. They outline the duties which the master owes his pupils, and the return which the pupils owe the master. They describe the proper plan and arrangements of the schools, their different divisions and locations. They are exceedingly minute in describing the curriculum, the number of years proper to the course of studies, the studies themselves, the varying learned degrees and the accomplishments they represent. We learn for example that a lay college comprised three distinct establishments, housed in three different buildings, grouped according to a custom that came down from pagan times. We find references to the college libraries, as in the case of Dallan Forgaill (sixth century), celebrated as the contemporary and elegist of Columcille, who in the Book of Leinster is represented as saying: "Among the schools with libraries (etir scoluib scripta) thou hast read the mysteries of the Ro-sualt."[2]

We learn that the master owed the student "instruction without reservation and correction without harshness" as well as gratuitous maintenance, if too poor to support himself. This hospitality was as liberally dispensed to the foreigner as to the Irish themselves. Thus Bede tells us, as before noted, that a great many of the higher and

[1] Sequel to Crith Gabhlach, Brehon Laws IV. Also Brehon Laws V, 27 (Small Primer) and II, p. 18 seq. See Joyce's Social History, Vol. I, Ch. XI, p. 417 seq., where details and references are copious.
[2] Silva Gadelica, 480. ii; 527.

lower classes of the English lived in Ireland in his day for the sake of study, and while some of them became monks, others preferred to give themselves over to getting an education, passing from one professor's house to another. These foreigners, Bede adds, were cheerfully received by the Irish, who provided them with food and shelter, books and teaching, without payment of any kind.[1] Doubtless most of these Anglo-Saxon students pursued their studies in the monastic colleges, but others must have studied in the lay schools as well. They would all carry a knowledge of Irish and of Irish poetry back to their own country and we have to keep facts such as these in mind in considering the early sources of English literature.

The masters, according to the old Irish law tracts, were also answerable for the misdeeds of the students, except in one case only, namely, when the scholar was a foreigner and paid for his food and education. The degrees of wisdom were given in the lay schools as in the monastic schools, and the laws describe these learned degrees minutely, giving the Irish name of each, and the number of years of study required to attain them. Thus the highest degree in poetry, as in other branches of study, was the ollamh (ollave), and then after one another, according to their rank, came the Cli, the Cana, the Doss, the MacFuirmeadh, and the Forloc. The students pursued their learning for twelve years or perhaps more. At last when a poet graduated as an ollamh he knew 350 kinds of versification and was able to repeat 250 prime stories and a hundred stories of the second rank. We still have the remains of the books from which the poets drew their knowledge.[2]

[1] Ec. Hist., Book III, XXVII.
[2] Book of Ballymote, H. 2.12, a parchment MS. in Trinity College, Dublin. See Hyde, MacTernan Prize Essays II, Irish Poetry, p. 65.

2. SYNOD OF DRUMCEAT, 575 A. D.

As students in Ireland, both Irish and foreign, who so desired, were not only taught but supported gratuitously, their numbers became in time so burdensome to the country—that legislation on the subject was found necessary as early as the imperial parliament and synod of Drumceat, A. D. 575. At this celebrated parliament, to attend which Columcille and King Aidan voyaged with numerous retinues from Scotland, lands were formally set apart for the endowment of some of the educational establishments, which survived as public institutions down to the English destructions of the seventeenth century.

The secular education of Ireland was reorganized by this parliament which erected a chief bardic seminary or college for each of the five kingdoms, and under each of these mother establishments a group of minor schools, one in each tuath or cantred, all liberally endowed. The heads of these schools were ollaves of poetry and literature and were all laymen.[1] The curriculum included law, history, antiquities, poetry, and other Irish studies and, as the arts and professions in Ireland were largely hereditary, these schools were often presided over by members of the same family for generations.[2]

At this same parliament, over which the High Monarch presided,[3] the Bardic Order in Ireland was largely deprived of its extraordinary privileges and wealth, which had begun to make it a burden to the people. At this time, Keating tells us, nearly a third of the

[1] O'Curry, Manners and Customs, I, 78.

[2] See, for example, Hy Fiachrach, 79 and 167, bottom; Keating, Hist. 455.

[3] Numerous other measures, including a grant of self determination to the Irish kingdom of Scotland, were enacted at Drumceat. Following the fall of Temhair or Tara, as the legislative capital of Ireland, the Irish parliaments held their sessions at various centers, such as Usnach, Tailtenn, and Drumceat.

men of Erin belonged to the poetic order, but the parliament reduced the numbers, allowing only to each provincial prince and to each lord of a cantred one registered ollave or professor. On these ollaves it was ordained that their patrons should settle an hereditary revenue.[1]

Despite restrictions the literary profession continued to enjoy great wealth. Some idea of the style of living of the learned professions may be gathered from the income enjoyed by the literati of Tir Conaill (present county Donegal). It has been computed that no less than the amount represented by two thousand pounds sterling or ten thousand dollars was set aside annually in this small state for the maintenance of the class.

It has been ascertained from the public legal records that the rental of the landed properties of several of these professors of literature would at the present day amount to upwards of four or five hundred pounds sterling or two thousand five hundred dollars annually, besides the guerdons they received from the ruling sovereigns and princes. Many of them are stated to have maintained three or four schools on their estates, at which pupils were boarded and educated gratuitously.[2] The Irish Triads mention as the "three coffers whose depth is not known" —"the coffers of a chieftain, of the church, of the privileged poet."

3. ORIGINAL AND INDEPENDENT CULTURE

The light thus shed on the prosecution of the ordinary studies of the schools, on the cultivation and transmission of the liberal arts, on the devotion to music and poetry and history and literature and the concomitant depart-

1 See Trans. Ossianic Society, Vol. V, xxxi.
2 See Trans. Ossianic Society, Vol. V, xxii.

ments of learning, will therefore be admitted as not lacking in clearness. But is there any evidence that the Irish intellectuals went further than this? Did their studies ever soar above the mechanical tradition of Bede and Rhabanus Maur in the West or of Choeroboscus and Photius in the East? Did they, like them, merely learn by rote what had been handed down to them by Greek and Roman teachers and pass it on to newer generations? Is there any evidence of an Irish independent culture, of a self-sustaining mental cultivation, of a development and expansion of knowledge, of any addition of learning, and of the employment of the varied powers of the mind in the investigation of new fields of thought, and the fertilization of new ideas? It would indeed be remarkable that an Ireland capable of improvising the habitations and paraphernalia of knowledge as no other land was able to improvise them and of maintaining its educational organizations through periods of time of which no other people before them could show a like record, should not have added to the stores of knowledge represented by Greco-Roman and Christian learning.

Undoubtedly Ireland so added. But we must remember that Ireland's main energies were directed along two important channels—namely, the preservation and development of her own immemorial culture and civilization, as distinct and unique as the civilization of Greece or Egypt, and the transmission to the newer peoples of Europe of Greco-Roman learning transfused by the doctrines of Christianity. Her devotion to her own culture has enriched the world with an heroic literature even in its fragments inferior only to the Grecian, and the example of that devotion probably preserved to the world such monuments of early literature as at this day belong to

68

England, to Germany, and to Scandinavia. Had Irish influence in the young ages of her faith been directed to the destruction of pagan literature and art, as it was directed in some other lands, the early literature of Ireland as of these other countries might have been lost to the world forever. But it was not so directed, and indeed it was in those very ages of faith, when Christian enthusiasm flamed throughout the island, that the Irish epics, having received their shaping in the mouths and minds of the people through unnumbered generations, were first committed to writing and to literary recension.

As to Ireland's cultivation of philosophy the great name of Johannes Scotus Eriugena constitutes a sufficient answer. His works have been preserved to us because they existed on the Continent. The works of the schools of thought he represented have been destroyed because those works remained in Ireland. Of the Irish philosophers and the Irish schools of philosophy contemporary with him he speaks indeed in a manner reminiscent of the interlocutions to which we are accustomed in the dialogs of Plato, and indeed it is on the strength of his verbal modes and his knowledge of Greek that the false tradition of his having been a student in Athens was built up. "I quitted," says he, speaking of his youth in Ireland, "no place or temple where the philosophers were accustomed to compose or deposit their secret works without inspecting it; and there was not one amongst such scholars, as might be supposed to possess any knowledge of philosophical writings, whom I did not question."[1]

We can compute the strength and originality of a Johannes Scotus Eriugena and his circle and the speculative activity of the schools that produced him by re-

[1] Wood's Hist. and Antiquit, Univers. Oxon. in fol. 1674, Vol. I, p. 15.

calling that the Byzantines with all the accumulations of Greek learning at their command were unable to produce anyone like him. Photius, the contemporary of Eriugena, and like him a tutor to emperors, despite his many-sided erudition and devotion to Aristotelian studies, which illumined a Constantinopolitan age of darkness paralleling the age of iron, of lead and of gloom (saeculum . . . . ferreum . . . . plumbeum . . . . obscurum) in the West, is more easily comparable to Rhabanus Maur or Servatus Lupus than to Eriugena. Even Psellus, whose very profession was philosophy and who revived the study of Plato as far as Arabia and the distant East, is dwarfed to the dimensions of a mere pedagog when tested by the standards of the mighty Irishman, who, in an age hopelessly bridled by authority and tradition, worked out a theory of the universe in the untrammeled spirit of Augustine and the noblest of the ancients unknown in that age save in the Irish schools.

4. COLUMBANUS AND GREGORY—"IRISH ANCIENTS WHO WERE PHILOSOPHERS"

Johannes Scotus Eriugena wrote late in the ninth century, but "philosophus" had become almost as synonymous as "peregrinus" for the Scotus or Irishman at a much earlier date. Midway in the sixth century when Columbanus was a youth we find the scientists of the Irish schools rating themselves as very much superior to those of Gaul or Italy. Thus Columbanus in one of the letters to Gregory, written at Luxeuil, tells the pope that the Irish astronomers and computists held in very low esteem Victorius of Aquitaine, whose cycle, drawn up in 497 A. D., had been adopted in the Gallican and other churches. "For know thou" he says writing

c. 598 A. D., "that by our masters and the Irish ancients, who were philosophers and most wise computists in constructing calculations, Victorius was not received, but held more worthy of ridicule or of excuse than as carrying authority."[1]

In this letter to Gregory, as elsewhere, the extraordinary self-assurance of the Irish schoolmen, which was so long to exercise the popes and the religious world of Europe generally, breaks out thus early despite the overflowing affection and reverence manifestly cherished by the wonderful old monk for the chair of Peter. With all the consciousness of a superior culture he tells the great pope, who was little accustomed to counsel so imperiously given, what would be the Irish attitude if Irish opinion on Easter observance was not endorsed by him: "For I frankly acknowledge to thee that anyone who goes against the authority of Saint Hieronymus will be repudiated as a heretic among the churches of the West; for they accommodate their faith in all respects unhesitatingly to him with regard to the Divine Scriptures." And he adds, "And if, as I have heard from thy holy Candidus,[2] thou shouldst be disposed to say in reply that things confirmed by ancient usage cannot be changed, error is manifestly ancient, but truth which reproves it is ever more ancient still." To Haureau the Latin poems of Columbanus "read like the works of an entire pagan" while his monastic rule "appears to have been composed by a league of philosophers."[3]

[1] St. Col. to Greg. Epist. CXXVII, Bk. IX Registrum Epistolarum, C. 598-9; also in Collectanea Sacra, Fleming; and Migne, Pat. Lat., LXXVII, 1061-6 LXXX, 263.

[2] Candidus was Pope Gregory's representative traveling in Gaul. He appears to have spent some time at the foundation of Columbanus at Luxeuil, as appear from their own words. Augustine and the other missionaries sent to England also stayed at Luxeuil. Columbanus and his Irish colleagues, who spent some time in England trying to reclaim the natives, appear not to have minimized the bad reputation of the Islanders in the mind of Augustine.

[3] Singularités, chap. 1.

Columbanus (543-615) in Ireland and Gaul was the contemporary of Cassiodorus (490-585) in Ravenna and Squillace. Cassiodorus, who showed a twofold devotion to the Christian and heathen classics, peculiar in that age to Irish scholars almost alone, was the contemporary in the East of the Emperor Justinian and of Priscian, and in the West of Odoacer, successor to Romulus Augustus, the last Roman emperor, and Boethius—"the last of the Romans whom Cato or Tully could have acknowledged for their countrymen."[1] Boethius and Cassiodorus were the final representatives of Roman learning as Columbanus was one of the first representatives of Irish learning in Gaul and Italy.[2] Thus the affiliation of Irish culture with the ancient Greek and Roman cultures is as visible and authentic as the position, revealed by Zeuss, of the Irish language in the inner shrine of the Indo-European group as sister to Latin and Greek. The Teutonic wedge of barbarism, thrust in the fifth century into a triple association that had been maturing for centuries, while it seriously impaired, did not destroy the continuity in the tradition of civilization.

[1] Gibbon, Bury's, IV, 197-204, C. 395.

[2] The activity of the continental Celt in Roman literature began early. Virgil was a native of Gallia Cisalpina—his name is cognate with the Irish Fearghil, anglicized Farrell. Livy, Catullus, Cornelius Nepos, the elder and younger Pliny, Domitius Afer, Marcus Aper, Favorinus, Ausonius, Numantianus, Sulpicius Severus, Sidonius Appollinarius were other Gauls or Celts who attained fame in Latin letters. The Celts also gave Rome several of its emperors—Claudius, Caracalla, Antoninus, Galba, Otto, Vitellus, Vespasian, Domitian, and Maximus, this last a Briton. The Celtic tongue died out in Gaul in the fourth century, but St. Jerome intimates that the Galatians in Asia Minor still spoke it in his day: "While the Galatians in common with the whole East speak Greek, their own language is almost identical with that of the Treviri." (Pref. Book II, Comment. on Galatians.)

CHAPTER VII

TRANSMITTING THE TREASURES OF ANCIENT LEARNING

1. High Culture of Ireland a Living Reality. 2. Destruction of Irish Libraries. 3. Irish Genealogy of Carolingian Schools. 4. Organizing the City and Christian Society.

1. HIGH CULTURE OF IRELAND A LIVING REALITY

WE have thus brought up before our eyes an Ireland whose authentic right to the varied titles traditionally bestowed upon her as the hearthstone of civilization, the school of the West, and the habitation of learning, is based on a living reality and not on an idle dream. There was hardly a city or clan in Ireland that had not its schools. There was hardly a valley, a hill, or an isle that did not resound to the voices of teacher and student. And all this ardor of learning, this everlasting contest of mind with mind, this endless catechizing and philosophizing and multiplication of books and succession of dynasties of hereditary teachers and of school on school was peculiar and unique to Ireland alone, save where Irishmen sought to reconstruct abroad and gradually succeeded in there reconstructing the intellectual life and world they had known at home. To the Irish in the West and the Byzantines in the East had Fate thus committed as trustees that Greco-Roman civilization in which had been summed up the heritage of all preceding ages.

It is a circumstance eloquent of the destructions that have been the rule in Ireland in modern times that of the varied mass of literature produced by her when her intellectual supremacy wielded undisputed sway and her writers were most prolific the merest fragments have been preserved in Ireland itself. A few examples of the Gospels in Latin, their unearthly beauty a slender passport to posterity, still remain to us from that age. One of them, the Book of Armagh, has continuous narratives in the Irish of the period, and others, like the Book of Deir, have Irish interlinear and marginal notes. But of the Irish literature dating from the sixth or seventh to the eleventh century the total is scanty in Ireland. Even the later monuments, the Book of the Dun Cow, the Book of Leinster and the others, were, like the Ardagh Chalice and the Tara Brooch, only saved by first being lost. These encyclopedic vellums contain many copies of works belonging to an earlier age, but we have to go, not to Ireland itself, but to the Continent for the earlier authentic literature in Irish and Latin produced in Ireland or abroad in the medieval period prior to the eleventh century.

The Irish libraries abroad, St. Gall, Rebais, Bobbio and others, almost all founded in the seventh century, proved the great treasure houses of the Roman classics. In Ireland itself the mother libraries of St. Gall, Rebais and Bobbio, went down in the common ruin of Irish civilization. On the Continent the Lombard and the Hun showed themselves less destructive than the Tudor and Cromwellian Englishman in Ireland. Eighty-one years before the English reformers sent by Henry VIII began the first war of conquest on Ireland that was to have a measure of success,[1] Constantinople fell before the Turk.

---

[1] The so-called "Norman Invasion" or "Conquest" of Ireland was in reality an emigration from Britain of Norman, French, Cambro-French, Flemish—all French-speaking—who began to become Irish as soon as they landed, tho a foreign colony or pale containing newcomers existed on the coast. This also tended to disappear.

But the Turk showed himself no Vandal in respect to
the Greek manuscripts of the Byzantine cities, which
must have been anathema to him. He sold them by the
cartload; he did not deliberately destroy them. But the
tradition of destruction which the Englishmen carried
with him to Ireland embraced everything except what
was capable of being turned to the use of the Englishman himself. The libraries attached to the great monastic
universities we know were very large. Their contents
were in the main in Irish and in Latin. There may
have been a goodly number of Greek manuscripts also,
for the evidence is that the Irish scholars were in possession of Greek works unknown on the Continent, for example, the Timæus of Plato, their quotations from which are
independent of the translation of Chalcidius.

The testimony is that the Irish were in possession of
Latin manuscripts that did not otherwise exist out of
Ireland. The Irish colony of literati in Liège in the
time of the Emperor Lothair II were in possession for
example of the In Pisonem of Cicero, a work of which
only one other copy existed on the Continent. The oldest
Horace is an Irish manuscript now at Berne. The oldest
Ovid is a Cambro-Irish manuscript now at Cambridge.
The oldest manuscript in Switzerland, which is an em-
porium of ancient manuscripts, is not a Roman or a Greek
manuscript, but an Irish manuscript. It is a biography
of a sixth century Irishman, written in Latin by a seventh
century Irishman, and transcribed by an eighth century
Irishman. It is certain that of the 628 Latin authors
whose works have been totally lost, and that of the 107
more Latin authors whose works only partially survive,
many examples must have existed in the medieval Irish
libraries. We have the testimony of Alcuin as to the

number of books in the library of York in his day. If a library so much superior to any on the Continent could have been gathered together in England with its ever insurgent barbarism which swept schools and libraries away in a night we can well imagine, apart from the evidence, how wealthy and numerous must have been the libraries in Ireland where the great academies grew in maturity from age to age in the midst of an ever-developing national civilization.

Ludwig Traube draws attention to the numerous hand libraries which the Irish schoolmen carried with them to the Continent and points to the probability that Sedulius Scotus, in making his remarkable collection of excerpts from the Roman classics in the manuscript originally owned by Nicolaus von Cues, used manuscripts written in Ireland, since many of these ancient works were unknown on the Continent. His copy of the De Re Militari of Vegetius was procured by him on the Continent, but he also quotes from almost unknown works of Cicero, Lactantius, Valerius, and numerous other authors. While it appears that Sedulius made excerpts from some of the manuscripts in Liège, it appears also likely that other excerpts were made by him as a student in the course of his reading in his alma mater in Ireland.[1]

2. Destruction of Irish Libraries

But it was, says Webb, "the object of the English government to discover and destroy all remains of the literature of the Irish in order more fully to eradicate from their minds every trace of their ancient independence." The men whom the English government sent on their mission of destruction and dispossession to Ireland in the

[1] Kl. Bay. Akad., Abhandl., 1891, p. 366.

sixteenth century were no more educated men than the
men she sent in the nineteenth and sends in the twentieth.
It is not likely that in days when not one Englishman
in a hundred could read or write that these emissaries
of barbarism would be able to discriminate between an
Irish and a Latin manuscript. To them they were both
Greek. Unlike "ye sinfulle jewelles" they were not car-
ried away or transmuted, but blindly destroyed. Had the
Irish manuscripts, the Hiberno-Latin and the Hiberno-
Greek manuscripts, now peacefully reposing in Switzerland and elsewhere, had the libraries of Bobbio, Rebais,
Fleury and St. Gall, been in Ireland, to-day hardly
a vestige of them would remain. Had Johannes Scotus
Eriugena, the greatest thinker in the West or East from
Augustine to Aquinas, written his books at home in
Ireland, they would have been destroyed and we would
never have known of his existence. We can measure the
loss to civilization now; we could not have measured it
then. The psalm-singing Englishman has been able to
give the heathen Vandal lessons in vandalism.

For these reasons the work of the people of Ireland in
the medieval age cannot be judged by the standards in
respect to number and quality of existing monuments as
in other lands. In no other land has there been a foreign
government established in power interested in the destruction of the memorials and monuments of the national
civilization. The Romans when they conquered Greece
did not destroy Greek architecture or Greek literature.
But the English in Ireland decided that the spoliation
and abasement of the Irish nation was a necessary condition of their own aggrandizement. We have to realize
therefore that the literary monuments that have come
down to us from medieval Ireland, noble and interesting

as they are, form but a very small fraction of what existed even as late as the sixteenth century. What remains is merely what escaped destroyers bent on the destruction of everything. If for example it is remarked that Irish manuscripts in Latin of the ninth century are numerous, while Irish manuscripts in Latin of the tenth century are rare, it does not follow that there were not a large number of Irishmen writing in Latin in the tenth as well as in the ninth century. It only follows that of the ninth century manuscripts more escaped the destroyer than of the tenth century manuscripts. If it is remarked that despite the medieval Irish knowledge of Greek the documentary evidences of that knowledge should be more conspicuous on the Continent than in Ireland, it does not follow that the Irish abroad were better Greek scholars than Irishmen in Ireland, it only follows that the Hiberno-Greek manuscripts abroad escaped the destruction to which they would have been doomed in Ireland. If it is a matter for comment that the Anglo-Saxons, despite their continued barbarism, produced an ecclesiastical historian like Bede, while the Irish, despite their superior and sustained culture, did not, it does not follow that there were not Irish ecclesiastical historians. That there were not such appears in the highest degree improbable.[1] We only know that whether one Irish Bede or more existed the probabilities are that his works would have been destroyed. The literary monuments that escaped the Danes in Ireland were later destroyed by the English in so far as they were able to discover them. We have historical narratives in Ireland belonging both to the seventh and eighth cen-

[1] Adamnan (624-703) is said to have written an historia Hibernorum ab origine ad sua tempora, mentioned by Ward, Vita Rumoldi, p. 218, Lovan, 1662. There were numerous other kinds of histories. In the "Annals of Ulster" we read at the year 439, "Chronicon magnum scriptum est"; at 467, "sic in libro Cuanach inveni"; at 482, "ut Cuana scripsit"; at 507, "Secundum librum Mochod."

turies. They are fragments representing a large historical literature that has perished.[1]

3. IRISH GENEALOGY OF CAROLINGIAN SCHOOLS

We shall see as we proceed in what manner and by what methods the medieval Irish trustees of civilization transmitted to the newer races the treasure in their keeping. But already one of the paths of that transmission lies open before us. Speculation has been rife as to the source from which Charlemagne and his contemporaries drew their inspiration in the establishment of the cathedral and monastic schools of their time. The speculation has invariably ended in a blind alley, for the average historian, knowing little of Ireland and her civilization, and seeking for his phenomena an ancestry in the easily accessible where no ancestry existed, has been content to construct a genealogy with its medieval generations dubious or missing. Yet the maternal relation of Ireland to the episcopal schools and seminaries of the Carolingian era is plainly as authentic as her relation of maternity to the men who conducted them. Whether all these men were Irish or not does not affect that relation. They were almost all Irish in any case, and such of them as were not, like Alcuin and Rhabanus Maur, were representatives of Irish learning.

We know that in the Carolingian era Irish scholars swamped Gaul and Germany and Italy. For over the two preceding centuries they had been sounding in European lands the evangel of a higher intellectual life. No thinker of the time could escape their influence and the

1 "The books of saga, poetry and annals that have come down to our day, though so vastly more ancient and numerous than anything the rest of western Europe has to show, are yet an almost inappreciable fragment of the literature that at one time existed in Ireland": (Hyde, Literary History of Ireland, 263).

effects of their work, and whether the personages were monarchs like Charlemagne, who was their life-long admirer, or were like Theodulph of Orleans, who was in constant conflict with them, or the monks of St. Gall, who associated with and were directed by them, or the bishops of France and Germany, who were incessantly investigating them in council, or the popes in Rome, who got all sorts of reports about them, to these Irishmen and to none other could they look as intellectual leaders and advisers.

It was while the Irish Ferghil was bishop of Salzburg, defending against less informed theologians his theory of the rotundity of the earth and the existence of the Antipodes, that the Council of Bavaria in 774 issued its first pronouncement on the establishment of schools. It was while Theodulph of Orleans was smarting under the rapier-like thrusts of the Irishmen at the court of Charlemagne of whose culture he gave voice to an envy less unsophisticated than Aldhelm's, that he issued his capitularies for grammar schools where the teaching was to be almost as hospitable and gratuitous as in Ireland itself. It was while all these influences were in the air that Pope Eugenius II for the first time in history issued in 826 A. D. bulls enjoining throughout Gaul and the rest of Christendom schools of the kind that had then been in existence in Ireland for centuries. It was when Louis the Pious, harking back to a less enlightened tradition among Christian governors, showed a disposition to disregard the counsel of the popes that the bishops of France, again for the first time on record, recalled and seconded the papal precepts on education and had them in turn confirmed by a later pope. It was in direct condemnation of the "negligence and indolence" of his father, the Emperor Louis, that Lothaire, King of Italy, pupil of the Irish Clement, issued in 825 A. D. his important edict assigning Pavia, Turin, Cremona, Piacenza, Florence and other places for central schools, some of them with Irish teachers like Dungal, to whom scholars from the surrounding districts, mentioned in detail, were to resort. Thus after centuries of unwearied effort Irish scholars who presided at the opening of the ninth century in Gaul, Germany and Italy, saw the flourishing of the seed which generations of Irishmen in those lands had been sowing before them.

Yet it is at the Irish foundation of St. Gall that we find the first indubitable evidence of the actual education not only of youth intended for the priesthood or the cloister, but of the Irish fashion of educating lay youths as well. Of the ideal of lay or secular schools with lay students taught by lay teachers, such as existed in Ireland, we have to come almost to modern times to find an example in other lands. But St. Gall at any rate made the nearest approach to it at this early period and that approach we see in actual working during a period of renaissance when Irish teachers like Moengal and Marcus were the life and soul of the celebrated center of learning and cradle of German civilization.

Thus the remarkable extant plan of the monastery of St. Gall, c. 820 A. D., which Dr. Ferdinand Keller unearthed in 1844,[1] shows an inner school of the novices or oblati, i. e., the boys offered to God, and an outer school, providing for about 150 boarders, for young gentlemen intended for civil and military life.[2] At the time

[1] There is a facsimile and description of the plan in the Archæological Journal, 1848, vol. 5. (London).

[2] Irish proficiency in the secular studies was well recognized on the Continent. Thus Walafrid Strabo (d. 849) says that Erlebald, of noble birth and abbot of Reichenau (822-838) was first instructed at Reichenau by Heito and afterwards was sent with a companion to some learned Irish instructor for training in the secular branches of the sciences and arts.

of its greatest activity both schools were presided over by the Irish scholar, Moengal.

It is to be noted that in this ancient pictorial description of the monastery of St. Gall, which was probably as near an approach to an Irish monastery as then existed on the Continent, the entire establishment resembles a town composed of isolated houses with streets running between them. The chief building was the basilica and on two sides of its semicircular atrium two Irish round towers lifted themselves into the air, with altars to the archangels Michael and Gabriel, and conical roofs and ornamental finials. In the basilica itself altars dedicated to St. Columbanus and St. Benedict were placed side by side, and a digest of the rules of both was observed by the cœnobites. The novices' school is shown as a replica of the monastery, complete in all parts, near the church and the infirmary of the monks, while the secular school was separated from the cloisters and was near the street and the guest hall. Close to the church were the library and scriptorium, the calefactory with dormitory over abbot's house, and refectory.

4. ORGANIZING THE CITY AND CHRISTIAN SOCIETY

But, as has been observed, the Irish monastery was a city in itself, often with a population of many thousands, not merely cultivating all the studies, but practising all the arts and industries. Here at St. Gall we find provision for all these things. There are kitchen, doctor's house, house for bloodletting, bakehouse, brewhouse, mills and factories with accommodation for all the mechanical arts. Then there are the outer departments with workshops, threshing floor, kiln, stables, cowsheds, goatsheds, pigsties, sheepfold, servants' and workmen's sleeping quarters, gardener's house, hen and duck house, poultrykeeper's house, baths and cemetery. There is also an immense garden with all sorts of medicinal herbs, and incidentally we learn from a Latin poem in the library the name of the Irishman who laid the gardens out. So the monastery was not merely a school, library and scriptorium, but a world of industry, a university in the large sense of to-day, a living metropolis, teaching the nation in which it was set the art of civic life and work.

Indeed Wattenbach assigns to the medieval Irish the leading place in the organization of Christian society, declaring them to have first supplied the defect in the organization of society which arose from the development of cities, for until their time monasteries had been founded only in the solitude of the country, excepting such as were attached to episcopal seats.[1] Wattenbach found the inspiration for this observation in the Irish foundations which Marianus Scotus and his countrymen established in Germany in the middle of the eleventh century. Thus the merchants from Ratisbon who founded Vienna knew no rest till a colony of Irish monks, whom Ratisbon citizens had helped in the building of their first monastery, had come and settled among them. But it is to be noted as part of the Irish contribution to modern civilization that just as at an earlier period Irishmen had founded cities like St. Gall by building on sites in the solitude, so at a later period they supplied the organizing element in cities in the origin of which they had at first no part.

[1] See the Ulster Journal of Archæology, Old Series, VII, 297.

CHAPTER VIII

WESTERN CIVILIZATION'S BASE OF SUPPLY

1. Military Strength of Medieval Ireland. 2. Land of Enormous Wealth. 3. Celtic, Greek, and Roman Europe. 4. Ireland's Abundance of Gold. 5. Exodus of Irish Scholars. 6. Parallel Promulgation of Civilization and Christianity.

1. MILITARY STRENGTH OF MEDIEVAL IRELAND

BEHIND the men engaged in the great work of rehabilitation abroad lay as base of supply an Ireland very different from the Ireland familiar to us in recent times. Medieval Ireland was not only the freest and most enlightened country on earth, but also the richest and almost the most compact and powerful. It is inconceivable that the men of Ireland could have done the things they did unless she was all these things. But we do not need to argue back from the work of Irish scholars and missionaries abroad. We have all the data necessary to a complete presentment of Ireland itself and the deeds performed by her. When the first Dane appeared on her coasts at the close of the eighth century Ireland could look back on an authentic history of at least a thousand years during which no foreigner had dared to violate her by attempted occupation. Dating from that very century there is still, as has been noted, extant a history in the old Irish tongue which speaks of the last invasion of Ireland by the Gaels themselves and of the establishment of the kingdom in the time of Alexander the Great.[1] From that time forward the Gaels of Ireland had never known any rule but Irish rule, administered through all the clans, under a single royal

1 See p. 29 supra.

84

dynasty and government, called in history the Milesian, that still endured from the time when the last migration of the Gaels entered the island.

The prolonged period of peace and prosperity did not enervate the Irish people. In 1014 A. D. at Clontarf they crushed the Danes who had conquered both France and England. Four years later at Carham the Irish forces inhabiting Scotland inflicted on the English a defeat more decisive than Bannockburn. Repeatedly the Irish had appeared in the way of conquering the entire British Isles. As the Roman forces in the fifth century withdrew from Britain Irish armies followed them to the foot of the Alps, Irish fleets held the western seas, and what is now England was almost entirely Irish ground. But Christianity came to Ireland in the very midst of these events and from that time forth no raiding expedition went forth from the island. Again, following the battle of Carham in 1018 A. D., the northern counties of England became ground so debatable that they were not included in the Domesday Book of the Conqueror. Had the Franks from Normandy and the contiguous French provinces not appeared in 1066 A. D. at Hastings to give the *coup de grâce* to the demoralized English the chances are that the finishing blow would have been delivered by the Irish of the north, and southern Britain, first British, then Roman, Saxon, and Danish, might like Wales and Scotland have become enduringly Irish.

The Norman French and the Flemings who began to emigrate to Ireland[1] about a century after their conquest of England came in contact with a people at least quite the equal in culture and manners of any on the Continent

[1] This French entry into Ireland is often spoken of as an "English" invasion and as signalizing the beginning of "English rule" in Ireland. The absurdity of this will be apparent.

and in whom an immemorial pride of family and birth and an unbroken sense of freedom had made obeisance to any conqueror inconceivable.[1] The newcomers speedily succumbed to Irish civilization and, dropping their French speech, dress and customs, sought matrimonial alliances with Irish families of equal station and became, in the old phrase, more Irish than the Irish themselves.

Very different had been the behavior of these Frenchmen in England. The Anglo-Saxon had not taken to civilization kindly. The vices, the brutalities, the indolences and sensualities of an intractable barbarism weighed him down, and despite six centuries of wandering among the habitations of Roman civilization, and despite almost five centuries of Christianity, the Englishman still remained the semi-savage, using his intervals of liberty from one oppression or another to alternate excesses of swinish self-indulgence with suicidal orgies of internecine strife.[2] To his French conqueror the medieval Englishman was simply an evil-smelling boor and hind, fit only for low and menial tasks; and to such tasks he was henceforth condemned.[3] Thus the Anglo-Saxon, trodden into resistless clay by the Dane, was trodden

[1] Nothing more surprized these French and Flemish settlers from Britain, accustomed as they were to the cringing servility of the English produced by long slavery and what contemporary Norman French writers call innate Saxon dulness, than the natural boldness and readiness of the ordinary Irish in speaking even in the presence of their princes and nobles. (Giraldus Cambrensis, "Description of Wales," b. i., C. 15; but the remarks apply to the Irish in a greater degree.)

[2] Green is more candid in his correspondence than in his history. Thus in writing to Freeman about his projected history to the Norman conquest, he remarks: "As I read it, the story isn't a pretty one, and the people are not pretty people to write about." Stubbs had told him that people would not read anything in English history before 1066. He refused to bow to this doom and managed to throw over the facts and absence of facts a veil of romance. (Letters of John Richard Green, 478.)

[3] "Who dare compare the English, the most degraded of all the races under Heaven, with the Welsh?" writes Giraldus Cambrensis (1147-1222). "In their own country they are serfs, the veriest slaves of the Normans. In ours (Wales) whom else have we for our shepherds, herdsmen, cobblers, skinners, cleaners of our dog-kennels, aye, even of our privies, but Englishmen?" (Opera, ed. by J. S. Brewer, vol. III, p. 27.)

down into a deeper well of degradation by the Frank, by whom he was classed with the cattle in the field and to whom he remained as much a stranger. We can judge in no clearer way of the military prowess of the Irish and of the strength and brilliancy of their civilization than by their contrasted effect on the all-conquering Frank from Normandy, Anjou and Aquitaine, whose name had become a terror in England, Sicily and in the East.

2. LAND OF ENORMOUS WEALTH

Ireland, however, was a country not only militarily powerful and highly cultured, but also a country of enormous wealth. This is evidenced, among other things, by her large population of English slaves. The English slave, as will later be shown, was as familiar a figure to the medieval Irishman as the negro slave to the southern planter in the United States in the early half of the last century. These English slaves were carried in cargoes to Ireland from English ports much as the negro slave was carried from Africa to America at a later epoch. Irish families of station had their Anglo-Saxon "fudirs," male and female, just as the family of the southern planter each had its "nigger." Many Irish families had large numbers of these English slaves, and herds of them were often included in the tributes, donations and stipends that passed between one Irish family of rank and another. These English slaves were not taken in war, as some historians try to make out, the tolerance which the medieval Irishman showed to the Englishman, and the almost savage worship which the Englishman manifested towards the Irishman, rendering hostilities almost impossible.[1]

[1] During the entire period before the French conquest and after the arrival of Aidan only one act of hostility is recorded as having been perpetrated by the English against Ireland, namely, the raid made by the order of Ecgfrith, referred to by Bede, and really directed, it would seem, against the protection there afforded to Aldfrid, his half-brother and rival, who succeeded him.

The slaves were purchased in England by dealers from the degraded fathers and mothers and other more powerful relatives of the unfortunates.[1]

Much of Ireland's wealth came to her in foreign commerce, carried on from the beginning with her kindred in Gaul. That wealth was well recognized abroad. We find, among others, Walafrid Strabo writing in the ninth century of "wealthy Hibernia."[2] Doncadh, or Donatus, of Fiesole, goes very much further and gives in Latin hexameters a glowing description in the same century of Ireland's exhaustless riches.[3] In the tenth century she remained "that very wealthy country in which there are twelve cities and wide bishoprics and a king and that has its own language and Latin letters."[4]

The impression has long prevailed that Ireland had from the beginning been widely removed from the main stream of European life and that her fate had been to move around in a backwater where only the fainter wash of the larger currents reached, neither giving nor receiving much from Europe. Her position in the extreme West has nurtured this view, but the enterprise of her sons, surpassing the energy of every other nation in the West, overbore in antiquity as in the medieval era the obstacles of nature.

[1] See Appendix A.

[2] In his life of Blaithmac, monk of Iona: Blaithmac, genuit quem dives Hibernia mundo (Poetae Lat. A. C., II, 297).

[3] Migne and Poetae Latini Aevi Carolini reproduce the poem; and translations in Irish and English are given in Flannery, "For the Tongue of the Gael." See also Ossianic Society, V. p. 75.

[4] Chronicle of Ademar, Monk of Angoulême.

3. CELTIC, GREEK AND ROMAN EUROPE

The truth is that Celt, Roman and Greek lived side by side from beyond the dawn of history,[1] and no foreign element drove a wedge between them till the Saxon and Anglian tribes invaded Britain in the fifth century separating the Celts of Ireland from their continental brethren. The Irish were thus always active in the interchange of knowledge and trade, keeping close to the heart of the developing civilization of the West, whether Carthaginian, Celt, Greek or Roman was in the ascendant.[2]

Europe was Gaulish, or Celtic, before it was Roman, and when history, as revealed by what are called classical writers, dawned, a single civilization and a single speech, shading off into various dialects, prevailed from the west coast of Ireland almost to the Black Sea.[3] Thus Celtic,

[1] Modern research seems to have shown that the master race of Greece, the Achaians, whose deathless glories are enshrined in the poems of Homer, were a fairhaired race of Celtic invaders, whom the discovery of iron made irresistible, and who, descending into the Peloponnesus from the head of the Adriatic, conquered the aboriginal Pelagians or Greeks proper, and, having made of them helots, adopted the language of the subject race, as appears to be the habit of invading conquerors, when they do not bring their wives with them. (Cf. Ridgeway, "Early Age of Greece.") In like manner the Patricians of Rome appear to have been a Celtic tribe of Umbro-Sabellians, who descended from the Alps into Central Italy, conquered the aboriginal Latins or Ligurians, later known to history as the Plebeians, and who then adopted the tongue of the subject people in place of the Celtic dialect they had brought with them (see Ridgeway, "Who Were the Romans?" British Acad., Proc., 1907-8.)

[2] Thus in 1831, two hundred Roman coins were found in Ireland near the Giants' Causeway, dating from 70 A. D. to 160 A. D. Bodies have been found near Bray Head, each with a copper coin of Trajan or Hadrian on his breast. Ptolemy gives a more accurate picture of Hibernia than of Britannia, enumerating several Irish cities, three being seaports, seven inland. Tacitus describes the ports of Ireland as better known to merchants and traders than those of Britain. Juvenal's Satires attest that Irish woolen goods were sold and worn in Rome.

[3] We are dependent on Irish literature for our knowledge of ancient Europe and its Celtic world, for Ireland, outside of Greece and Rome, is the only country that has preserved a record of its life during the period of antiquity. In the Tain, the chief Irish epic, we find depicted an Irish world contemporaneous with the Rome of Sulla and Cæsar. Thus the Irish champions have much in common with the warriors of Gaul described by the Greek traveler, Posidonius, while their equipment and armor correspond with the La Tene types on the Continent. The Irish heroes, for example, still fight in chariots, war-dogs are employed, whilst the heads of the slain are carried off in triumph and slung round the necks of the horses. (See Ridgeway, First Shaping of the Cuchulain Saga, Proc., Brit. Acad., 1905-6.)

the mother of the Irish language, was sister to Latin and
Greek, and the Celtic dialects spoken in Gaul appear to
have shaded so gradually into the Italic or Latin languages spoken in the South that there hardly seems to
have been a frontier line between them.[1]

The continued intercourse of the Irish with their
Gaulish kindred soon filled Ireland with the refinements
of a luxurious civilization. "From various sources we
learn," says Gilbert, "that in those ancient times the native
dress was costly and picturesque and the habits and modes
of living of the chiefs splendid and oriental. The high-born
and wealthy wore tunics of fine linen of immense width,
girdled with gold, and with flowing sleeves after the eastern fashion. The fringed cloak, or cuchula, with a hood,
after the Arab mode, was clasped on the shoulders with
a golden brooch. Golden circlets of beautiful and classic
form, confined their long, flowing hair, crowned with
which the chiefs sat at the banquet, or went to war. Sandals upon the feet, and bracelet and signet rings, of rich
and curious workmanship, completed the costume. The
ladies wore the silken robes and flowing veils of Persia,
or rolls of linen wound round the head like the Egyptian
Isis, the hair curiously plaited down the back and fastened
with gold and silver bodkins, while the neck and arms
were profusely covered with jewels."

Thus the relics of a civilization 3,000 years old may

---

[1] The names of the chiefs of Gaul who fought with Cæsar are comprehensible in Irish: For example: Vercingetorix, Irish—Fear cinn gacha toruish,
"the man at the head of every expedition;" Dumnorix, Irish—domadh an torus,
"second person of the expedition;" Orgetorix, Irish—orra, "chief," gacha, "of
every," torus, "expedition;" Eporedorix, Irish—ab urra torus, "sire and chief
of the expedition;" Andecumborius, Irish—an te cum bothar, "ambassador,"
"man for the road;" Bellovesus, Irish—bealach fiosach, "man acquainted with
the highways;" and so on. The case is the same with the names of places:
Garonne, Irish—garbh amhan, "rough river;" Alps, Irish—ailp, "mountain;"
Sequana, Irish—seach amhan, "dividing river." The names are written down
by Cæsar as they sounded to Roman ears. (See Holder, Alt-Celtischer
Sprachschatz, Leipzig, 1896; "Irish Names in Cæsar," Catholic World, New
York, 1882.)

be still gazed upon by modern eyes in the unrivaled antiquarian collection of the Royal Irish Academy at Dublin. The circlets, lunulæ, fibulæ, torques, gorgets, tiaras, diadems, necklaces, bracelets, rings, there to be seen, nearly all of solid gold, worn by the ancient Irish, are not only costly in value, but often so singularly beautiful in the working out of minute artistic details, that modern art is not merely unable to imitate them, but is even unable to comprehend how the ancient workers in metals could accomplish works of such delicate, almost microscopic, minuteness of finish. This single Irish collection contains some five hundred ornaments of gold, a scanty remnant, miraculously recovered, of what has been lost, carried out of the country, and melted down: their weight is five hundred and seventy ounces, as compared with a weight of twenty ounces—much of it considered to be originally Irish also—in the British Museum from all England, Scotland and Wales.

4. Ireland's Abundance of Gold

These remarkable jewels, detritus rescued from great destructions, lend an air of perfect reality to the numerous passages in ancient Irish literature in which the various personages are described as wearing ornaments of gold and other precious materials. The Book of Ballymote, for example, contains a striking and almost contemporary description of Cormac, son of Airt, high monarch of Ireland (d. 266 A. D.), presiding over the parliament at Tara, in which gold ornaments figure: "Flowing and slightly curling was his golden hair, a red buckler with stars and animals of gold and fastenings of silver upon him, a crimson cloak in wide descending folds around him, fastened at his neck with precious stones, a neck torque of gold around his neck, a white shirt with a full collar and intertwined with red gold thread upon him; a girdle of gold, inlaid with precious stones, was around him; two wonderful shoes of gold with golden loops upon his feet; two spears with golden sockets in his hands, with many rivets of red bronze, and he was himself, besides, symmetrical and beautiful of form, without blemish or reproach." The passage is but typical of many in the Irish tales relating to habiliments, vestiture, weapons, and armor, which, in the case of the higher classes, were costly and splendid.

Ireland's former wealth in gold was nothing short of extraordinary. "For hundreds of years Ireland was an enormously rich country, supplying not only herself but also Britain and part of the Atlantic seaboard with gold. Such natural wealth must have produced a marked effect on the relations and culture of the Irish."[1] Giraldus Cambrensis testifies to the abundance of gold in Ireland. Montelius remarks that "Ireland's wealth of gold in the Bronze Age is amazing." "No other country possesses so much manufactured gold belonging to early and medieval times," says E. A. Smith.[2] "Ireland's original wealth of gold must have been so vast as scarcely to be credited," says an authority already quoted.[3] It has been repeatedly remarked that in the literature of no other country are there as many references to gold, as an ordinary possession, as in Irish literature. This Irish wealth of gold is one of the unsolved mysteries of Irish history. The mere extant remains exceed the known medieval quantity of gold of any country, save perhaps equatorial Colombia alone.

[1] Reid, Archæology, En. Brit. 11th ed.
[2] Of the Royal College of Mines (London).
[3] Reid, loc. cit.

. In 793 the Danes made their first descent on the English coast. Lindisfarne suffered severely at their hands as well as south Wales. They also visited France. But thereafter for a generation they forgot both France and England and for thirty years confined their attention to the spoliation of Ireland. In that they showed good judgment, for, tho Ireland was a more powerful foe than other countries and was eventually destined to down them, it was also the citadel of Christian civilization and was very much richer than both France and England.[1] A national development, free from foreign intrusion, going back to the point almost contemporary with the founding of Rome, had made her the treasure-house of the West. Her accumulation of precious metals, heaped up from a vast antiquity, had been poured into innumerable shrines on islands and in valleys, and these the martial cupidity and cunning of the Danes, by ceaseless surprize attacks and thieving raids, were concentrated on rifling. The wealth borne from Ireland in those distant times is still attested to by the quantity of Irish metal work in Scandinavian lands. What they could not steal, what they were unable to understand or appraise these Danes destroyed, and against nothing did they evince a greater destructive vandalism than against Irish books, to which, in common with the English, they ascribed superstitious powers. But after each considerable attack—and the attacks continued till the Battle of Clontarf, 1014—Ireland shook herself together again and repaired the damage. She did not succumb to Danish power, as eventually En-

---

[1] In 1285, more than a hundred years after the so-called Norman "conquest" of Ireland we find Ireland described as rich and powerful, and the English in comparison as poor; Item, Hibernenses sunt divites, potentes, et Anglici pauperes, quod vix illi Anglici qui potuerunt in sexdecim . . . . eisdem in equitatura contra Hibernenses; modo non habent quod manducent. (Calendar of Documents, Ireland, ed. Sweetman, iii., p. 15; Mrs. Green, "The Making of Ireland and Its Undoing," p. 13.)

gland and part of France succumbed, but finally crushed it utterly so that Irish sovereignty was not irremediably impaired.

These things are given in order that we may add to our conception of the land from which the Irish builders of European civilization went. Its wealth and its strength, as well as its culture, were assets in their work. A knowledge of these facts helps us to a clearer analysis of their motives. Not poverty or strife or hope of betterment carried them to other lands. The occasions and purposes of their exiles and journeys were altogether different.

5. EXODUS OF IRISH SCHOLARS

That Ireland should have been the retreat and nursery of learning and the center of intellectual activity while the rest of Europe was the prey of barbarism would appear to have been distinction enough. Little reproach could have been cast upon her had she been content to enjoy the fruits of her own civilization, sharing those fruits the while with such foreign visitors as sought them on Irish soil. But the fact remains that she was not so content.

At an early period, as one French writer puts it,[1] Irish sanctity and culture became animated by an ardent spirit of proselytism and missionary zeal. The converts of one generation became the apostles of another. Fervent monks longed with a great longing to carry beyond the sea their methods of asceticism. Their voluntary exile appeared to them in the light of a supreme immolation sovereignly fitted to perfect the work of renunciation which they had undertaken. They left the land of their birth, radiant with tender associations, blooming like a garden with the

[1] Gougaud, Les Chretientés Celtiques, p. 135.

cultivation of the arts and sciences, to become "monks and exiles for the sake of Christ," "for the love of God," "for the name of the Lord," "for the love of the name of Christ," "for the benefit of their souls," "for the gaining of the heavenly land," as "pilgrims for the kingdom of God"—such are the formulae which the biographers of these consecrated pilgrims preferably employ. Pro Christo peregrinari volens enavigavit—"Desiring to go abroad for Christ he sailed away" are the words of Adamnan concerning Columcille. "My country," said Mochona, one of Columcille's disciples, "is where I can gather the largest harvest for Christ." The three Irishmen who after tossing on the seas for days arrived at the English coast and were received by King Alfred had left Ireland, the Anglo-Saxon Chronicle tells us, "because for the love of God they would be on pilgrimage they recked not where." They called themselves, and were called by others, "peregrini," that is to say, pilgrims, strangers, voluntary exiles. They interdicted themselves for a prolonged period—often for their whole life—from returning to their own land. The hagiographers, for this reason, often compare them to Abraham. It seemed as if they had all heard the voice which said to the Patriarch: "Go forth out of thy country and from thy kindred."[1]

To continental people there was something baffling in the sustained energy of these medieval Irishmen. Writers of the time make note of the impression of wonder produced by the Irish passion for traveling and preaching. How strongly the Alemanni of the ninth century, who never left their own country, were imprest, as Zimmer notes, by this trait of the Irish, is perceived in the remark

[1] Compare on this subject the reasoning from insufficient evidence of John Henry Newman, Hist. Sketches, Vol. III. Yet Newman compares very favorably with some later English Catholic writers, who have had opportunities of knowing better.

of Walafrid Strabo (d. 849) when in allusion to it he says: "The habit of traveling to distant lands has become a second nature to this people."[1] Men of education in Britain likewise make note of it. Thus we have the remark of Alcuin that "it has long since been a custom for very learned teachers to come from Ireland to Britain, Gaul and Italy."[2] The frequent testimony of Alcuin to the state of learning in Ireland is valuable because of his close association with Irishmen.

To leave home and kindred for the inaccessible crag, the high mountain, the bare desert, the ocean-swept isle, seemed to these ascetic Irishmen the literal following in the footsteps of the Lord. To seek out remote tribes, and work among them, preaching, teaching, spending themselves in behalf of them, building them up into Christian nations, was again work such as Christ commanded and his disciples performed. "Going, teach all nations!" was an admonition they ardently took to heart and to which many of them consecrated their lives. And they communicated this spirit to their disciples and thus set going a moral energy that carried Europe forward for centuries and made Christianity synonymous with civilization.

Ireland succeeded in retaining the heroic spirit of its pagan youth and accommodating it to its later Christian ideals. The fierce courage of a Cuchulain was changed into the spiritual heroism of a Columcille. The superterrestrial zeal of the missionary and monk is foreshadowed in the unyielding resolution of the pagan warrior. The valor of death in the midst of labors of so many devoted

[1] Nuper quoque de natione Scottorum, consuetudo peregrinandi jam paene in naturam conversa est. Vita S. Galli, Mon. Germ. Hist., Script. Rer. Germ. IV, 336. See also his poem Ad Probum Presbyterum, Poetae Lat. Car., II, 394. Osbern of Canterbury has something similar to say: quod aliis bona voluntas in consuetudinem, hoc illis (sc. Hibernis) consuetudo uertet in naturam (Stubb's Dunstan, p. 74).
[2] Mon. Ger. Hist. Epp., IV, 437.

Irishmen found its secular parallel in the intrepidity of the death-hour of Cuchulain: "Beir leat me d'ionnsaigid na carraige cloice ud tael ar do comair gurab ann dogeubad bas agus deirig m'airm orm, agus an fead do-cifid fir Eireann mar sin me, ni leigfi an eagla doib teact im ionnsaigid dom diceannad." "Carry me and stand me against yonder rock, and put my weapons in my hands, and when the men of Erie shall see me in such guise sheer fear will deter them from approaching to behead me."

Somewhat later than the cycle to which Cuchulain and his fellow champions belonged there was an order of chivalry in ancient Ireland called the Fianna or Fenians, whose heroic accomplishments are sung by Oisin, or Ossian. Than the Fianna, whose chief was Fionn, there were no stronger, straighter, bolder, nobler men in all Eire. Each member had to vow never to refuse hospitality, never to turn his back in battle, never to insult a woman, nor to accept a dowry with his wife. He had to be able to ward off with his shield the spears of his adversaries hurling them simultaneously, to be able to fly through forests without loosing his braided locks, or breaking a branch, to jump over a branch as high as his forehead and stoop under one as low as his heel while running at full speed, and to pluck a thorn from his foot while so doing.

All this spirit of high and vehement endeavor, mirrored in the wonderful poems of Oisin, was carried over from pagan into Christian Ireland. It animated the eremite monks who looked for solitude in the center of the ocean, in the heart of desert wastes, on the high mountain, or in the cold of arctic islands, and it animated the missionaries and schoolmen. They looked on life as a warfare, and themselves as soldiers, trained and armed for spiritual combat, and they responded to the spiritual call of religion, of learning and of liberty, as they had before answered to the martial call of bard and king. They were called ascetics, or athletes, which is the very meaning of the Greek word, and they loved to "make a record," and records they made in abundance, as we shall see as we proceed.

Behind the going from Ireland of some of these passionate pilgrims often lay a romance of high passion such as is depicted in Irish literature with wonderful purity, tenderness and charm. There is for example the ninth century tale of "Liadain and Curithir," which, by its pathos and rare knowledge of the human heart, recalls the other great love stories of the world's literature. It tells of the love of a poetess who has taken the veil for a young poet from whom her vows separate her forever. Thus the plot is a conflict between love and religion. The lovers seek the direction of one of the saints who gives them the choice between seeing each other without speaking or speaking without seeing.

"Talking for us," says the poet. "We have been looking at each other all our lives." So they converse, while one is enclosed in a cell and the other wanders around it. Passionate words of love and longing and regret are exchanged:

> "Beloved is the dear voice that I hear
> I dare not welcome it.
> 'Tis this the voice does to me,
> It will not let me sleep."

At length the poet is banished by the saint and, renouncing love, takes up the pilgrim's staff. The hapless Liadain follows, seeking him and wailing:

> "Joyless
> The bargain I have made:

The heart of him I love I wrung.
I am Liadain
Who loved Curithir.
It is true as they say.
. . . The music of the forest
Would sing to me when with Curithir,
Together with the voice of the purple sea."

But he crosses the sea and Liadain returns to die on the flagstone on which he had been wont to pray. "Her soul went to Heaven, and that flagstone was put over her face upon her tomb."

6. PARALLEL PROMULGATION OF CIVILIZATION AND CHRISTIANITY

We know the names of a great many of these missionary Irishmen, but thousands perished in their work unknown to fame, for their numbers were great. "They overflowed the Continent with their successive migrations" remarks St. Bernard,[1] who, though a poor authority on Ireland, could speak with knowledge of what passed on the Continent. The dangers that beset them were manifold. Europe was then in the remaking.

Famine, invasion, earthquake, pestilence, floods, and civil war had almost blotted out the landmarks of the ancient world. From the cities, which are the seats of civilizations, the remnants of ancient learning had sought refuge in the caves and woods. But even there the savagery and rapacity of successive invaders sought them out to burn and demolish. In a period when men thought mainly of rapine and murder and the vilest passions were aroused in sustained racial conflict, these spiritual Irishmen intervened between the warring elements with their prophetic evangel of peace, good will, love of kind, self sacrifice, asceticism, and renunciation of all unnecessary

[1] Vita Malach.

material things in a laborious ascent to the higher spiritual and intellectual life. For something over five hundred years, from the sixth to the twelfth century, the Irish mission continued. It was a work of singular fruitfulness. There has perhaps been nothing like it in the world beyond those other two great apostolates by which civilization on the one hand and Christianity on the other were introduced into the minds and souls of men. It was the singular merit and fortune of the Irish mission that it was at once an apostolate of Christianity and an apostolate of civilization.

Strange parallels will indeed be noted by those who care to compare the methods by which the work of the Irish mission was accomplished and the results that sprang from it, with the methods and results by which Christianity was first promulgated and consolidated and by which the condition of civilization was gradually superinduced upon the western world. The growth of civilization was slow and arduous. Homer may have been its first visible apostle, but unnumbered ages and a legion of lesser Homers were necessary before Homer himself was possible.

Measuring the growth of civilization from Homer we note that knowledge was dispensed and promoted through the lands bordering the Mediterranean by the precise missionary and colonizing methods employed by its Irish exponents at a later epoch. But the Irish missionary had a twofold character which the Greek had not. We have to add the Christian confessor to the Athenian sophist before we have a Columbanus, or an Eriugena. In them Christianity was the inspiration and in large part the medium by which they communicated their culture; and as in the one case their work followed the natural methods of the old pagan teachers, so in the other they consciously modeled their apostolate on the pattern provided by the early Christian teachers. When Christianity came into the world the soil had already been prepared to receive it and from Peter and Paul to Constantine the grafting of the revealed doctrine upon the civilization of the Roman world was a comparatively brief process. Then Christianity and civilization went down in common ruin and it was left to a new race of men, children of the farthest western isle, to renew and restore both. The two had traveled from East to West by different routes and at different times. They journeyed back from West to East not separately, but entwined in an inseparable union. No jeweler's product resulting from the fusing of precious metals, for which Ireland was then famous, could compare with this masterwork of spiritual smithing represented by the union through the force of the active Irish intellect of Christianity with the ancient learning. The process of developing that union went on till it appeared to reach its full expansion in the thirteenth century, but the ideal of Christian civilization first became a reality on Irish soil and it was out of that realized ideal that the vast organization of Christendom grew.

CHAPTER IX

THE IRISH KINGDOM OF SCOTLAND

1. Two-fold Invasion and Conquest. 2. Ireland of the Sixth Century. 3. Ancient Pagan and Medieval Christian Ireland. 4. The Military Conquest of Scotland.

1. TWOFOLD INVASION AND CONQUEST

THE conquest which the invading Gael had set on foot in Ireland in the sixth century B. C. and which he had sealed with the establishment of the Gaelic monarchy over the island in the third century B. C. had already thrown its powerful tides over the western coasts and islands of what is now called Scotland when the curtain lifted over the northern scene and authentic history began. The successive steps by which the Celts from the Continent established their authority over what later came to be called the five kingdoms, or provinces, of Ireland are veiled by the uncertainty and conjecture that precede our era. But the processes by which the men of Ireland carried that authority northward over the sea and added to the five kingdoms the Irish kingdom of Scotland fall well within the historic period and can be followed by us with tolerable clearness.

This later Irish conquest was not merely military and national. Civilization has moved from the beginning by devious paths and these first tides of conquest that received their immediate impulse from Tara and Dalriada carried with them an accompanying impulse from Athens, Jerusalem and Rome. The power of Roman arms that had enveloped first the Celts of Cisalpine Gaul, then Gaul itself and then Britain, stopped short at the Irish

Sea, but that sea presented no insuperable obstacle to the diffusion of Roman learning. That diffusion was made more easy by the settlement of Irish colonies within the nominal confines of the Roman Empire itself. What is now Wales was, as will later be shown, an Irish colony during the great part of the period of the Roman occupation of Britain. An exiled Irish prince, presumably with a retinue, sojourned at the camp of Agricola in Britain.[1] Irish legions fought side by side with Roman legions in Gaul and Germany. Thus numerous channels of intercourse were opened up between Ireland and the empire long before the official mission of Patrick and his colleagues.

To the distinctive civilization which Ireland therefore had developed within herself as the most clearly patterned and defined entity within that empire of the Celts whose limits were deeply merged in an incessant ebb and flow with the empires that followed each other on the Mediterranean coasts, Ireland was able to add to her store from the indescribable wealth of the Greco-Roman mind almost in the very hour of its ultimate perfection. To that store she added incessantly till with the entire Christianization of the island Ireland became a partaker in the full illumination that produced a Constantine and a Boethius, an Augustine and a Chrysostom.

No slight interest therefore attaches to the twofold invasion and conquest which brought the northern half of Britain simultaneously within the empire of the Gael and the empire of Greco-Roman civilization. In its way it was an extension of that process of envelopment by which Rome had brought most of the known world

---

[1] "Agricola, expulsum seditione domestica, unum ex regulis gentis, exceperat, ac specie amicitae in occasionem retenebat." (Tacitus, Life of Agricola.)

within the orbit of its influence. It was an emanation from an Ireland that had succeeded Italy as the home of the liberal arts and that alone enjoyed the homogeneity and repose necessary to their highest cultivation. It represented the first chapter in that prolonged cultural enterprise which was in course of time to take in the greater part of Europe. It exhibited in action abroad an Ireland glowing in all her first young-eyed enthusiasm, her mind enraptured by the wonders of the ancient classics, her heart thrilled and overcome by the revelation of the Christian mysteries.

2. IRELAND OF THE SIXTH CENTURY

No close student of Irish history but must feel that in the Ireland of the sixth century he is in the presence of one of those movements or crises rare in the history of civilization and destined to affect its whole subsequent course. Something of the kind—and it is the supreme example—ran its course in Athens in the fifth century B. C. There was a similar manifestation in Rome during the century that preceded our era, and the thirteenth century saw parallel movements in France and Italy. Their similitudes may be noted in the crucial stages that occur in the life of the individual dividing one portion of his life from another. Something emotional comes to a head, there is a coalescing of forces, a chemical explosion, a parturition, a blossoming and a subsequent illumination or alteration of vision that is enduring. In the case of nations there is a sudden appearance of a group or procession of great minds, such as in the ordinary course appear only at long intervals, whose works mold the national tongue and are subsequently appealed to as the national classics, the holy writ and depository of their revelations, or whose work results in the foundation of great institutions that endure for centuries.

In the Ireland of the sixth century we feel ourselves in the presence of the phenomena of some such crisis. Had we the full literature of Ireland or even so much of it as has been proportionately spared in other countries, we would probably find therein a manifestation of the human spirit with few parallels in history. But even the precious fragments left to us give clear indications of what we have lost, as stray pieces of Greek sculpture or Egyptian masonry indicate the proportions of the statue, or temple, to which they belonged.

In the case of Ireland we note a sudden grouping of men who from one cause or another—by the magic of their personality or the strength of their intellect or by the prestige acquired through the establishment of great institutions, or the initiation and guidance of great movements set influences in motion that gather momentum even after their deaths. The sixth century in Ireland was indeed prolific in great men. Towering above them all we may gaze with studious eyes on the mighty Columcille, a figure for all its strangeness as familiar and human as any during the whole Middle Ages. Almost contemporaneous with him is Columbanus, the most energetic and scholar-like character in the Europe of his day, whose work on the Continent proved as fateful and fruitful as the work of Columcille in Ireland. In the early years of both of them the "Twelve Apostles of Erin," in whose company Columcille is numbered, lived in the land. Ciaran[1] who founded Clonmacnois, Finnian who founded

1 Ciaran is credited in bardic compositions with the first literary recension of the Tain. The Leabar na h'Uidre or Book of the Dun Cow, the oldest big book in the Irish tongue, which also contains much Iliadic literature, including the Tain, is said to have been made from the skin of the dun cow that provided the student Ciaran with milk, but is probably copied from a book so made.

Moville, Comgall who founded Bangor, Brendan[1] who founded Clonfert, Finnian who founded Clonard, Brendan of Birr and Cainnech of Ossory who figure so prominently in Adamnan as the personal friends of Columcille —they are but leading figures in a company every individual member of which stood forth as a burning beacon to subsequent ages. Nor was Ireland deficient in great kings during this era. Diarmid II who occupied the throne of Tara for a score of years and Aedh who was sovereign for more than another score both made their reigns memorable in Irish history.

It was in the course of the sixth century that Ireland's most celebrated schools started on their full career. It was in that century that her ancient heroic literature, maturing towards perfection during the preceding ages, was cast in its fulness into the literary form in which we now know it, and that the literature of the new era, transformed and awakened by the new ideas of Christianity, blossomed into its first springtide.[2] It was towards the close of the century that the spiritual and material forces of the nation came together at Drumceat and set on foot a new epoch, reforming the bardic institution, reorganizing the entire educational system of the kingdom, and establishing a free Scotland in union with the motherland. It was during this century that the overflowing energy of Ireland began to deluge Europe with a missionary activity that read the Irish ferocity of enthusiasm and self-abnegation and the eloquence and daring of the

---

[1] The copies of Brendan's Legend, which are preserved in Ireland and on the Continent, are numerous. It is still disputed whether in his famous Navigatio he reached part of the American continent.

[2] Tho valuable fragments have been preserved from the sixth century, the more striking specimens of the new literature left to us, in Latin rather than in Irish, belong to the seventh. Thus Cummian wrote his paschal epistle in 634; the Irish Augustin or Ængus wrote his striking work on miracles, apparently in Carthage, in 659; while Adamnan brought out his extant works in the last decade of the seventh century.

sinewy Irish intellect into the early history of every country in Europe.

It has been noted that the pedigrees of the leading families of Ireland converge most of them in the fourth century and in the family of Niall of the Nine Hostages. The monarch Niall died in the fifth year of the fifth century leaving a numerous progeny and the record of a life filled with exploits at home and expeditions abroad. His reign marked the beginning of an epoch. For six hundred years the descendants of Niall, with three or four exceptions, succeeded each other in the sovereignty of Ireland, a marvelous phenomenon in tumultuous Europe. Three of the sons of Niall[1] founded respectively the kingdom of Meath and the principalities of Tyrconnell and Tyrone, which combined to form the kingdom of Ulster. The descendants of Brian, the brother of Niall, delimited the kingdom of Connaught. It is clear that in the fifth and the sixth century Ireland had reached a condition of political development that no other country in Europe was to reach for centuries later. When during the reign of Diarmuid the triennial or septennial parliament of Ireland was held in Tara for the last time the curtain was rung down on a drama that had been enacted in the royal city from a date almost contemporaneous with the establishment of the Irish monarchy itself. The reign of Diarmuid, who died in 563, lights up for us a clear picture

---

[1] They were Conaill Crimthann; Conaill Gulban (from whom Tyr [Lat. terra] Conaill, "Country of Conaill"); and Eoghan (from whom Tyr Eoghan or Tyrone, "Country of Eoghan"). Conaill Gulban gave the clan name to his descendants the Cinel Conaill, the family to which Columcille belonged. The terms: Clan, Cinel, Muintir, Cin, Ui or Hy, are all affixes signifying kindred, race, family, descendants—as Cinel Airt, race of Art; Ui or Hy Maine descendants of Maine. They were the forms in use in Ireland and Scotland before the establishment of surnames in the tenth and eleventh centuries. Mac means "son"; Ua or O, "grandson"; Ni, "granddaughter."

in Irish history. Diarmuid himself[1] bears in our eyes the lineaments of a modern constitutional sovereign, wielding power with justice as well as energy, meting out the law to high and low alike, building up a modus vivendi with the church, and recognizing instinctively the checks and balances which defined his authority in the Gaelic state. His interest in education is demonstrated by the munificence and support he extended to the foundation of Ciaran at Clonmacnois[2] which later rivaled Armagh as the national university. His conflict with Columcille during the session of the national parliament at Tara which led to the battle of Culdreimhne reveals the monarch rather than the churchman as the upholder of the law. His conflict with Ruadhan, who, like Columcille, is numbered among the Fathers of the Irish church and whose ceremonial cursing of Tara figures in Irish history as an element in the decline and fall of the royal city, likewise shows up to us the saint rather than Diarmuid as the fount of trouble and discord. It seems to have been at the instance of Diarmuid that the Synod of Tailtenn was called, which sought to excommunicate Columcille for the bloodguiltiness of Culdreimhne. It is impossible to follow the events of the reign of Diarmuid and the consequences that issued from the convention of Drumceat without feeling that Ireland during this period with its ancient parliament, its system of fivefold sovereignty with the high monarch as the head of all,

[1]There is an ancient Irish life of King Diarmuid II, MS. H. 2.16, Trinity College, Dublin. His reign is remarkable as the one in which Tara ceased to be the legislative capital. His father was Fergus Cerbaill, son of Conaill Crinthann, and grandson of Niall of the Nine Hostages. After his death his head was conveyed to Clonmacnois and his body was buried at Connor. See Reeves, Life of St. Col., by Adamnan, p. 67.

[2]In one of the panels of the great cross at Clonmacnois (A. D. 916), the clean-shaven Ciaran in his long robe and the bearded prince Diarmuid in short tunic are clearly shown in the act of setting up the tall cross, which was the first post of the founder.

with the kings of Leinster, Connaught, Ulster and Munster directly beneath him, with its lower aristocracy of princes, nobles and chiefs, all bound up with the free population and clans by ties of close kindred, all recognizing the national laws, synods and parliaments, all speaking the same tongue and delighting in the same literary heirlooms, had evolved a political state as superior to anything then known as her culture was superior.

The ancient safeguards which restrained the power of the sovereign, so often cited as a reproach by foreign critics, merely show that the individual unit in the medieval Irish state had developed a sense of personal responsibility and freedom which the secularly opprest subjects in other lands did not acquire till modern times. Compare for example the political civilization of Ireland in the sixth century with the political civilization of England in the sixteenth, three centuries after the passing of Magna Carta.[1] In the sixteenth century the lawyers of Henry VIII gravely debated whether the English people were the personal property or merely the subjects of the sovereign. In sober fact they were his personal chattels. Abject and terrorstricken slaves, neither whose bodies nor souls nor thoughts were legally their own, watching in panic eagerness the mere nod of king or queen, anxious only to obey the royal will, which was the actual fount of law, of honor and of punishment, the helplessness of the English under the Tudors turned the kingdom into a worse than Oriental despotism. Within the space of a single generation the English people— every one of whom was, by the laws of Henry VIII, to which their parliament assented, theoretically a traitor,

[1] The value of the Magna Carta was more apparent to the kings' jesters than to anybody else. Few kings paid much attention to it. See p. 296.

liable to the death penalty, by the mere act of living and thinking—at the command of the sovereign changed their religion three different times. The popular agitation furnished a spectacle of national and individual cowardice that set neither form nor limit to its servility. It is to the honor of Ireland that not even in the sixth century could absolutism thus ride roughshod over the national spirit. Even at that early period the individual in the clan and in the kingdom, claiming kinship with its rulers, recognized himself as a unit in a great patriarchal organization, and yielded obedience to the law and honor to the head of the State, while holding inviolate his personal sense of freedom and dignity.

3. ANCIENT PAGAN AND MEDIEVAL CHRISTIAN IRELAND

Ireland is the only one of the northern nations that was not first civilized by Christianity and indeed it is one of the boasts of Irishmen that there has never been a period in their ascertainable history when they were not a civilized people. The distinctive old Irish civilization grew out of the same soil and was fed by the same sap that gave life and birth to Greco-Roman civilization. Its inner strength and soundness are illustrated by the carrying forward from a remote antiquity to the age of Greek and Roman letters the masterpieces of Irish literature on which the subsequent literature of Ireland levied constant tribute. This was a tremendous feat. It placed Ireland at a single bound among the literary nations of antiquity, and in the field of heroic literature side by side with Greece alone. For Ireland's literature is not like Roman literature, a reproduction and imitation of Greek literature, but a parallel growth. In her ursgeula, or sagas, she has what even Rome has not, a literature of heroic Iliads that is the independent, unadulterated, original creation in antiquity of the heart and lips of her people. The northern nations, apparently as free as she, as unmolested by Roman power, failed to accomplish this tour de force. It invests Ireland with a supreme glory. It marked her from the beginning as a nation of destiny and served as a fitting prelude to that medieval work which was to continue as an enduring foundation to subsequent civilization.

By the sixth century Greco-Roman and the old Irish culture had become inseparably blended and a new Christian polity had given breadth and stature to the older national entity which unassisted Irish experience had created. In Ireland alone are we enabled to look on the old life and the new—on that ultra-world which knew neither Roman nor Greek and on that world again transformed by Greek and Roman learning.

Classical writers and the unknown authors of the old Irish epics reveal to us the unity of the civilization of the Celts, more clearly developed and defined in Ireland than elsewhere. We see them eating, drinking, playing and fighting. We note their great numbers and powerful physique; the magnificence of their funerals; their use of the chariot; their splendid horsemanship; their races and cattle-spoils; the ferocity of their onset in battle; the retinue around their princes; their astonishing apparel— dyed tunics, flowered with colors, fantastic, flaming cloaks, breeches, and wondrous buckles and ornaments of gold. We note their haughty self-confidence, as in the colloquy with Alexander, their chivalry in combat, their figurative rhetoric, and their belief in an Elysium and the immortality of the soul.[1]

It is a changed world into which the literature of medieval Ireland ushers us. The old magnificence is there, but it is a secondary theme. The great military encampments have been eclipsed by the sudden mustering of new legionaries—champions of wisdom, milites Christi, athletes of asceticism, sages, prophets and saints. Armagh has taken the place of Tara of the Kings, Bangor has become the rival of Tailtenn, Clonard has out-gloried Emain-Macha. A living voice from out of the new strongholds comes to us across the space of 1,100 years:

"Tara's mighty burgh perished at the death of her princes: with a multitude of venerable champions the great height of Machae (Armagh) abides.

"Right valiant Loigure's pride has been quenched—great the anguish: Patrick's name, splendid, famous, this is on the increase.

"The Faith has grown: it will abide till Doomsday: guilty pagans who are carried off, their raths are not dwelt in.

"Rathcroghan it has vanished with Ailill offspring of victory: fair the sovereignty over princes that there is in the monastery of Clonmacnois.

"Choirs lasting, melodious, around Ciaran, if thou shouldst mention him; with the victorious tumult of great Clonmacnois."[2]

New ideals have taken the place of the old. Cattle-spoils give way to contests of dialectical valor. Searches for deserts in the ocean succeed to martial expeditions abroad. The new literature is both in Irish and in Latin,

---

[1] The chief epics of the Irish Heroic cycle are: The Tain; Deirdre and the Sons of Uisneach; Conchobar's Vision; The Battle of Rosnaree; Conchobar's Tragedy; The Conception of Cuchulain; The Training of Cuchulain; The Wooing of Eimer; Death of Conlaoch; Cuchulain's Adventure at the Boyne; Intoxication of the Ultonians; Bricriu's Banquet; Eimer's Jealousy; Pining of Cuchulain; Conaill's Red Rout and the Lay of the Heads; Capture of the Sidh; Phantom Chariot of Cuchulain; Death of Cuchulain; Recovery of the Tain Through the Resurrection of Fergus. The Heroic or Cuchulain cycle took its shaping in the first century, B. C. It is later than the Mythological cycle and earlier than the Fenian cycle of epics.

[2] Felire of Ængus (c. 800 A. D.), edited by Whitley Stokes, pp. 24-5.

and the alteration of outlook and purpose is fundamental. While the old literary tradition marches forward, drawing perpetually from the original fountain, the new literature talks the accent and thought of the empire. It has become practical: the purpose is not any longer primarily to thrill, to terrify, or to amuse, but is a call to action, to reformation and to sacrifice. Its heroes are not gods and fighting men. They are monastic founders and scholars, poets and philosophers, legislators and saints. The biographies of the distinguished Irishmen of the epoch constitute in themselves a volume of literature that reconstructs for us the old Irish world and peoples it with living men and women in whom legend and wonder commingle with ripe scholarship and complete intellectual integrity.

4. THE MILITARY CONQUEST OF SCOTLAND

It was from the midst of an Ireland thus intimately known to us and thus carrying on the tradition of Irish as well as Greek and Roman culture that the men who conquered, colonized and Christianized the northern half of Britain went forth to their work. Little more than an outline is necessary to delineate the steps by which the military conquest of Scotland was completed.

Irish Scots had crossed the Strath-na-Maolle of the Gaels, the northern arm of the Mare Hibernicum of the Romans, and the North Channel of modern days, and settled in that part of Caledonia which the Romans called Vespasiania, some hundreds of years before Angle, or Saxon, or Jute, had appeared on the rim of civilization. The Venerable Bede refers to the migration: "In course of time Britain, besides the Britons and Picts, received a third nation, Scotia, who, issuing from Hibernia, under the leadership of Riada, secured for themselves, either by friendship or the sword, settlements among the Picts which they still possess."[1]

From at least the second century onwards Irish expeditions crossed from Ireland into North Britain and gradually conquered and colonized the southwestern parts of the country. From the fourth century onwards stronger Irish forces crossed over and gradually extended the conquest of the country, the larger part of which was in the hands of the Picts. Towards the close of the fifth century, to follow the chronology of Tigerneach, a powerful Irish expedition crossed over into Caledonia under three brothers, the princes Fergus, Loarn and Angus, sons of Erc, of the royal house of Ireland, and established themselves in what is now Argyleshire, Bute and the Hebrides. The Gaelic form of Argyle is Airer-Gaedhil, that is the territory of the Gael, or Irish, and the name is therefore a living record of these early colonizations.

Fergus Mor became first king of the Gaels or Irish now settled in Caledonia and his death is recorded by Tigerneach, the Irish annalist, at the year 502. Fergus was succeeded by a long list of kings, the most conspicuous of whom was Cinead, or Kenneth, mac Alpin (surnames were not in vogue at that early time and the "mac" here,

[1] Hist. Eccl. This account by Bede is true only in so far as it indicates that the Irish migration to Scotland was gradual and did not begin under the sons of Erc. No Irish leader named Riada headed an Irish migration to Scotland. Riada, the ancestor of Fergus, lived three centuries earlier. It was about the year 470, according to Tigerneach, when the sons of Erc, Fergus and his brothers went from Ireland to Scotland. Fergus was king of Dal Riada in the northeast corner of Ireland. The crossing meant that the princes established their rule over the Irish settlements of that region. Irish genealogies show that the same dynasty and the same kings ruled Dal Riada in Ireland and the Irish colonists in Scotland till the Norse occupied Cantyre and thus cut off the Irish territory from the Scottish territory in which the kings of Dal Riada had become resident. When this separation took place, the title of "King of Dal Riada" was abandoned. The last king who bears the title in the annals is Donn Coirci, 792; and in 794, the same annals record "the devastation of all the islands of Britain by the heathen." (MacNeill, Phases of Irish History, 195.)

without the capital, means the "son" of Alpin literally), who in the year 842 conquered the whole kingdom of the Picts, carrying his victorious Irish forces as far north as Caithness and to the south over the Tweed and well into England. In the reign of Stephen, King of England, the Irish Scots in Britain held three northern countries of what is now England, while such names as that of Gospatric, Earl of Northumbria, show how deeply the Irish invasion had penetrated to the south.

Sixty kings of the Irish race reigned in Alba, or Scotland, during a period of nearly eight centuries, from the time of King Fergus, A. D. 502, to the death of Alexander III in 1286 A. D. During that period Irish culture and the Irish language became established over all Scotland, and the intercourse between Scotland and the other Irish provinces of Munster, Connaught, Ulster, Leinster and Meath, was as constant as was the intercourse between the inland provinces themselves.

So Scotia Major, as Ireland was sometimes called, and Scotia Minor formed a single country and nation of six provinces, or kingdoms, each with separate kings, of whom one was the high-king, or Ardrigh, each speaking the same tongue, and each looking back on a national history common to them all. In course of time the influence of the Francii, or Norman and Angevin French who under William the Conqueror had made themselves masters of England crossed the English border northwards into the Scot Lothians, with first the French and later the English language as medium, just as Norman French influence almost simultaneously crossed the sea westward into Leinster. But centuries had yet to pass before English was to displace Irish as the language of the Scottish people.

CHAPTER X

COLUMCILLE, APOSTLE OF SCOTLAND

1. Archpresbyter of the Gael. 2. A Christian Cuchulain. 3. The Facts of His Life. 4. His Career as Monastic Founder.

1. ARCHPRESBYTER OF THE GAEL

IN this conquest of the northern half of Britain the rôle of spiritual proconsul was played by the famous Columcille, "the high saint and high sage, the son chosen of God, even the archpresbyter of the island of the Gael, the brand of battle set forth with the divers talents and gifts of the Holy Ghost." Marvelous indeed are the characterizations which the skilled medieval writers apply to this prince of the Irish royal line, who appears to have been born also to the natural purple of intellect and spirit that has marked from the beginning the born leader of men. Sage, prophet, poet—dove of the cell— lovable lamp, pure and clear—silvery moon—a diadem on every train—a harp without a base chord—a child noble, venerable, before God and man—a child of the King of Heaven and earth—man of grace—physician of the heart of every age—manchild of long-sided Ethne —there never was born to the Gael, we are told, offspring nobler or wiser or of better kin than he—there hath not come of them another who was meeker or humbler or lowlier. "Noble insooth was Columcille's kindred as regards the world; for of the kindred of Conaill, son of Niall, was he. By genealogy he had the natural right to the kingship of Ireland and it would have been offered to him had he not put it from him for the sake of God."

"Angelic in appearance, graceful in speech, holy in work," as Adamnan describes him, it is clear that this remarkable figure made a deep impress on the imagination of his age. With a score of streamlets from Ireland's bluest blood uniting in his veins,[1] richly endowed in body and mind, of great height and powerful in physique, with hair curling like the ringlets of a Greek god, with face broad and comely, eyes gray, large, and luminous, a voice resonant, musical and deep, that could be heard at the distance of fifteen hundred paces, a lionhearted being whose energy, glowing with steady fire, would not permit him to spend even the space of an hour without some occupation, Columcille left an astonishing record of performance behind him and still looms over the fourteen centuries that divide us as one of the most impressive figures of the Middle Ages.

In his character and in his extraordinary career we seem to see embodied, more than in any other figure, the aspiration, the passion, the exaltation, the energy of the Ireland of the sixth century. Romance and poetry speedily made him their own. Columbanus was a contempo-

[1] A member of the reigning family in Ireland and closely allied to that of Dalriada in Scotland, he was, as Reeves notes, eligible to the sovereignty of his own country. His half-uncle, Muircertach, was on the throne when he was born, and he lived through the successive reigns of his cousins, King Domnaill, King Fergus, and King Eocaid; of his first cousins, King Ainmire and King Baedan; and of King Aed, son of Ainmire. His immediate lineage stands as follows:

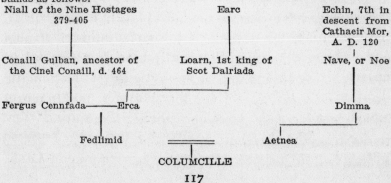

rary of Columcille, and outside of Ireland accomplished a work paralleling that of Columcille within the Gaedhaltacht. He was Columcille's junior by twenty-two years. He was twenty years old when Columcille set out for Iona. He sailed for the Continent when Columcille was twenty-two years in Iona. He himself was, like Columcille, the embodiment of the spirit and striving, the awakened heart and developing intellect of his country, and he made an extraordinary impression abroad on the age in which he lived. But Columbanus, remarkable as his personality was, remained totally unknown in Ireland. Marvelous as were his gifts, he cut absolutely no figure in Irish history and his career and personality appear commonplace compared with the career and the personality of Columcille. We have a life of Columbanus, written by one of his immediate disciples,[1] just as we have such a life of Columcille. We have Latin epistles written by the hand of Columbanus, as well as Latin poems, rules, instructions, sermons, directions, wonderful for their age. From the authentic voice of Columcille himself there is little that does not touch on the unearthly or that is not in meter, Irish or Latin. In the stories that have come down to us concerning him the poetical element is almost always put forward in front of the practical, and in few episodes of his career is he ever shown as playing a subordinate part. He is ever the high hero, the victor, the champion, the darling of the gods, the idol of men and women, the child of fortune, born to command in heaven and in hell as well as upon the earth. Columcille represents the poetry, as Columbanus may be said to represent the prose, of the Ireland of the sixth century.

[1] Jonas in Migne, Pat. Lat., LXXXVII, Cols. 1009–46. Both Columbanus and Columcille were more fortunate than St. Patrick in respect to their biographers' nearness to their own time. The earliest reference to St. Patrick is in the paschal epistle of Cummian (634)—"Sanctus Patricius papa noster."

2. A Christian Cuchulain

The atmosphere of idolatry which wrapped Columcille round in life crystallized into something of an apotheosis in death. He became the Christian Cuchulain of the Irish race, the wonder-working miles Christi, whose exploits performed against the powers of darkness rivaled those of the pagan hero who in an earlier day had been chief among "the curled and rosy youth of the kingdom." The legends that grew around his name took the epic note and form as they passed from mouth to mouth and found credence even in the ears of the scholars. Adamnan, the chief biographer of Columcille, was a man of cultivated judgment, steeped in Roman learning. In preparing the life of his celebrated kinsman he took painstaking care, he tells us, in endeavoring to sift the false from the true.[1]

But the popular apotheosis of Columcille also took captive the imagination of a man as capable as Adamnan. After the battle of Troy the poets in the Greek-speaking towns collected the traditions and adventures of the heroes and made a diversion of them for the public. From such material and through such processes was the Iliad born and from parallel materials and processes were developed the epics of the Irish heroic cycle, in which the youthful hound of Ulster plays the high rôle. Adamnan's life of Columcille, despite its intentionally historical character, occupies in the Christian field a place comparable to these stories in the pagan field. His work is a Christian epic in which the accomplishments of Columcille as scribe, statesman, missionary, monastic founder

[1] In the second preface to his work he tells us that it is the substance of narratives learned from his predecessors and is founded either on written authorities anterior to his own time or on what he learned himself from ancient men then living. He talks of "witnesses, as the law requires."

and scholar are indeed revealed to us, but only incidentally and in the background and environment of the story. In the foreground we see Columcille performing in the miraculous rôle in which that age loved first to view him, and indeed if in the pagan literature of Ireland we recognize the introduction here and there, by the hand of the Christian literateur of a later age, elements foreign to its first shaping, it may be said with truth in the narrative of Adamnan we find in the formation of character and episode that love of romance and high superhuman exploit cultivated by pagan epic from a remote antiquity.

In the Tain we watch the high and vehement Cuchulain accomplishing prodigies of valor. Single-handed he holds the ford against the army of Queen Maeve. Hovering around them unseen all day he kills as many as a hundred of them in the night with his sling. His anger at the boiling-point melts the snow around him. With his vigorous edge-stroke he could at will take off all the hair of an opponent from poll to forehead and from ear to ear as clean as with a razor without drawing blood. With his oblique transverse stroke he could divide an antagonist into three equal segments falling simultaneously upon the ground. He conquers the bird-shaped demons of the air, the monstrous plaguing forms of the war-goddess Morrigan, and the spells of the magician Cailtin and his twenty-seven sons. The tracks of the wheels of his chariot circling round the Connaught army rise up like fortifications as he spreads havoc amid the uncounted host.

Hardly a whit inferior to Cuchulain in his own field as wonder-worker Columcille is pictured in the pages of Adamnan. His wisdom was supernal like the valor of Cuchulain. "Through a wonderful experience of his inner soul he beheld the universe drawn together and laid open to his sight as in one ray of the sun." He healed diseases. He raised the dead to life. He subdued the furious rage of wild beasts. He expelled by a word and sign hosts of malignant demons. He calmed the surging waves and changed the direction of the winds. Celestial light played around him and celestial legions descended to keep him company. He saw the souls of men ascending to the highest heavens, or descending among the demons of hell. He looked into the future and foretold the destinies of men. His voice breathed incessant prophecy and preternatural revelation.

Yet beneath all this aura of legend and wonder there is a solid accompaniment of fact and historic reality which has preserved Columcille to us as a living, breathing, human personality, whose course from the cradle to the grave is laid bare to us with a distinctness lacking in any other career during the early Middle Ages. No legendary dim figure is Columcille but a great and striking historical character whose work constitutes a fact in history as enduring and indissoluble as that of Cæsar. Legend made Columcille its own as it made Charlemagne its own. But as Charlemagne had his Einhard as well as his Trouvère, so Columcille had numerous witnesses to the realities of his life as well as to its supposed wonders. Nobody can doubt that Adamnan, for example, described the phenomena and incidents of his patron's life as they appeared to those who were living observers. It is only in the supernatural agencies to which he ascribes natural acts and processes that he goes beyond the record. The facts themselves and their environments may be accepted; the explanation of the facts often indicates the line where pious fancy has superimposed the element of legend on reality.

3. THE FACTS OF HIS LIFE

Hardly does Columcille appear to have been in his grave before his friends and admirers began to set down the facts of his life for the benefit of posterity. Even in his life Dallan Forgaill, the poet laureate of Ireland, wrote a poetic eulogy of his work at Drumceat, still with us in its archaic form and heavily annotated.[1] Mura, his companion, and Baithene, his intimate and immediate successor, wrote memoirs of him. Cuimine, seventh abbot of Iona (657-669) wrote a treatise on his virtues which has been preserved.[2] The work of Adamnan, who wrote c. 691-3, has been described as "the most complete piece of such biography that all Europe can boast of, not only at so early a period, but even through the whole Middle Ages."[3] To this succeeded a life by John of Tin-

[1] Amra Choluim Chilli by Dallan Forgaill, ed. and transl. by O'Beirne Crowe, Dublin, 1871.

[2] It is partly included in the third book of Adamnan's work, but has been independently preserved.

[3] Pinkerton, Enquiry, Pref. Vol. 1 p. xlviii (Edinb. 1814). A copy of this work of Adamnan, written by Dorbene, who was elected abbot of Iona in 713, and who died in that year was discovered by Dr. Ferdinand Keller in 1854 at the bottom of an old chest in the public library of Schaffhausen. It proved to be the identical MS., formerly at Reichenau, copied by the Irish Jesuit Stephen White, and from his copy used by John Colgan for his Trias Thaumaturga published in 1647, and the Bollandists in 1698, and to-day it is the oldest MS. in Switzerland. It was edited in 1857, by Dr. William Reeves with a perfection of scholarship and painstaking research, which puts his work on a level with O'Donovan's edition of the "Annals of the Four Masters." Reeves showed himself familiar not merely with the main stream of Irish history, but with its numerous accessories and tributaries. In concentrating his varied information and resources on any desired point and presenting his material in vivid order, he writes with the accurate knowledge almost of an eye-witness and contemporary and the Ireland of the sixth and seventh century passes before us as though a world in which the modern actors were still living. The original MS. has a colophon which ends thus: "Whoever readeth these books on the virtues of St. Columba, let him pray to the Lord for me Dorbene that after death I may possess eternal life." The title page of Reeves' edition reads: "The life of St. Columba, Founder of Hy. Written by Adamnan, ninth abbot, of that Monastery. The text printed from a MS. of the eighth century: with the various readings of six other manuscripts preserved in different parts of Europe. To which are added copious notes and dissertations, illustrative of the early history of the Columbian institutions in Ireland and Scotland." "The Historians of Scotland." Vol. 6, reproduces the work of Reeves with an English translation of the life. A new edition founded on that of Reeves, with a new translation, by J. T. Fowler, appeared in 1894. "St. Columba of Iona," by Lucy Menzies (1920) has also some new features.

mouth and the old life of unknown authorship written in Irish and contained in the Book of Lismore, as well as another independent Latin memoir. The Book of Leinster, the Leabar Breac, or Speckled Book, and other Irish compilations have notices concerning him, while Bede, Alcuin, Walafrid Strabo and Notker Balbulus likewise refer to him. They are but the vanguard of a procession that has endured to our day.[1] Of all the influential personages born in Ireland in her long prime, men distinguished by high birth, lofty talent, and accomplishing eminent work in Ireland and abroad, to Columcille alone, by a singular destiny, has been allotted through the ages his fair meed of fame. He still stands before us a commanding, aged, inscrutable and yet familiar figure, surrounded by a crowd of men, who assisted or succeeded him in his work, and who are known to us chiefly because of him.

Columcille was born in 521 at Gartan close to the Atlantic shore in the beautiful territory of the Cinel Connaill of which his father, Fedhlimidh, was a ruling prince. The reigning high monarch of Ireland was his half-uncle, while his mother Ethne was the direct descendant of the line of Cathaoir Mor which gave Leinster its kings. Reared at Kil-mac-nenain, celebrated later as the site of the inauguration of the O'Donnells as Princes of Tyr-Connaill, Columcille received some preliminary teaching at the hands of Finnian in his famous foundation at Moville. The strictly lay element in his education was next acquired in the Leinster school of the bards presided over by the aged Gemman. The old

[1] The last and most copious of the manuscript lives of Columcille is a compilation of all existing documents and poems both in Latin and Irish, made by the order of his clansman, Manus Ua Domnaill, Prince of Tyrconnell, in 1532. It is preserved in a large vellum folio in the Bodleian Library at Oxford and has not yet been printed.

Gaelic life has a number of delightful anecdotes relating to this early period and from one of them we learn that the old Roman practice of teaching the alphabet by means of lettered cakes, alluded to by Horace,[1] had taken root in Ireland. "Now when the time of reading came to him (Columcille) the cleric went to a certain prophet who abode in the land to ask him when the boy ought to begin. When the prophet had scanned the sky he said: 'Write an alphabet for him now.' The alphabet was written in a cake. And Columcille consumed the cake in this wise, half to the east of the water and half to the west of the water. Said the prophet, through grace a prophecy: 'So shall this child's territory be, half to the east of the sea and half to the west of the sea; that is, in Ireland.' "[2]

From the school of Gemman, Columcille went to Finnian's great establishment at Clonard, where he began to study for the priesthood, and where he had the society of the remarkable group of men, both young and old, who with himself became later celebrated as the "Twelve Apostles of Erin." The old Irish life tells us that each man of the future bishops there used to grind a quern in turn. "Howbeit an angel from heaven used to grind on behalf of Columcille. That was the honor which the Lord used to render him because of the eminent nobleness of his race." A fellow student and particular friend of Columcille at Clonard was the celebrated Ciaran, later founder of Clonmacnois. The Lismore life tells us that once there appeared to Finnian a vision concerning them, to wit, two moons arose from Clonard, a golden moon and a silvery moon. The golden moon went into the

[1] Sat. I. ii 25. See Gaidoz, Les gateaux alphabetiques, Paris, 1886.
[2] Anecdota Oxoniensia, Med. and Mod. Ser. 5 (Lives of the Saints from the Book of Lismore), ed., Whitley Stokes, p. 172.

north of the island and Ireland and Scotland gleamed thereby. The silvery moon went on till it stayed by the Shannon and Ireland at her center gleamed. That, we are told, "was Columcille with the grace of his noble kin and his wisdom, and Ciaran with the refulgence of his virtues and good deeds."

From Clonard Columcille passed on to the school of Mobhi at Glasnevin, near Dublin, whither he seems to have been accompanied by Ciaran, Comgall and Cainnech. There on one occasion, the Book of Lismore life tells us, the clerics were considering what each of them would like to have in the great church which Mobhi had built. " 'I should like,' saith Ciaran, 'its full of church children to attend the canonical hours.' 'I should like,' saith Cainnech, 'to have its full of books to serve the sons of Life.' 'I should like,' saith Comgall, 'its full of affliction and disease to be in my own body to subdue me and to repress me!' " Then Columcille chose its full of gold and silver to cover relics and shrines withal. "Mobhi," the story goes on, "said it should not be so, but that Columcille's community would be wealthier than any community in Ireland or Scotland."

The plague of 544 visited Ireland while Columcille was at Mobhi's foundation and it fell heavily on the community, which numbered about fifty members. Columcille as a precautionary measure went northward and shortly after received from his cousin, Prince of Aileach and later monarch of Ireland, the site of a monastery on the coast covering some 300 acres and clad by a splendid forest of oak trees which gave to that beauty spot the name of Daire, or Derry. Here in 546, when he was twenty-five years old, Columcille founded the famous church and school which remained so dear to him in after life. A generation later, when Iona had become his home, he often reverted to it in his talk and occasionally allowed his feeling to find expression in poetry. "He loved that city greatly," says the Lismore life, "and said:

> For this do I love Derry,
> For its smoothness, for its purity,
> Because it is quite full of white angels
> From one end to the other."[1]

4. HIS CAREER AS MONASTIC FOUNDER

About 553 he founded the school of Durrow in the present King's County which attained great celebrity. Durrow (Irish, Dairmagh, oak-plain) was like Derry named from the beautiful groves of oak which were scattered along the slope of Druim-Cain, and, as Columcille's chief institution it is mentioned by Bede. He appointed as its abbot Cormac, the son of Dima, who figures in the pages of Adamnan as an indefatigable voyager in the northern ocean, repeatedly visiting Iona and going as far north, it would appear, as Iceland. Cormac was a Momonian of the race of Heber and not of the kin of Columcille, and as a result he does not appear to have got on well with the southern Ui Niall with whom he found himself. This fact may account for his travels abroad. Columcille in one of his poems upbraids him for abandoning so lovely an abode:

> "With its books and its learning
> A devout city with a hundred crosses."

During the sixteen years interval between 546 and 562, when Columcille departed for Iona, he established a

---

[1] Anecdota Oxoniensia, ser. 5, p. 175. A more eloquent translation is given in Hyde, Literary History of Ireland, p. 169. The full poem in Irish was copied from a Brussels MS., by Michel Ua Clerigh for Colgan. It has been modified in transcription.

great number of other monasteries and schools in Ireland, of which thirty-seven are clearly marked, among them Kells, Swords, Drumcliff, Screen, Kilglass and Grumcolumb. He was at this time at the height of his powers and enjoyed a reputation second to none in Ireland. His activity was prodigious and opposition appears to have kindled it into a fiercer flame. There is at this period little evidence of the Columcille described by Adamnan,[1] "beloved by all" in whom "a holy joy ever beaming on his face revealed the joy and gladness with which the Holy Spirit filled his inmost soul." That seems to have been a later development. Columcille during this period displays all the ardor, the passion, and the self-will of his masterful character and is credited by Irish writers with having been the prime instigator of three bloody wars.

The events which led to the battle of Culdreimhne, which was fought in 561 and which is traditionally assigned as a cause of Columcille's exile to Iona, cast a dramatic light on the feelings and aspirations of the epoch, the union and clash of barbaric passion and the highest culture, culminating on the lofty stage set by the Irish nation in parliament assembled under the ancient Truce of God at Tara. Finnian of Moville, with whom Columcille had first studied, had visited Rome and returned with a copy of the Psalms, probably the first translation of the Vulgate of St. Jerome that had appeared in Ireland. Finnian apparently valued his treasure so highly that he did not want anyone to copy it, but Columcille, who was a

[1] The commentator on the Felire of Ængus describes Columcille as "a man well formed, with powerful frame; his skin was white, his face broad, and fair and radiant, lit up with large, grey, luminous eyes; his large, well shaped head was crowned, except where he wore his frontal tonsure, with close and curling hair. His voice was clear and resonant, so that he could be heard at the distance of 1,500 paces, yet sweet with more than the sweetness of birds." He himself in one of his poems speaks of his "grey eye that looks back to Erin."

skilled scribe, succeeded by sitting up several nights, in making a secret transcription which Finnian, when he learned of it, claimed as his property. Columcille refused to surrender his transcription and the matter was brought up for decision at the court of the High Monarch, Diarmuid II, at Tara. The decision is the first we know of in the law of copyright and as such is extremely interesting, tho it is condemned by most of the Irish annalists. Appealing to the precedent of the old Irish laws that *le gach boin a boinin* "with every cow her calf!" the monarch decided in favor of Finnian, adjudging that "as with every cow her calf, so with every book its son."

The decision greatly offended Columcille, to whom books were a passion, and fuel was added to his resentment by another event. It happened during the great Feis, or Parliament, of Tara, that the son of the King of Connacht, in violation of the law of sanctuary which was universally held as sacred on these occasions, slew the son of the High King's steward and, knowing the penalty was certain death fled to the residence in the royal city of the northern princes, Fergus and Domhnaill, who immediately placed him under the protection of Columcille. The offense was too grave, however, for temporizing, and King Diarmuid, who was a strenuous upholder of the law, had him immediately seized and put to death. The action exasperated Columcille to the last degree. Shaking the dust of Tara from his feet he sped northward and called on his kindred for vengeance. A great army was collected, led by Prince Fergus and Prince Domhnaill, two first cousins of Columcille, and by the King of Connacht, whose son had been put to death. The High King marched to meet the combination with all the troops he could muster, with the result that a furious battle was fought between Benbulbin and the sea in which he was defeated with the loss of 3,000 lives.

It was in the year following this battle that Columcille decided to leave Ireland. He had filled Ireland with arms and bloodshed and he seems not to have been insensible to the cloud that lay upon him. Adamnan tells us that a synod assembled at Tailtenn in Meath for the purpose of excommunicating Columcille. The assembly, however, was not unanimous. Brendan of Birr protested against any condemnation and later Finnian of Moville testified his sense of veneration for the accused, who had been his pupil.

There is much evidence that Columcille's exile to Iona was assumed as a sort of penance, imposed on him by St. Molaise of Devenish, who, according to several Irish accounts, made the penalty one of perpetual exile. Other testimony would seem to indicate that the missionary enterprise was voluntary. "Pro Christo peregrinari volens, enavigavit," the common formula of missionary enterprise, is Adamnan's statement of his motive; with which Bede's expression "ex quo ipse praedicaturus abiit" is in keeping. That Columcille returned to Ireland repeatedly and took an active part in civil and religious transactions is demonstrable from Adamnan.

In 563 Columcille, now in his forty-second year, set sail with a number of associates from his well-beloved Derry, determined, according to popular tradition, to convert in Scotland as many souls as had fallen at Culdreimhne. The parting was bitter and the lament ascribed to him reveals his feeling:

> Too swiftly my coracle flies on her way;
>   From Derry I mournfully turned her prow;
> I grieve at the errand which drives me today
>   To the land of the Ravens, to Alba, now.

How swiftly we glide! there is a grey eye
Looks back upon Erin, but it no more
Shall see while the stars shall endure in the sky
Her women, her men, or her stainless shore.

The missionary labors of Columcille in Scotland, in collaboration with his devoted colleagues, extended over the remaining period of his life. The island of Hy was donated to him by King Conall, his kinsman, and there he established his celebrated monastery of Iona. The Scoti or Irish already in Scotland were nominally Christians; the Picts were not. Hence the conversion of these latter formed the grand project for the exercise of missionary exertion and Columcille applied himself with characteristic energy to the task. He visited the Pictish king in his fortress, won his esteem, overcame the opposition of his ministers, and planted Christianity in the province. He lived thirty-four years at Iona, and it is with his work with the island as a center and with his life after he had gone there that the biography of Adamnan mainly deals.

CHAPTER XI

COLUMCILLE AND BRETHREN AT IONA

1. The Moving World of Ireland and Britain. 2. Ritual and Ceremonial. 3. Literary Work and Other Occupations. 4. Columcille and His Friendships.

1. THE MOVING WORLD OF IRELAND AND BRITAIN

IN turning over the pages of Adamnan, we have brought home to us one of the precious functions which literature serves. Had we no Roman literature, the material monuments of Rome would be almost as meaningless to us as the Pyramids and the Sphinx. Had we no Grecian literature, the marvels of Greek architecture would tell us a story as broken almost as the cryptograms conned by archeologists from Babylonian mounds. Had we no pagan Irish literature, the Europe of the Celt, the Galatian and the Gaul would be as dead to us as an Egyptian mummy; its monuments would be as insoluble as the sentinel stones of Stonehenge and Carnac; and old wives' foreign tales would take the place of the authentic witness of antiquity. Had we no medieval Irish literature, medieval Ireland would be as incommunicable as medieval America. But the living literature of ancient and early medieval Ireland is more copious and authoritative than the literature of all the rest of western Europe put together, and of its medieval monuments there is hardly any work more informative and interesting than Adamnan's biography of Columcille. Regret is sometimes exprest that Adamnan did not write in Irish rather than in Latin; that he wrote the history of an

individual rather than of a church or nation. But it
is enough that the work is a masterpiece of its kind. It
holds up for us as in a mirror the living soul and mind
of the Ireland of the sixth and seventh centuries. It
reveals to us the inmost thought, the breathing life, the
spontaneous speech and gesture and the interior spiritual
mechanism of the men who swung Europe from barbarism back to civilization, and it is doubtful whether
it could have gained in comprehensiveness without losing
its priceless wealth of intimate disclosure and camera-
like detail. Enough for us that through Adamnan and
the other Irish authors of his time, we are permitted to
gaze with entranced eyes on the moving world of Ireland
and Hibernicized Britain bathed in the morning light of
heroic pristine faith and culture.

It is no static world of placid contemplation on which
Adamnan throws the casement but an ever-shifting popu-
lous scene of unflagging movement and varied occupation.
Guests, distinguished and undistinguished, are perpetually
coming and going. At Derry and Iona fleets of ships lie
at anchor with crews not far away, ready to start on short
notice either for Ireland or Britain. Occasionally at Iona
one of the sailors is missing and there is a delay, but if
the breeze is favorable, Columcille bids the traveler
depart with confidence. We hear of voyages into the
North "beyond the bounds of human enterprise," of huge
sea monsters and swarms of smaller amphibians, of poach-
ers among the young seals bred at Iona, and of Gallican
sailors bringing news of an earthquake in Istria. The
building of ships, houses and churches goes on incessantly.
At Iona long boats are drawn loaded with hewn pine
and oak, and fleets of twelve vessels carrying oak trees
for building row out to sea with sailyards raised in the

form of a cross. We hear of plowing, sowing, reaping and threshing; of the cultivation of oak groves and apple trees; and of salmon fishing. Strangers signal across the sound from Mull by shouting or lighting fires and are ferried over the mile of water.

The yachts, freightships and ferries on the water have their counterpart in the curri and chariots on the land. Columcille journeys forth in his chariot both in Iona and Ireland, on one occasion with the chariot unsecured by linchpins. A rich cleric mounted in a chariot drives pleasantly along the Plain of Breg (Magh Bregh, Meath) and Columcille prophesies that he will die lying on a couch with a prostitute and choked with a morsel of meat from his neighbor's cattle that had strayed within his walled enclosure. Most of Columcille's long journeys, covering in some cases hundreds of miles, were made however on foot with no greater help than that given by a staff. Tho the danger from wild beasts must have been imminent, Columcille and his companions do not seem to have carried any weapon. On one occasion it is stated that by prayer and the power of the eye he procured the death of a huge wild boar pursued by the hounds.

The majority of the houses built by the brethren were apparently of wood, of heavy timber or wattles, while others were of stone, and that some of them were not small is made clear by the anxiety displayed by Columcille over the severe labor of the brethren on one of the buildings marked out by him at Derry. Many of the houses of the time were in fact white timbered mansions, glistening in the sunlight on the summit of great duns, chambered and unchambered, thousands of which continue to this day. We hear of a magna domus and a monasterium rotundum—clearly Round Towers, as Petrie notes, were not unknown in the sixth century. The size of the monastery and school was limited by the demand, and grew with it. The cell of Columcille at Clonard became the portal to the later church; his royal birth may have housed him in a chamber larger and more ornate than the retreat of the other students. Iona was a small community compared with the more renowned establishments in Ireland, but the references to guest chambers, kitchen, refectory, church, sacristy, and other chambers, and out-buildings give the impression of an extensive household.

2. RITUAL AND CEREMONIAL

The reception of guests and the deportment of the brethren towards one another were distinguished by a ritual and ceremonial as precise as the motions at a royal court. When a stranger arrived he was sometimes introduced at once to the abbot by whom he was kissed, and sometimes the interview was deferred. When an expected guest arrived Columcille and the brethren went to meet and welcome him. He was then conducted to the oratory and thanks returned for his safety. From this he was led to a lodging, hospitium, and water was prepared to wash his feet. If a visitor happened to arrive on an ordinary fast day of the week, the fast was relaxed in his favor, and a consolatio cibi was allowed. If the guests numbered more than one, as in the case of the arrival of Comgall, Cainnech, Brendan and Cormac, all "holy founders," on one occasion, the celebrations, sacred and profane, were in accord with their rank. On this occasion the four illustrious guests agreed that Columcille should consecrate the mysteries of the Eucharist. Almsgiving was practised and valuable presents, under the name of "Xenia," were sent on one occasion to a man in need. Itinerant beggars, who went about with wallets, had only a cold welcome, and grievous transgressors were excluded.

Adamnan, himself an aristocrat belonging to Columcille's own line, and an intimate friend of at least three kings, Finnachta of Ireland, Aldfrid of Northumbria, and Buite of Pictland, shows in his narration of facts a lively sense of difference in rank. He refers habitually to the station of visitors and mentions whether they are of high or lowly position, and birth. He Latinizes into tigernes the Irish word "tigherna," lord. The type of historian who takes comfort in the delusion that the monarch of Ireland was a merely nominal figure-head, will find little consolation in Adamnan. He is a distinct believer in the divine right of kings. The high monarch is "the king of all Ireland." He is "by divine appointment (ordinatus a Deo) king of all." It is Adamnan indeed who gives us the story of the first Christian inauguration of a sovereign.[1] But there is a proper honor and rubric pertaining to each rank, spiritual and secular. A bishop for instance is received in the conventional hierarchy with the sort of honor which one officer of a state might extend towards another. Marked respect is shown to him by the abbot, who in his turn receives the homage of those of inferior spiritual rank. Fintan, for example, arriving at Iona and being presented to Baithene, the cousin and immediate successor of Columcille, kneels and remains in that posture until ordered by the abbot to rise and be seated.

[1] This was Columcille's inauguration of Aidan as King of the Irish Scots to succeed Conaill in 575. The Irish coronation service used by Columcille was introduced by Irish missionaries into England and was thenceforth used for the inauguration of the English kings. It has been continued in large part in England to this day. The stone beneath the throne at Westminster Abbey, brought from Scone, is likewise supposed to have been Irish.

The authority of the abbot was almost absolute. He was wont on extraordinary occasions to summon the brethren to the oratory even in the dead of night and there address them from the altar and solicit their prayers. Occasionally he instituted a festival, proclaimed a holiday and enjoined the celebration of the Eucharist. As occasion offered he dispensed with a fast, relaxed the penitential discipline, or regulated its intensity. He gave license of departure which he signified with his benediction. He was saluted by prostration.

He forbade at pleasure admission to the island. When he thought fit he dispatched a chosen brother on a distant mission or for monastic purposes. He had control of the temporalities. When at home he was attended, except when he signified his wish to be alone. When abroad he was accompanied by a retinue, the members of which were styled viri sociales. Columcille inaugurated the first independent king of Scot Dalriada in Iona, and the ceremony was probably continued as an honorary function by the abbots who succeeded him. Columcille named his own successor and in the election preference was always given to the kin of the founder.[1]

3. Literary Work and Other Occupations

Details wanting in Adamnan are often filled in by the biography in the Book of Lismore,[2] of later medieval

---

1 The tradition of the high birth and princely connections of the governors of Columcille's foundations was well known abroad, and in the verses which Walafrid Strabo wrote concerning the life and death of Blaithmac of Iona, "whom wealthy Hibernia gave to the world," who was killed in a Danish raid on the monastery, reference is made to his kinship with the Irish kings:
Regali de stirpe natus summumque decorem.
Nobilitatis habens florebat regius heres (Poetae Latini Aevi Carolini II, p. 297).

2 Anecdota Oxoniensia. Lives of Saints from the Book of Lismore, edited with a translation, notes, and indices, by Whitley Stokes, D. C. L., Oxford, the Clarendon Press, 1890. Mediæval and Modern Series 5. Betha Choluim chille, pp. 20-33; transl., pp. 168-181.

origin. Apart from the larger occupations connected with farming and building, we observe the brethren engaged in innumerable smaller occupations. Columcille himself was skilful with his hands and an adept at making "crosses and writing tablets and book satchels and other church gear." His favorite occupation seems to have been writing, sometimes transcriptions, sometimes composition. His last occupation in life was copying the scriptures and his ejaculation, "Let Baithene write the rest," was taken as an indication of his will in respect to his successor, whose ability as a scribe was a primary consideration. The total number of the works written by Columcille must have been great. The Lismore life credits him with 300 books—"many were the churches he marked out and the books he wrote, to wit, 300 churches and 300 books." Allowing for round numbers, it is certain he left many works behind him. Bede tells us that "writings of his life and discourses are said to be preserved by his disciples" (Lib. III, C. 4), and the medieval tradition is that he left a book to every church founded by him.[1] He was prolific as a poet as well, tho of the enormous number of extant poems attributed to him, few can be genuine even in part. But the poetic mood was a frequent visitation: "Then he went to Clonmacnois with the hymn he made for Ciaran. For he made abundant praises for God's households, as said the poet:

"'Noble thrice fifty, nobler than every apostle,
The number of miracles are (as) grass,
Some in Latin which was beguiling,
Others in Gaelic, fair the tale.'"

[1] Adamnan relates that after Columcille's death, and fourteen years before the date at which Adamnan himself wrote, during a drought at Iona, the brethren walked around a newly plowed and sowed field, taking with them the white tunic of Columcille and some books written by his own hand, which they raised in the air, shaking the tunic three times, and opening the books and reading them on the Hill of the Angels (now called Sithean Mor).

But to a being so strenuous the writing of poetry could only have been a diversion and a relaxation. "He could not," says Adamnan, "spend the space of even one hour without study or prayer, writing or some other holy occupation. So incessantly was he engaged night and day in the unwearied exercise of fasting and watching that the burden of each of these austerities would seem to be beyond the power of all human endurance. And still in all these he was beloved by all; for the holy joy ever beaming from his face revealed the joy and gladness with which the Holy Spirit filled his inmost soul."

"Surely," adds the Lismore life, "it was great lowliness in Columcille that he himself used to take off his monks' sandals and wash their feet for them. He often used to carry his portion of corn on his back to the mill and grind it and bring it home to his house. He never used to put linen or wool against his skin. His side used to come against the bare mold. A pillarstone used to be under his head for a bolster and he slept only so long as Diarmuid his fosterling was chanting the three chapters of the Beatus. He would arise up at once after that and would cry and beat his hands together, like a loving mother lamenting her only son. He would chant the three fifties on the sand of the shore before the sun would rise. In the day he attended to the hours. He offered Christ's Body and Blood. He preached the Gospel, he baptized, he consecrated."

The culminating period in Columcille's career seems to have been reached following the parliament or convention of Drumceat, held in 575. The primary object of that parliament, which had been called together by the High Monarch Aedh, was the dissolution of the order of the bards, who had developed through the centuries

138

an organization so powerful as to be a menace both to the State and the Church, and whose insolence and exactions had become an oppression to every man and woman enjoying wealth and rank enough to draw their poetic satire. Columcille's eloquent defense of the men who, despite their offenses, had served as guardians of the literary memorials of the kingdom, mitigated the sentence of extinction, and turned the current of opinion in the direction of a general reorganization and reduction in numbers. His counsel in respect to the lay education of the country, which was largely in the control of the bards, led to the establishment of head colleges in each of the provinces with subsidiary colleges under them. He likewise, in union with Aidan, King of Scot Dalriada, who had accompanied him to the parliament, succeeded in relieving Scotland of the tribute which it had hitherto been obliged to pay to the High Monarch and giving it the status of a self-governing kingdom in union with the motherland.

Following the parliament, the proceedings of which furnished a striking manifestation of his influence,[1] Columcille was acclaimed by multitudes and countless gifts from the people of the Eilne (Magh Elne on the Dann) were laid out on the paved court of the monastery. Visiting Clonmacnois from Durrow some years later, from the famous monastery of Ciaran and all the grange farms around, the populace, headed by the Abbot Alithir, flocked with enthusiasm to meet him, "as if," says Adamnan, "he were an angel of the Lord. Humbly bowing down their faces to the ground they kissed him most reverently and, singing hymns of praise as they went, they conducted

[1] An extremely dramatic account of the proceedings and of the reception given to Columcille at Drumceat, where he faced old enemies, is given in the Edinburgh MS., p. 22b; reproduced by Stokes, Anecdota Oxoniensia, Mediæval and Modern, Series 5, pp. 309-315.

him with all honor to the church. Over the saint as he walked a canopy made of wood was supported by four men walking by his side lest the holy abbot, St. Columcille, should be troubled by the crowds of brethren pressing upon him." The luster and glory of his work in Scotland had then thrown a halo around him and sentiment had changed greatly since, following Culdreimhne a quarter of a century earlier, the Synod of Tailtenn had sought to excommunicate him.

4. Columcille and His Friendships

Like Adamnan, Columcille had, despite the impulsive and vehement temper that precipitated fierce wars even after his departure to Iona, a true genius for friendship. His passionate devotion to his own family and clan gleams alike in Adamnan and the other medieval literature that abounds concerning him. This excess of affection he imputed to himself as a fault. "So then Baithene related to him the famous vision, to wit, three chairs seen by him in heaven, even a chair of gold and a chair of silver and a chair of glass. Columcille explained the vision: 'Ciaran the Great, the wright's son, is the chair of gold, for the greatness of his charity and his mercy. Molaisse is the chair of silver because of his wisdom and his piety. I myself am the chair of glass because of my affection: for I prefer Gaels to (the other) men of the world, and the kindred of Conall to the (other) Gaels, and the kindred of Lugaid to the (rest of the) kindred of Conall.' "[1]

His extraordinary solicitude for the brethren who peopled his foundations, which Adamnan so signally illus-

[1] Lebar Breac or Speckled Book, p. 236, col. 2; Anecdota Oxoniensia, Med. and Mod., Series 5, p. 302.

trates, was an element and development of his partiality
for his own kin who figured so largely in their composition. But his friendships did not on that account run
in narrow confines. He was on terms of intimacy with
most of the great men of his day. Ciaran of Clonmacnois
acted the part of an elder brother at Clonard and their
friendship remained warm till Ciaran's early death in
548. Comgall, founder of Bangor, and Cainnech of
Ossory were not merely intimate friends but on occasion
the companions of some of his long missionary journeys.
Both these great men, along with Brendan of Clonfert,
and Brendan of Birr were frequent visitors to Iona and
other of his foundations. On one occasion Columcille
foretells the coming of Cainnech in the midst of a tempest
and orders the brethren to prepare the guest chamber and
draw water to wash his feet. He never forgot his cham-
pionship by Brendan of Birr before the excommunicating
Synod at Tailtenn and when the latter died in 573 he
instituted a festival at Iona in commemoration of his day.
In his later days all Ireland longed to see him. "When
Columcille had been thirty years in Scotland anxiety (?)
seized the men of Ireland as to seeing him and as to
communing with him before he went to death."[1]

Among the numerous company whom Columcille honored with his friendship, many of them famous on their
own account, standing out in a vivid lineament and life-
like detail lacking in many a modern statesman, a strange
attachment united Columcille to Cormac, the descendant
of Lethain. He was of the line of Olliol Olum, King of
Munster and pivotal ancestor of its nobility, and was
thus far removed from kinship with Columcille, who nev-

[1] Edinburgh MS., p. 22b, apparently taken from the introduction to some
copy of the Amra Choluim chille, Dallan Forgaill's poetic eulogy of Columcille's work at the convention of Drumceat (Anecdota Ozon., Ser. 5, p. 309).

ertheless set him over his loved Durrow in the midst of his own kin of the southern Hy Niall, who showed little toleration to the stranger. Under the circumstances it is not strange that Cormac should show that strong liking for travel and the sea which was his most distinguishing characteristic. Two extremely ancient poems in Irish embody the expostulations of Columcille to his friend for his abandonment of Durrow and the resultant colloquy. The opening passage of one of them touches on Cormac's navigations:

> Thou art welcome, O comely Cormac
> From over the all-teeming sea;
> What sent thee forth; where hast thou been,
> Since the time we were on the same path?
> Two years and a month to this night
> Is the time thou hast been wandering from port to port
> From wave to wave; resolute the energy
> To traverse the wide ocean. [1]

Columcille's thoughts appear to have been continually with Cormac, and on one occasion he suddenly calls on the brethren to pray for the indefatigable navigator who "sailing too far hath passed the bounds of human enterprise." On another occasion the brethren were talking about Cormac. He had taken boat some time before for the Orkney Islands and they were speculating from appearances whether or not he had had a prosperous voyage. The voice of Columcille breaks in on their colloquy. They shall see Cormac that very day and have the

---

[1] Copies of these poems are preserved in the Burgundian Library at Brussels in a volume of manuscript collections made in 1630, by Michel Ua Clerigh, one of the Four Masters. Both the poems are found also in a MS., of the Bodleian Library, Laud 615 (pp. 34, 117), which contains a large collection of Irish poems, 136 in number, for the most part ascribed to Columcille. Reeves' Life of St. Columba, by Adamnan, gives both Irish poems with English translations, by Eugene O'Curry, from which the above passage is taken. Their titles are given in Colgan's list of the reputed writings of Columcille (Trias Thaum., p. 472a, num. 15, 16).

CHAPTER XII

DEATH OF COLUMCILLE

1. The Last Scene at Iona. 2. Illuminated Manuscripts and Latin Poems. 3. By the Time of Adamnan. 4. The Hibernicizing of North Britain.

1. THE LAST SCENE AT IONA

IT is characteristic of the meticulous accuracy of Irish records that we know not merely the year and the month, but the very day and almost the very hour and minute of the night in which Columcille passed away.[1] It was just after midnight between Saturday the 8th and Sunday the 9th of June, in the year 597, that there took place at Iona a scene, the story of which is as moving and humanly interesting as any that has come out of the North.

The story is told in the last chapter of Adamnan, where he describes "How Our Patron Saint Columba Passed to the Lord." On the eve before his death the great man, having inspected the granary and the barn of the monastery and having exprest satisfaction that the brethren would be well supplied for the year, confided to his attendant Diarmuid that his end was near. A touching dialog then follows, which leaves Diarmuid weeping bitterly, while later on is depicted the oft-quoted incident of the white horse, "the obedient servant that used to carry the milk-vessels between the monastery and the byre," which wept

[1] On the subject of the accuracy of Irish annals, etc., consult Reeves, Proceedings of the Royal Irish Acad., Joyce, Social History of Ireland, I., pp. 513-21; War of the Gaels with the Galls, ed., Todd, Introd. XXVI; Hyde, Literary Hist. of Ireland, 38-43; Kuno Meyer's "Early Relations between the Gael and Brython," read before Society of Cymmrodorion, May 28, 1896.

into Columcille's bosom and which he blest. Adamnan goes on:

"And going forth from thence and ascending a small hill, which rose over the monastery, he stood for a little upon its summit, and, as he stood, elevating both his palms, he blessed his community and said, 'Upon this place, however narrow and mean, not only shall the kings of the Scots (i. e., the Irish) with their peoples, but also the rulers of foreign and barbarous nations (i. e., the Picts, English, etc.) with the people subject to them, confer great and no ordinary honor. By the saints of other churches also shall no common respect be accorded it.'

"After these words, going down from the little hill and returning to the monastery, he sat in his cell writing a copy of the Psalms, and on reaching that verse of the thirty-third Psalm where it is written, 'But they that seek the Lord shall lack no thing that is good:' 'Here,' said he, 'we may close at the end of the page; let Baithin write what follows.' Well appropriate for the departing saint was the last verse which he had written, for to him shall good things eternal be never lacking, while to the father who succeeded him (Baithin), the teacher of his spiritual sons, the following (words) were particularly apposite, 'Come, my sons, hearken unto me. I shall teach you the fear of the Lord,' since, as the departing one desired, he was his successor not only in teaching but also in writing.

"After writing the above verse and finishing the page, the saint enters the church for the vesper office preceding the Sunday; which finished, he returned to his little room, and rested for the night on his couch, where for mattress he had a bare flag and for a pillow a stone, which at this day stands as a kind of a commemorative monument beside his tomb. And there sitting he gives his last mandates to his brethren, in the hearing of his servant only, saying, 'These last words of mine I commend to you, O little children, that ye preserve a mutual charity with peace, and a charity not feigned among yourselves; and if ye observe to do this according to the example of the holy fathers, God, the comforter of the good, shall help you, and I, remaining with Him, shall make intercession for you, and not only the necessaries of this present life shall be sufficiently supplied you by Him, but also the reward of eternal good, prepared for the observers of things Divine, shall be rendered you.' Up to this point the last words of our venerable patron (when now) passing as it were from this wearisome pilgrimage to his heavenly country, have been briefly narrated.

"After which, his joyful last hour gradually approaching, the saint was silent. Then soon after, when the struck bell resounded in the middle of the night,[1] quickly rising he goes to the church, and hastening more quickly than the others he enters alone, and with bent knees inclines beside the altar in prayer. His servant, Diarmuid, following more slowly, at the same moment beholds, from a distance, the whole church inside filled with angelic light round the saint: but as he approached the door this same light, which he had seen, quickly vanished: which light, a few others of the brethren, also standing at a distance, had seen. Diarmuid then entering the church calls aloud with a voice choked with tears, 'Where art thou, Father?' And the lamps of the brethren not yet being brought, groping in the dark, he found the saint recumbent before the altar; raising him up a little, and sitting beside him, he placed the sacred head in his own bosom. And while this was happening a crowd of monks running up with the lights, and seeing their father dying, began to lament. And as we have learnt from some who were there present, the saint, his soul not yet departing, with eyes upraised, looked round on each side, with a countenance of wondrous joy and gladness, as though beholding the holy angels coming to greet him. Diarmuid then raises up the saint's right hand to bless the band of monks. But the venerable father himself, too, in so far as he was able, was moving his hand at the same time, so that he might appear to bless the brethren with the motion of his hand, what he could not do with his voice, during his soul's departure. And after thus signifying his sacred benediction, he straightway breathed forth his life. When it had gone forth from the tabernacle of his body, the countenance remained so long glowing and gladdened in a wonderful manner, by the angelic vision, that it appeared not that of a dead man but of a living one sleeping. In the meantime the whole church resounded with sorrowful lamentations."

So went to his death the founder of the Scottish nation, the father of civilization and Christianity both in Scotland and England, and after Cæsar perhaps the most majestic being that has ever trod the isle of Britain.

[1] The saint, as Reeves notes, had previously attended the vespertinalis Dominicae noctis missa, an office equivalent to the nocturnal vigil, and now at the turn of midnight the bell rings for matins, which were celebrated according to ancient custom a little before daybreak.

2. ILLUMINATED MANUSCRIPTS AND LATIN POEMS

If Columcille was the author of both the Book of Kells and the Book of Durrow as was long believed the title of consummate artist must be added to the other characterizations that have been lavished upon him.[1] The famous copy of the Psalter known as the Cathach,[2] long the most valuable heirloom in that branch of Columcille's clan that issued in the Ua Domnaill family, Princes of Tyrconnail, is accepted as being his handiwork and indeed as the very transcription from Finnian's set of the Vulgate over which 3,000 warriors fell at Culdreimhne. Of the Latin poems attributed to Columcille and believed to be genuine wholly or in part three have come down to us.[3] They are the Altus, In te Christe and Noli Pater. The Altus is the most celebrated and was quoted in the ninth century by Rhabanus Maurus. It describes the Trinity, the angels, the creation of the world and the fall of man, the deluge, and the last judgment. The poem, which is a sort of early Paradise Lost, consists of twenty-two stanzas, each beginning in order with a letter of the alphabet. The first two lines run as follows:

Altus prosator, vetustus dierum et ingenitus,
Erat absque origine primordii et crepidine.

[1] Both these miracles of beauty are at Trinity College, Dublin. The colophon on the Book of Durrow bears the name "Columba."

[2] The Cathach or Battler, contained in a shrine made for it in the eleventh century by the order of Cathbar Ua Domnaill, was carried to the Continent in the seventeenth century by the exiled Domnaill Ua Domnaill. It was recovered in 1802 by Sir Niall Ua Domnaill and was opened by Sir William Betham soon after. Within was found a mass of vellum hardened into a single lump, which, when the leaves were separated, was found to contain part of a Psalter written in Latin in a "neat, but hurried hand." Fifty leaves remained, containing from the 31st to the 106th Psalm, and an examination of the text showed it to be part of the second revision of the Psalter by St. Jerome.

[3] They are contained in an eleventh century manuscript, the Liber Hymnorum.

The poem has been variously rendered into English, the following being a specimen:

> Ancient of Days; enthroned on high;
> The Father unbegotten He,
> Whom space containeth not nor time,
> Who was and is and aye shall be;
> And one-born Son and Holy Ghost,
> Who co-eternal glory share,
> One only God of Person Three,
> We praise, acknowledge and declare.[1]

Curious conceptions of the physical origins of clouds, rain and tides are given in the stanza beginning with the letter I:

> In three quarters of the sea
> Three mighty fountains hidden lie
> Whence rise through whirling water-spouts
> Rich-laden clouds that clothe the sky;
> On winds from out his treasure House
> They speed to swell bud, vine and grain;
> While the sea-shallows emptied wait
> Until the tides return again.

3. BY THE TIME OF ADAMNAN

By the time of Adamnan (624-704), the Christianization of Scotland had been pretty well completed, tho a century and a half had yet to pass before its thorough Hibernicization. Adamnan became ninth abbot of Iona and was perhaps after Columcille the greatest of that distinguished and enduring line. His celebrity as a literary man in a period when there was very little literature in Europe outside of Ireland and its intellectual dependencies has overshadowed his accomplishments in politics, in diplomacy and in the Church. He is known and will be known through the ages as primarily

[1] By the Rev. Anthony Mitchell. An excellent translation is also given by Alfred Percival Graves in the Contemporary Review (London), Sept., 1920.

the biographer of St. Columcille, yet this was a work performed during the intermittent leisure hours of a life filled with action. Adamnan belonged to Columcille's own family and was born twenty-seven years after the death of his great kinsman. Adamnan, like Columcille, whose life became a model to the youth of Erin, studied in a number of Ireland's great seats of learning, then in the meridian of their fame and influence, and in a bardic composition embodying a memoir of the High Monarch Finnachta there is given a story of his student days which is valuable for the glimpse it gives into the Irish university life of the period.

Finnachta, although of the blood royal, was in his youth quite poor. He had a house and wife but only one ox and one cow. Now the king of Feara Ross strayed to the neighborhood of Finnachta's house; and his wife and a crowd of retainers were with him. Finnachta struck the ox on the head and the cow on the head and feasted all the king's people sumptuously, so that no one was hungry. Then the king and queen of Feara Ross gave large herds of cattle to the generous Finnachta and made him a great man. Shortly after this, Finnachta, not yet king, was coming with a large troop of horse to his sister's house, and as they rode along they overtook Adamnan, then a student, traveling the same road with a vessel full of milk on his back. Anxious to get out of the way Adamnan stumbled and fell, spilling all the milk and breaking the jar to pieces. He ran after the cavalcade and said: "O good man, I have reason to be sad, for there are three good students in one house and they have us as two messengers—for there is always one going about seeking food for the five, and it came to my turn to-day. The gathering I made is scattered and, what I grieve for far more, the borrowed vessel has been broken and I have no means to pay for it." Then Finnachta declared he would make it alright and he kept his word. He not only paid for the vessel but he brought the scholars to his own house and their teacher along with them; he fitted up the ale-house for their reception and gave them such abounding good cheer that the professor, the annals say, declared Finnachta would one day become king of Ireland, "and Adamnan shall be the head of the wisdom of Erin, and shall become soul's friend or confessor to the king."

Adamnan became abbot of Iona in 679 when he was fifty-five, five years after Finnachta became king of Ireland. The monarch had never lost sight of the boy with the jar, whose bearing had indicated a youth of promise. Adamnan was invited to the court and was ultimately made the king's spiritual adviser or anamchara.

The friendship that united Adamnan and King Finnachta was duplicated in the intimacy between Adamnan and Aldfrid, king of Northumbria,[1] who had an Irish mother and who was educated in Ireland and was at one time apparently a schoolfellow or pupil of Adamnan. The esteem in which he was held by the two kings bore fruit on the occasions on which he acted as ambassador between them. One of these diplomatic missions undertaken by Adamnan brings into relief the only occasion in Anglo-Saxon history, after the mission of Aidan, on which an act of hostility was perpetrated by the English against the nation that had been to them so remarkable a benefactor. This was an attack on Meath by Ecgfrith, the predecessor, brother and enemy of Aldfrid, whose presence in Ireland appears to have been its inspiring

[1] He talks of visits to "my friend, King Aldfrid, in Saxonia" (V. Columbae, I, XLVII).

motive, and the carrying away of a number of prisoners. In 686, following the accession of Aldfrid, Adamnan undertook at the instance of Finnachta a mission to Northumbria and brought back to Ireland sixty captives.

Two years later he again visited Aldfrid's court in Northumbria, and also, it appears, visited the monasteries of Wearmouth and Jarrow. Bede appears to have known him well and greatly reverenced him. On the occasions of his visits to England a great plague, to which Bede movingly alludes, was ravishing the country, but the Irish and the Picts appear to have been remarkably spared by it. Adamnan attributes his own immunity and that of his countrymen to the intercession of Columcille, but the personal habits induced by a superior civilization doubtless played their part.

4. THE HIBERNICIZING OF NORTH BRITAIN

In 692 Adamnan resided in Ireland and he was there again in 697—it was round the earlier of these two dates that he seems to have composed the major part of the life of Columcille. He seems to have been the influential figure at the Parliament of Tara held in 697 and caused to be reenacted a law exempting women from fighting, which Columcille had caused to be passed, but which the passions of the time had disregarded. From that date the edict was strictly enforced and came to be known as the Lex Adamnani or Cain Adhemhnain. It appears to have been at this Parliament that the questions in respect to the observance of Easter, which then agitated so many minds, were discussed and that the Roman views and usages, which Adamnan greatly favored, were generally adopted, though as early as 634 they began to be

Death of Columcille

the vogue over a great part of Ireland. Adamnan seems to have dwelt in Ireland from 697 to 701; and Bede observes that he crossed from Ireland to Iona the summer before he died; and alluding to the variance between himself and his brethren at Iona, who could not be induced to forsake the observances sanctioned by the devotion of Columcille, adds: "For it came to pass that before the next year came round he departed this life: the Divine Goodness so ordering it that, as he was a man most earnest for peace and unity, he should be taken away to everlasting life before the return of the season of Easter he should be obliged to differ still more seriously from those who were unwilling to follow him in the way of truth."

Adamnan, though, like Columcille, of noble, and even of royal birth, led a life of solid hard work, not disdaining, any more than his great predecessor, to assist the brethren in the manual labor of building, rowing, and dragging overland ships laden with the hewn pine and oak needed in their operations. In spite of this, his literary work must have been extraordinarily voluminous.[1] Latin was his favorite medium of expression, and he seems to have had a good working knowledge of Greek and Hebrew. His "De Locis Sanctis," from which Bede quotes, and which has happily been preserved, is the earliest account coming from modern Christian Europe of the condition of Eastern lands and the cradle of Christianity.[2] It was compiled from the conversation

[1] In the prologue to his "De Locis Sanctis" he tells us how he worked, writing the first rough drafts of his compositions on waxed tablets (tabulae ceratae) and later transferring the finished copy to the membranes. Columcille and his companions, when traveling, also carried such tablets with them for the purpose of making notes.

[2] The reticences of Adamnan are as remarkable as what he says. He has, for example, in his extant works no reference to the work of the Irish missionaries in England, though the chief of them, Aidan, Finan, Colman and the others, were among the brethren of Iona in his time. Never was there a great work done in the world with less trumpeting on the part of those who did it. Were it not for foreign testimony we would know very little of the work of medieval Irishmen abroad, and indeed we know of only a very small part of it.

of Arculf, a Gallic bishop who visited Iona after he had been in Palestine, and Adamnan presented a copy of the work to King Aldfrid. Adamnan is credited with a life of St. Patrick as well as with poems reproduced by Tighernach, the Annals of the Four Masters, and the Book of Lecain. He is said to have written a history of the Irish nation up to his own times and an Epitome of the Irish Laws of Metre. In the Liber Hymnorum there is a poem in Gaelic called Adamnan's Prayer. In the Leaber na h'Uidhre or Book of the Dun Cow is the famous Fis Adhamhnain or Vision of Adamnan attributed to him, a truly remarkable precursor of Dante's Divina Commedia, in which the "high scholar of the Western World" visits heaven and hell. His fame endured in a degree only inferior to Columcille's. Contemporaries like Coelfrid offered their tributes to his character and learning. Bede calls him "a good and wise man, most nobly versed in the science of the Scriptures."[1] While Alcuin classes him with Columbanus and other distinguished Irishmen as "renowned brothers, masters both of manners and of life."[2]

A line of forty-nine abbots, of whom Adamnan was the ninth, succeeded Columcille at Iona, ending with Giollacrist who died c. 1202.[3] In course of time the spiritual authority of Iona passed eastward with the success of Irish arms to the more central seat of government which the Irish kings of Scotland established at Dunkeld. The Danish descents on Iona in the ninth century and

---

[1] "Vir bonus et sapiens, et scientia scripturarum nobilissime instructus."
[2] "Patricius, Charanus, Scottorum gloria gentis,
Atque Columbanus, Congallus, Adamnanus atque,
Praeclari fratres, morum vitaeque magistri.
Hic pietas precibus horum nos adjuvet omnes."—(Migne, LXXXVIII, col. 777.)
[3] Reeves, Life of St. Columba, by Adamnan (pp. 269-413), gives a list of the forty-nine abbots with a brief biography of each and a chronicle, compiled from the Irish annals, of the chief events under the encumbency of each.

the rise of Kells in Ireland caused a diversion in the administration of the Columbian brotherhood, and when soon after the Pictish nation yielded to Irish rule and Kenneth mac Alpin, c. 847, transferred the sovereignty to the eastern side of Scotland, Dunkeld became the spiritual and political capital of the united kingdom of the Irish and the Picts. From that time Iona continued to decline[1] and Dunkeld, which is numbered among the fifty-three known foundations of Columcille and his disciples in Scotland, took its place as the capital and center of the national life.

Of the multitude of other men—missionaries and kings, soldiers, statesmen and scholars—who aided, supplemented and succeeded Columcille in the work not merely of Christianizing but of colonizing and Hibernicizing Scotland, little can here be said. There were noble figures among them—Modan in Stirling; Drostan in Aberdour; Molurg in Lismore; Ciaran in Kintyre; Mun in Argyle; Buite in Pictland; Moohar on the eastern coasts; Fergus in Caithness and Buchan with Maelrubha of Skye and the other apostles of the Western Isles—these are but leading names in a great host that Ireland gave to Scotland. There were none of them that were not wholly Irish. The missionaries of civilization in other countries have been of diverse nationalities. In England they were Irish, Roman, and Greek. In France they were Greek, Roman, Hebrew, and Irish. Scotland had no saint, no

---

[1] It remained the favored burial place of the kings of Scotland, as Shakespeare evidences:
"Ross: Where's Duncan's body?
"Macduff: Carried to Colmekill (Iona)
    The sacred storehouse of his predecessors
    And guardian of their bones."
"Ross: . . . . That now
    Sweno, the Norway's king, craves composition;
    Nor would we deign him burial of his men
    Till he disbursed at Saint Colme's Inch
    Ten thousand dollars to our general use."—(Macbeth, Acts I and II.)

prophet, no king, no leader among the people, who was not an Irishman. Irish speech and Irish civilization were to put the seal of Irish authority so completely on Scotland that even in modern eyes it remains in many respects more Gaelic and Irish than the inland provinces of the motherland. To other lands medieval Irishmen brought Christianity and culture. To Scotland they brought the whole Gaedhaeltacht, and, dividing Britain almost into halves, added the northern portion as a fifth Irish province to the five other provinces of Ireland, and called the whole Scotia.[1]

1 See appendix B. p. 314, for additional details concerning the Irish kingdom of Scotland.

CHAPTER XIII
IRISH PRINCIPALITY IN WALES

1. Gael and Sassenach in Britain. 2. Irish Clans in Britain. 3. Irish Military Expeditions Abroad. 4. Irish Kings in Britain. 5. Wales Medieval Irish Colony.

1. Gael and Sassenach in Britain

WHILE Irishmen in North Britain were bending their energies to the work of conquering, colonizing and civilizing Caledonia, another conquest was going forward, chiefly under the direction of Irishmen of the center and south, which has received less attention from historians. Had there been no Anglo-Jute-Saxon conquest of Great Britain these two Irish conquests would in all likelihood have been decisive of the future of the island. They would have issued in a British Isles almost entirely Irish, with the Irish tongue the prevalent speech from Kerry to Lincoln and from the Orkneys to the Isle of Wight, and with the equivalent of what is now Wales pushed eastwards and southwards and confined to a jutting headland between the estuary of the Thames and the Wash, or more probably absorbed in the kindred Irish population. But there was an Anglo-Jute-Saxon invasion, so that the Gael and the Sassenach met on the broad moors of Britannia and fought their destiny out. The issue lay for centuries in doubt, but eventually the Sassenach proved the stronger, not in individual prowess indeed, for the Irishman is superior in physique to the Englishman,[1] but primarily then as later because the Gael had only the

[1] The Irish are probably the strongest, tallest, and most athletic race on earth, and their record in the world of sport seems to make this abundantly clear. But see "The Irish People; Their Height, Form and Strength," by F. E. Hogan (Dublin, 1899). Irish hatters stock larger sizes than hatters in England. The English made a remarkably poor comparative showing in the recent war measurements.

small island of Hibernia behind him, while the Sassenach drew his strength from the teeming population of northern Europe.

Thus Nennius says the invaders were constantly being reinforced—"the more the Saxons were vanquished the more they sought for new supplies of Saxons from Germany. Kings, commanders, and military bands were invited over from almost every province, and this practice they continued till the reign of Ida." A statement by Bede implies that practically the entire Anglic people emigrated from the Continent en masse—men, women and children—no one being left to cultivate the land, for, he says, the land "which is called Angulus" remained a desert till the day in which he wrote. And then there was another reason and a potent one. It was at this period that the Gaels of Ireland were turning their backs on the mirage of military glory and were preparing to spend themselves in the nobler engagement against the forces of ignorance and heathenism. From the time of Patrick there is no record of any raiding expedition going forth from the Gaedhaltacht. The military organization of the Fiana, whose exploits are celebrated in the poems of Oisin, still continued to exist, but it gradually disappeared, and the great military encampments, like Tara, Aileach and Cruachain, in which the Irish kings were accustomed to dwell surrounded by permanent fighting forces, lost their military character around the seventh century.[1]

[1] Kells, originally a military stronghold, later the head of the Colombian foundations, is an example, as the dialog between Columcille and the prophet Becc indicates:

"O Becc, tell thou to me
Kells, the wide, pure grassed,
Whether clerics (will) dwell in it,
Whether warriors (will) abandon it?"

So Becc said:

"Trains who are amidst it
Shall sing praises of the Lord's Son;
Its warriors shall depart from its threshold;
There will be a time when it will be secure."—(Leabar Breac, p. 32 a-b; Anecdota Oxoniensia, Ser. 5, p. 306.)

In this long contest nothing appears more remarkable than the lack of grit in the Britons themselves. Even the simple-minded English dwell on it: "They then sent to Angel, bade them send greater help, and bade them to say the Brito-Welsh's nothingness and the land's excellencies."[1] Three centuries of Roman dominance had deprived the Briton, originally an excellent fighting man, of his military virtue. The main fight centered around the ambitions of the Gael and the Sassenach, and the "Brito-Welshman" appears as little better than a pawn in a game between stronger rivals. The chief Brito-Welsh resource appears to have been flight. Thus from 460 to 550 a continual stream of British fugitives crossed over from Britain to Armorica and there established a smaller Britain that has endured to this day.[2]

The Saxons came to England according to the traditional account, invited to aid the Briton against the Gael and Pict by Vortigern, whom some consider to have been an Irish prince ruling the Britons.[3] Three distinct wars of conquest thus came to be waged simultaneously in the island. The Irishmen of the north were engaged in reducing Caledonia, a conquest subsequently completed by them. The Angles, Saxons and Jutes were successfully invading Britain from the east. And Irish tribes, chiefly of Munster stock, were taking possession of Britannia Secunda and part of Britannia Prima, establishing a colony or dependency that included present Wales as well as Somerset, Devon and Cornwall. This last conquest and settlement have, as I have said, received relatively small attention from historians, chiefly because their visible

[1] Anglo-Saxon Chronicle.
[2] Great Britain is so called in contradistinction to this smaller Britain (now called Brittany) in France. It is to be noted that the English have no right to the name Briton, which belongs to the former Celts of the country, now represented by the Welsh.
[3] Rhys, in "The Welsh People," gives reasons for this view.

effects have not endured to our day. Roughly the dominion of the Gael in West Britain or Wales lasted for four centuries—from the third to the seventh or eighth, during the latter part of which period it passed from being an Irish-speaking to being a Welsh-speaking country.

2. IRISH CLANS IN BRITAIN

Zeuss[1] demonstrated that the Irish and Welsh languages were one in their origin; that their divergence began only a few centuries before the Roman period; that the difference between them was very small when Cæsar landed in Britain—so small that an old Hibernian was still understood there; and that both nations, Irish and British, were identical with the Celtae or Galli of the Continent—namely those of Gaul, Spain, Lombardy and the Alpine countries—thus asserting the intrinsic unity of the Celtic family. By the seventh and eighth centuries of our era, however, the Irish and "Brito-Welsh" languages had diverged very considerably, and that divergence has continued and increased to the present time. The Irish in Wales, divided from the homeland by a broad and turbulent sea, became absorbed in the kindred British population around them or returned to Ireland. Meanwhile the Irish in North Britain, in unceasing close contact with the motherland, carried their arms, culture and speech over all Caledonia or Scotland and even into northern England. So French or English speech did not even begin to make headway among the Irish Scots of Caledonia till the thirteenth or fourteenth century, a period when Norman-French was the prevailing language throughout England, except among the lower orders.

[1] In his "Grammatica Celtica," published in 1854.

The conquest of North Britain or Caledonia had been achieved by the Irishmen of Ulster, the kinsmen of the princely clans of the O'Donels and O'Neills. The conquest of North Wales appears likewise to have been achieved by the Ultonians. South Britain, including south Wales and the Cornish peninsula, appear to have become Irish through the efforts of the men of Munster. During the historic period there appears to have been no fundamental difference in the Irish nation. All the governing clans, septs and races, equivalents of the Roman gens, point to a common origin, all are Irish and Gaelic. The Irish carried their pedigree to an incredible antiquity. The immediate eponym of the race was Galamh, from Gal, valor, a name which might be exprest by the Latin miles, a knight, whence came the names Milesius and Milesian. All the Milesian families traced their names to Galamh or Milesius. From three of the sons of Milesius, namely, Heber, Ir and Heremon, who invaded Ireland, are descended all the Milesian Irish of Ireland and Scotland, and the reputed descent from these sons colors all Irish history. From Heber, the eldest brother, the provincial kings of Munster (of whom thirty-eight were high monarchs of Ireland) and most of the noble families of Munster were descended. From Ir, the second brother, all the provincial kings of Ulster (of whom twenty-six were high monarchs of Ireland) and all the old and noble families of Ulster, and many noble families in Leinster, Munster and Connaught, derive their pedigrees.

From Heremon, the youngest of the three brothers, and the chief of them from the number and distinction of his descendants, according to Irish genealogical compilations, were descended one hundred and fourteen monarchs of Ireland, the provincial kings and Heremonian nobility and gentry of Leinster, Connaught, Meath, Orgiall, Tirowen, Tyrconnell, and Clan-na-boy, the three kings of Dalriada, and all the kings of Scotland from Fergus Mor, son of Earca, down to the Stuarts. The issue of Ithe is not accounted among the Milesian Irish or Clanna-Mile as being descended not from Milesius but from his uncle Ithe, of whose posterity there were also some monarchs of Ireland and many provincial or half-provincial kings of Munster. That country upon its first division was allocated to the sons of Heber and to Lughaidh, son of Ithe, whose posterity continued there accordingly.[1]

The points to be dwelt on are that the Munster Irish are in the main the reputed descendants of Heber, as distinguished from the reputed descendants of the other two sons of Milesius, Ir and Heremon, in most of the rest of Ireland, and that these Munster Irish had certain characteristics that distinguished them. They were among the first to receive the Christian faith before St. Patrick. Roman-British missionaries were among them, it would appear, at the beginning of the third century.[2]

[1] The pedigrees of the old Irish families that have been saved from the wreck of ages are among the most curious and valuable historic records in our possession. Their accuracy and genuineness have been fully demonstrated as far as it has been possible to trace and test them, which appears to be where they all converge round the fourth century—beyond that is uncertainty. There is no country in Europe, with the exception of Italy perhaps, that has anything that in any way approaches them. There are families in Ireland that can trace their pedigrees back to a point farther in history than the whole English nation. Irish pedigrees are one of the indisputable evidences of ancient Irish culture, for it is inconceivable that a family could cherish and preserve its family records from generation to generation, as the Irish families and clans are shown to have done, without a considerable degree of social self-consciousness and mental cultivation. The accumulation of those that have been preserved is extraordinary. The best handbook on the subject is O'Harts' "Irish Pedigrees" (2 vols.); Douglas Hyde has an interesting chapter on them in his "Literary History"; while Eoin MacNeill illuminates their use as historic signposts in a series of articles in the New Ireland Review (1904-5).

[2] See Zimmer, Pelagius in Ireland (Berlin).

The Ogham and other stone inscriptions found in Ireland are far more numerous among them than elsewhere. Distinguishing marks such as these have enabled investigators to differentiate between the Irish clans that peopled West Britain, and the conclusion has been that the Cornish peninsula and South Wales were in the hands of the Munster men, while North Wales and Scotland went to the more northerly Irish people.

3. Irish Military Expeditions Abroad

The foreign expeditions from Ireland coming within the historic period may be said to begin with the reign of the celebrated Cormac, son of Art and grandson of Conn of the Hundred Battles—who reigned over Ireland for forty years (226-266 A. D.), for the Annals of the Four Masters, quoting the Annals of Tighernach, tell us that in the year 240 A. D. Cormac, the high king, sailed across the high sea and obtained the sovereignty of Alba (Britain).

Frequent accounts, which Roman writers amplify, are given in the legends of the Irish kings and in Irish literature generally, of warlike expeditions from Ireland to Alba and Gaul and of settlements and intermarriages in those countries. The Glossary of Cormac, mac[1] Culinan, a production of the ninth century, tells us that "great was the power of the Gael over Britain, and they continued in this power till long after the coming of Patrick" and that "Crimthann Mor (or Criffan the Great), who reigned for thirteen years, was king over Ireland and Britain to the British Channel."[2] Keating tells us that

[1] "Mac" means son or descendant; "Ua" (O) means grandson or descendant; "Ni" means granddaughter or descendant. Where "mac," as in this case, is used before the establishment of surnames (tenth and eleventh centuries) the initial letter is in lower case preceded by a comma.

[2] Sañas Chormaic, ninth century, edited, Stokes, 1868.

it was this Crimthann who gained victories and extended his sway over Alba, Britain and Gaul, as the Shanachie tells us in the following rann:

> "Crimthann, son of Fidach, ruled
> The Alban and the Irish lands,
> Beyond the clear blue seas he quelled
> The British and the Gallic might." [1]

It was during the reigns of Eochaidh Muighmeadhoin (358-366), of Crimthann Mor (366-379), and of Niall of the Nine Hostages (379-405), that the Irish invasion and conquest of a large portion of Britain became consolidated. More than one of the Irish kings assumed the title of King of Alba (Britain); and of one of them, Miurchartach, son of Earca, who died in 533, it is reported that, in addition to his Irish titles, he was styled king of the Britons, Franks and Saxons.[2]

Readers of history are familiar with the Roman accounts of the blows dealt the empire in Britain by the Picts and the Irish Scots. The ancient chroniclers are generally assumed to represent that the Irish military taking part in these invasions all came, like the Picts, from the north. But Ammianus Marcellinus, "an old soldier and a Greek" as he calls himself, writing 380-390, expressly states that the Picts and the Irish arrived by different ways (per diversa vagantes). Bede has a passage to a similar effect, indicating that the Irish naval forces invaded Britain from the west, that is directly from Ireland, for the Irish or Scoti did not then inhabit present Scotland in any great number.

The invasion was organized and persistent. At the year 360 we find one of the earliest Roman references to the Irish "Scoti" as cooperating with the Picts in raids

1 Forus Feasa na h-Eireann (History of Ireland).
2 Irish Nennius, pub. of I. A. S., 180.

on the regions of the northern stations, and as they were accused of having by so acting broken the peace that had been agreed upon there had evidently been earlier fighting: "The affairs of Britain became troubled in consequence of the incursions of the Picts and Irish, who, breaking the peace (nupta quiete condicta) to which they had agreed were plundering the districts on their borders, and keeping in constant alarm the provinces (i. e., of Britain) exhausted by former disasters. Cæsar (Julian the Apostate, 360-363), proclaimed emperor at Paris, having his mind divided by various cares, feared to go to the aid of his subjects across the Channel (as we have related Constans to have done) lest he should leave the Gauls without a governor, while the Alemanni were still full of fierce, warlike intentions."[1]

Four years later the same writer tells us the "Picts, Irish, Saxons and Attacotti prest the Britains with incessant invasions." And again at 368 he says: "Valentinian (the emperor) having left Amiens and being on his way to Treves, then the capital of the western prefecture, received the disastrous intelligence that Britain was reduced by the ravages of the united barbarians to the lowest extremity of distress, that Nectarides, the count of the sea coast, had been slain in battle, and that the commander Fultofondes had been taken prisoner by the enemy in an ambuscade. Jovinus applied for the aid of a powerful army. Last of all, on account of the many formidable reports, Theodosius (the elder) was appointed to proceed to Britain and ordered to make great haste. At that time the Picts, the Attacotti, a very warlike people, and the Irish were all roving over different parts of the country and committing great ravages." In

---

[1] Ammianus Marcellinus, XX, I.

the battle that immediately followed, Theodosius drove back the Irish and the Picts from the city "which was anciently called Lugdun (Celt. the fort of Lug) (London), but is now known as Augusta." Then "he (Theodosius) established stations and outposts on the frontier and he so completely covered the province which had yielded subjection to the enemy that it was again brought under its legitimate rule and by the desire of the emperor called Valentia," that is the part above Hadrian's wall.

Claudian, the Alexandrian poet, adds to this by telling us that Theodosius "followed the Irishman with wandering sword and clove the waters of the northern ocean with his daring oars," treading "the sands of both the tidal seas," so that "Icy Ireland weeps for the heaps of Irish slain."[1]

4. IRISH KINGS IN BRITAIN

Among the Irish kings daring enough to attack the Roman armies in their own strongholds the most formidable appears to have been Niall of the Nine Hostages (d. 405), who in his last years practically brought the greater part of Britain under Irish rule. The Romans never entirely conquered Britannia Secunda, as what is

[1] Two passages in Claudian illustrate the campaigns of Theodosius. 368, 369. In the Panegyric on the Third Consulship of Honorius (A. D. 395) we read, vv, 54-6:

 Ille leues Mauros nec falso nomine Pictos
 Edomuit Scottumque uago mucrone secutus
 Fregit Hyperboreas remis audacibus undas,

and in the Panegyric on the Fourth Consulship (A. D. 397) vv, 28 seq.:

  debellatorque Britanni
 Litoris ac pariter Boreae uastator et Austri.
 Quid rigor aeternus, caeli quid frigora prosunt
 Ignotumque fretum? maduerunt Saxone fuso
 Orcades; incaluit Picorum sanguine Thyle;
 Scottorum cumulos fleuit glacialis Hiuerne.

The first of these passages suggests that Theodosius pursued the Irish across the sea, or at least made a naval demonstration in the Irish Channel, and this is perhaps supported by a passage in Pacatus, Panegyric, C. 5: attritan pedestribus praeliis Britanniam referam? Saxo consumptus bellis naualibus offeretur redactum ad paludes suas Scotum loquar?

now Wales was then called,[1] and strong legionary stations at Chester, the Roman Deva, and at Caerleon, the Roman Isca Silurum, were established by them as barriers against the Irish invaders.

Against King Niall in the closing years of the fourth century Rome sent, in the person of Flavius Stilicho, her ablest general. The organized strength of the Irish attacks, on the land and on the sea, is mirrored in the glowing words of Claudian, who, speaking in the person of Britannia, says of Stilicho: "By him was I protected when the Irishman moved all Ireland against me and the sea foamed under his hostile oars."[2]

From another of the poet's eulogies it appears that the fame of the Roman legion, which had guarded the frontiers of Britain against the invading Irish and Picts, procured for it the distinction of being one of the bodies summoned to the banner of Stilicho when the Goths threatened Rome: "There arrived also the legion spread out over the furthermost Britons, which bridles the fierce Irishman and examines on the dying Pict the hideous pictures punctured by the steel."[3]

With the withdrawal of the Roman forces from Britain at the beginning of the fifth century the Irish appear to have extended their sway over the whole of what is now

1 No legion appears in the western district of Britain in the Notitia Dignitatum, which represents the state of civil and military services in the Empire in the first years of the fifth century.

2 Totam cum Scotus Iernem movit,
  Et infesto spumavit remige Tethys.
  Illius effectum curis ne tela timerem
  Scottica ne Pictum tremerem, ne litore toto.
  Prospicerem dubiis uenturum Saxona uentis. (De Consulatu Stilichonis, ii, 247 seq., composed A. D. 399.)
St. Patrick himself appears to have been one of the captives of Niall's fleets operating in the mouth of the Severn, for concerning this very period he writes in his "Confession": "I was about sixteen years of age when I was brought captive into Ireland with many thousand persons."

3 Venit et extremis legio praetenta Britannis,
  Quae Scoto dat froena traci, ferroque notatas
  Perlegit examines Picto moriente figuras. (De Bello Gothico, 416-8.)

England. "The barbarians drive us into the sea, the sea throws us back upon the barbarians" is the purport of one of the "Groans of the Britons" as those groans were directed towards Aetius and Rome. Gildas, writing in the first half of the sixth century, says that the Irish "wafted both by the strength of oarsmen and the blowing wind break through the boundaries and spread slaughter on every side, and like mowers cutting down the ripe corn, they cut up, tread under foot, and overrun the whole country."[1]

During the reign of King Dathi (405-428), the nephew of Niall of the Nine Hostages and his immediate successor on the throne of Ireland, Irish forces penetrated beyond Britain into Gaul, either as the opponents or the allies[2] of the Romans. King Dathi was himself killed in the region of the Alps, whither he appears to have gone for the purpose, among other things, of avenging the death of his uncle, Niall, who had been killed on the banks of Loire.[3] Dathi was carried by his legionaries back to Ireland and was buried in the royal cemetery at Rath Croghan, where the great red monumental pillar stone, raised according to tradition above his remains, still defies the waste of ages.

> "And there was buried
> Dathi, the last renowned high-king who reigned
> Ere Faith came to Erin; he at warfare
> In far-off Latin lands had burned the home
> Of a most holy hermit and had died,
> Slain by God's lightning on the Alps."[4]

[1] De Excidio et Conquestu Britanniae, Migne, Pat. Lat., LXIX, col. 329; Mon. Germ. Hist., Auct. Antiquiss., 13.

[2] S. Hieronymi Epist. 11. adv. Jovin and context. St. Jerome, writing from Treves, is voucher for the existence of an Irish legion there.

[3] The book of Lecain says of the monarch that after fighting many battles in Eire and Alba "Dathi went with the men of Eire to Leatha (i. e., Letavia or Brittany) until he reached the Alps to avenge the death of Niall." For the legend of the Slaying of Niall of the Nine Hostages (Oruin Neill Noigiallaig) see the version edited by Prof. Kuno Meyer (in Otia Merseiana, ii, 84 seq.)

[4] The Tain, Epil. (Writing of the Tain), translation by Hutton, p. 448. See the poem of Torna-Eices on the famous men and women, who lay at Rath Croghan, published by de Jubainville in Revue Celtique, 17, 280, seq. A reproduction of Dathi's grave and pillar stone is given in Proceedings, Roy. Irish Acad., 1879, p. 117.

Gildas talks of the Britons eventually overthrowing the Irish enemies "who had for so many years been living in their country," by which he means not Wales but Britain. However, it is certain that the Irish formed a still strong military and colonizing power in Britain in the days of Gildas. The historian of the Britons says that after the departure of Maximus and his death in the year 388 at Aquileia, Britain "utterly ignorant as she was of the art of war groaned in amazement for many years under the cruelty of two foreign nations—the Irish from the northwest, and the Picts from the north." From other passages it would really seem as if the Romans succeeded in driving the Irish over the Mare Hibernicum on some occasions: "So did our illustrious defenders (the Romans) vigorously drive the enemies' band beyond the sea, if any could so escape them; for it was beyond those same seas that they transported, year after year, the plunder which they had gained, no one daring to resist them."

Their departure was, however, only for a brief space. When the Romans had gone "they hastily land again from their boats in which they had been carried beyond the Cichican valley" (Irish Sea). "Moreover having heard of the departure of our friends and their resolution never to return, they seized with greater boldness than before on all the country towards the extreme north as far as the wall."[1]

From 407, when the tyrant Constantine crossed with the Roman armies to Gaul, to 446 (the third consulship of Aetius) Irish power seems to have been consolidating over all Britain. It appears to have reached its high-water mark round the middle of the fifth century. As it receded

[1] De Excidio Britanniae, Liber Querulus, Migne, Pat. Lat., LXIX, cols. 329-92; Monumenta Germ. Hist., Auct. Antiquiss., 13.

in the south before the combination of Briton and Saxon, it took a wider sweep in what is now Scotland, completely conquering and incorporating it within the empire of the Gael.

5. Wales Medieval Irish Colony

And now with regard to the permanent results of these Irish expeditions and what remained of the Irish occupation of Britain as the Angles and Saxons overran the country.

There remained two distinct settlements of the Irish in Britannia Secunda or Wales: (1) of the Munster tribes in South Wales, Somerset, Devon and Cornwall; and (2) of other Irish in the Isle of Man, Anglesey and other parts of Gwynedd or North Wales.

Early writers pointed to a Gaelic element in the topographical nomenclature of West Britain and concluded that the country was once occupied by Irish people, whence they were supposed to have been driven into Ireland by the advancing Britons or Cymri, as they came later to be called, and as the Welsh call themselves in the Welsh tongue. This was the natural and reasonable conclusion at the time, but our present knowledge compels us to adopt a different view, namely, that, without prejudice to the existence at an anterior period of Irish tribes in West Britain, the numerous traces of Gaelic names found there are derived from the Irish invasions and occupations in the Roman period which I have just been describing.

The Rev. W. Basil Jones, bishop of St. David's, summing up his researches on the subject in his "Vestiges of the Gael in Gwynedd" (North Wales), came to the conclusion that the Irish occupied the whole of Anglesey,

Carnarvon, Merioneth, and Cardigan, with a portion at least of Denbighshire, Montgomeryshire and Radnorshire, and that the same clans that occupied Anglesey and Gwynedd also occupied the Isle of Man, which, as is well known, was an Irish possession before the Norman invasion.

Dr. Jones's work was brought out in 1851 and in it he showed that Irishmen were in possession of North Wales at the time of the collapse of Roman rule in Britain. Since the appearance of his work our knowledge on this subject has widened very considerably and we are now in possession of evidence which shows that not only North Wales but South Wales as well were Irish dependencies. The invasion and extent of the settlement of the Irish in South and West Britain are established by the discovery of Ogham inscriptions.

Ogham is a purely Irish form of writing and Ogham inscriptions have been found only in Ireland, the Isle of Man, Scotland, Wales and the southwest of England. More than five-sixths of the known inscriptions have been found in Ireland itself, and it is to be noted that more Oghams have been found in Wales than in Scotland, the character of which as an Irish province has never been lost sight of. The total number of known inscriptions appears to be about 360 and of the Irish inscriptions, numbering about 300, five-sixths have been found in what are now the counties of Kerry, Cork and Waterford. Scotland has 16 Oghams; the Isle of Man has 6; in Devon and Cornwall there are 5; Wales has over 30 Oghams, of which 13 are in Pembrokeshire, 4 in Breeknock, 2 in Glamorgan, 1 in Cardigan, 6 in Carmarthen, and only 1 in North Wales. In Hampshire there is 1, and this is interesting as showing the extent of the Irish military colonization across Monmouth, Gloucester, Somerset and Wilts into what is regarded as purely English territory; in the rest of England none.

No Oghams have been found on the Continent, but at Biere in Saxony there are stone tablets bearing unintelligible syllables traced in Ogham characters, possibly the work of some·traveling Gael who knew just a little of the craft. All the inscriptions that have been deciphered and interpreted belong to the same language—an early form of Irish—except a few in northeastern Scotland, which are said to be in the Pictish language. The distribution of the inscriptions clearly corresponds to the region of Irish influence in the period that followed the withdrawal of the Roman legions from Britain. The bulk of the Ogham inscriptions are ascribed to the fifth and sixth centuries, and their disuse appears to have come about consequent on the spread of Christianity and Latin learning and letters.[1]

The Ogham inscriptions, which are engraved on stone pillars in various parts of Wales, were discovered after Dr. Jones had written his book and they constitute unquestionable evidence of the prolonged presence of Irish people in Wales. They confirm Dr. Jones's original conclusions but show that he did not go far enough. They show that practically the whole of Wales was long an Irish possession. The Ogham inscriptions are mostly of an obituary or mortuary character, connected with religious motives, pagan or Christian. No list of Irish nobles or kings or fact of great historical value is found in them.

The Welsh inscriptions, like the others, are couched in the Irish language. Over twenty of them have a Latin rendering, a thing rare in Ireland. There have been

[1] MacNeill, Royal Irish Acad., 1907-9.

found over the same region in south Britain seventy other
non-Ogham inscriptions in Latin—all of them judged to
be Irish, for the pillar stone with an inscription is a distinguishing element in Irish archeology. The Latin
inscriptions in the main are in Irish minuscules of the
period, which appear indeed to have been the only form
of writing known and practised either in Wales or
England till the Normans introduced the Caroline characters.[1]

It is made clear then that at a time judged to be during
the third and fourth centuries, when Roman power was
still strong in Britain, the western regions were invaded
and settled by Irish colonists and soldiers with their
families. Thus is explained the presence in Wales and
the Cornish peninsula of a substantial Irish-speaking
element in the population. On the other hand, evidence
of the activity of the Romans in South Wales in the fourth
century is of the scantiest. Between the Irish in Wales
and Ireland there was maintained a regular intercourse,
an intercourse testified to, among other things, by the
great abundance of Roman coins found on the east coast
of Ireland.

Hereditary family names did not come into existence
till the eleventh century, but clan or sept names existed
from the beginning. Some of the Irish people in south
Wales were known by the same clan names as those in
Ireland, as in the case of Ui Liathain, an Irish family, or
gens, settled in ancient Desmond, between Cork and Lismore, having also a branch in Wales.[2] Cormac, son of

[1] The epitaph of Cadvan, Irish king of Gwynedd or North Wales in the
seventh century, at whose court Welsh tradition says the exiled Edwin of
Northumbria was brought up, is at the Anglesey church of Llangadwaladr.
The inscription says: "Catamanus rex sapientissimus opinatissimus omnium
regum."

[2] "Filii autem Liethan in regione Demetorum et in allis regionibus id est
Guir (et) Cetgueli" (Hist. Britt. c. 14).

Culinan, in his ninth century Glossary also places a "Dind map Letani" among the Cornish Britons.[1]

It has been shown that from 270 A. D. onward there were many expeditions from Ireland directed against the Britons. The suggestion that such evidences of the Gael as exist in south Britain might be derived from the Irish wave that is supposed to have preceded the arrival of the Britons in the island appears to have been disproved. "Whether we take history for our guide or native tradition or philology, we are led to no other conclusion than this: that no Gael ever set foot on British soil save from a vessel that had put out from Ireland."[2] The eighth century tale of Indarba mna n Dese tells how the Desii,[3] a powerful Irish family, having been defeated by the high king, Cormac, mac Art ('226-266 A. D.), left their old holdings in Deece, near Tara, and, dividing, went part to Decies in Munster, which still bears their name, and part under the leadership of Eochaid, son of Artchorp, to Dyfed or (south Wales) and remained there permanently. These Irish invaders appear to have displaced or conquered the native Silures, of whom the famous Caractacus, made prisoner by the Romans, had been king. In the eighth century Tewdor ap Rhain, king of south Wales, was claimed by the Deisi of Munster as a descendant of one of their ruling chieftains, Eochaid Allmuir, whose second appellation points him out as one who had sought his fortunes across the sea.

1 S. v. Mugeime.
2 Irish tale, ed. by Kuno Meyer for Vol. XIV of the Cymmrodor.
3 The Welsh form of the pedigree is to be found in Harl. MS. 3859 (Cymmr. IX, 171) and Jesus College (Oxford) MS. 20 (Cymmr. VIII, 86).

CHAPTER XIV

IRISH CHRISTIANITY IN WALES

1. Power of the Gael in Britain. 2. Wales Less Enduringly Irish than Scotland. 3. Irish Foundations in Wales. 4. Irish Intellectual Intercourse with Britain. 5. Ireland's Imperial Status and the Council of Constance.

1. POWER OF THE GAEL IN BRITAIN

IRISH noblemen and their families often owned two territories or estates, one in Ireland and the other in west Britain, visiting and living in each by turns. The heads of Irish clans often crossed over to receive the tributes due to them from their British possessions. This is made clear from the ancient work of Cormac, son of Culinan, already referred to, from which it appears that so extensive were the settlements of the Gael in Britain that the Irish territory beyond the channel was almost equal in extent to Ireland itself, and Irish princes parceled out the land of Britain, taking each one his share, building up strong forts and noble habitations, so that not less did the Irishman dwell on the east coasts of the sea than in Ireland. This record, overlooked by most historians and absolutely unknown, like most Irish records, to the average English historian, is referred to by O'Donovan as "one of the most curious and important" preserved relating to early Irish and British history.[1] It was after visiting his family and friends in their estates in Wales that Cairbre Musc, son of Conaire, brought the first lap-dog into Ireland, it would seem from the same

[1] Battle of Magh Rath, Pub. I. A. S., 339.

record. The passage from Cormac's Glossary is so valuable and so little known that it is here given as it stands:

"Mug Eime—that is the name of the first lap-dog that was in Eire. Cairbre Musc, the son of Conaire, brought it from the east from Britain; for then great was the power of the Gaels in Britain, they divided Alba between them into districts and each knew the residence of his friends, and not less did the Gael dwell on the east side of the sea than in Scotia (i. e., Erie, or Ireland), and their habitations and royal forts were built there. There is (a fort) called Dun Tradui, i. e., triple fossed fort of Crimhthann, the great son of Fidach, King of Eire and Alba, to the Ichtian Sea, and there is Glastonbury of the Gael, i. e., a church on the border of the Ichtian Sea, and it is on that part is Dinn map Laethain, in the lands of the Cornish Britons, i. e., the Fort of Mac Leithan, for mac is the same as map in the British. Thus every tribe divided on that side, for its property on the east was equal to that of the west, and they continued in this province till long after the coming of Patrick."[1] "Alba" here applies to southern Britain, tho more frequently applied to northern Britain. Both are called the land of the "Albiones" by Avienus.[2] Bede is also circumstantial about the power of the Irish in Britain.

In various parts of Wales the word Gwyddel, meaning Gael, or Irishman, enters into the composition of local names. Dr. Jones, in the work already referred to, enumerates twenty-five instances; and there are numerous references to the Gael in the traditions of the Cymri, who claimed to be the earliest inhabitants of the country. They

[1] Sanas Chormaic, i. e., Cormac's Glossary, ninth cent., edit. by Stokes for I. A. S. 1868, p. 110.

[2] Holder, Sprachschatz, sub voce, Albion.

complain of invasions of their territory time and again by the Gaels from Eire.[1]

The ancient Irish work, Leabhar na g-Ceart, or Book of Rights, has numerous entries attesting the existence of considerable commerce and intercourse between Britain and Ireland. We are told that under the pagan Irish kings 300 vessels traded with Britain. Welsh merchants returned from Dairius, an island in Wexford Haven, to St. David's; and Welsh harbors, like Porthmawr, are mentioned as points of departure for Ireland. Irish princes made frequent matrimonial alliances with families of equal station in west Britain. The superior wealth and influence of Ireland are shown in the constant mention, particularly in the fifth and sixth centuries, of Britons, both male and female, living as slaves in Ireland. Thus we read of St. Ailbe (d. 541) that he was given in fosterage to certain Britons who were in servitude in Ireland, in the east of Munster. All this gravitates in the direction of proving that Wales was then a vassal state in respect to Ireland. Monks passed to and fro between Ireland and west Britain, residing on both sides of the sea. To a British monk, working as a cartwright in an Irish monastery, S. Fintan tells the story of his visit to the Land of Promise. British princes fighting the Angles and Saxons found not only food and shelter but also soldiers and ships in Ireland.

Thus the Irish, who had subdued the war-like Picts of north Britain, not only established their authority over the people of south Britain "Even to the Ictian Sea" (English Channel), as Cormac tells us, but may be considered the chief agency in the expulsion of the Romans themselves from Britain. Numerous places in Britain

[1] Book of the West Cornwall, by S. Baring Gould, also Devon, by same author (1899).

are still called after the Irishmen who formerly occupied them, as in the case of Holyhead, of which the Welsh appellation is Cerrig y Gwyddell, meaning "Rocks of the Gaels." "Irish Road" was the name applied to Watling Street, the Roman highway running from Richborough in Kent to Holyhead. The Irish, wherever they settled in Britain, built for their families circular raths and forts. Many remain, particularly in Anglesea, and are called Cyttie r'Gwyddelod, or the "Dwellings of Irishmen."

The present spoken Welsh language contains a number of Irish words, relics of the former Irish domination, as the numerous Latin words in Welsh speak of the still earlier Roman conquest.[1] Investigation has likewise revealed that early Welsh legends originated in Ireland. Thus the story of the flooding which caused the Lake of Glasfrya Uchaf is modeled on the more celebrated Irish account of the forming of Lough Neagh.[2]

2. Wales Less Enduringly Irish than Scotland

We cannot quite tell at what period the Irish hold over Wales ceased. At the beginning of the seventh century the Saxon Chronicle tells us that Irish in Britain contended with Ceolwulf, king of the West Saxon. The passing of Irish rule must have been gradual, and there are evidences of it even in the eighth century. An Irish bishop of Britain, Sedulius, signed the decree of the Roman council of 721, where he is put down as "Episcopus Britanniae de genere Scotus." "Fergustus episco-

[1] Rhys. Revue Celtique, XVII, 102.
[2] The earlier portion of the Annales Cambriae (444-954 A. D.) seems to be derived from an Irish chronicle used also by Tigernach and the compiler of the Annals of Ulster. During its first century it contains hardly anything relating to Britain. Its first reference to English history is in relation to the mission of St. Augustine.

pus Scotiae Pictus" is also mentioned. If any considerable area remained at that time Irish it had remained such for over four centuries.

Wales had an Irish ruler as late as 1080. He was Gruffyd, the son of Cynan, or Caionain, or assuming the name was actually a surname, for surnames were then being established in Ireland, he is in Irish, Gruffyd Mac Caionian, and in Welsh, Gruffyd ap Cynan. He is so presented in the annals, and is styled King of Gwynedd or north Wales by right of inheritance. He left, among other donations, "a gift of twenty shillings to Dublin, that city being his native place," and like gifts to other churches in Ireland.

The international connections of Irish schoolmen are indicated in the case of Gildas (not to be confounded with the earlier historian of the Britons), who was born in 820 in Wales, "Whose parents were Irish," and who went to get his education in Ireland. He blossomed out as an author and one of his works is dedicated to Rhabanus Maurus of Fulda, who had studied under Alcuin at Tours.[1]

Briton and Gael were often confounded. Pelagius, to give a well known instance, is described both as a Briton and an Irishman. Mochta, described as disciple of St. Patrick and as a Briton, studied in Rome. Being taunted in the city about Pelagius, he replied: "If for the fault of one man the inhabitants of a whole province are to be banned let . . . . Rome be condemned, from which not one but two, three or even more heresies have started."

[1] The earlier Gildas, who wrote the Epistola, had many Irish connections and lived part of his life in Ireland. He is said by some authorities to have had an Irish mother, and was at Armagh, both as student and professor. Irish schoolmen visited him in Wales. St. Cadroc, who is a distinguished figure in Welsh history and legend, is described by Colgan as an Irish Scot, in other words as an Irishman born in Ireland. Mabillon, the Bollandists, and Lanigan judge him to have been a British Scot, that is, an Irishman born in Britain.

How it came about that Caledonia, or Alba, or North Britain or Scotland, as it is variously called, remained an Irish speaking country while west Britain became first Irish-speaking and then Welsh-speaking is a question that cannot be fully answered. Scotland was of course easier of access, and intercourse between Ireland and its northernmost province was regularly maintained. A broad and turbulent sea on the other hand divided Ireland from southern Britain. This made it less easy for the Irish colonists in Wales and the southern peninsula to bring their families with them, and the settlement was as a result of a more military character.[1] The proximity of the Romans and later of the Saxons would in any case have made it such. In this case, therefore, the rule, maintained by certain historians, that invaders eventually intermarry with, and adopt the language of, a conquered people when they do not bring their women folk with them, would appear to apply. Doubtless the Irish element in west Britain, at first the governing race, intermarried with the native British, and in that manner passed from the use of Gaelic to the kindred Cymric tongue.

The determination of the fact that west Britain was for centuries Irish ground has a direct bearing on the controversies that have from time to time arisen regarding the provenance and nativity of such men as Pelagius, Sedulius, Boniface and others, who have been called Irish, but who have also been said to have been born in Britain. Thus Boniface was born in what is now called Devonshire when it was distinctively Brito-Irish territory and many years before it fell to the West Saxons.

[1] When Brandoff, powerful king of Leinster, c. 597, heard that Prince Cummuscacg was coming to Leinster on "a youthful free circuit" he did not wait to receive him personally and said: "Let a messenger be sent to them and let them be told that I have gone into Britain to levy rent and tribute." —(Silva Gadelica, 408.)

3. IRISH FOUNDATIONS IN WALES

During the latter part of the Irish occupation that part of Britain now denominated Wales was largely Christian. Christianity had been gradually diffused amongst the ancient Britons during the Roman occupation and with the accession of Constantine was introduced into those parts of Britannia Secunda already colonized. The efforts of Roman priests were supplemented during the fifth, sixth and seventh centuries by the devoted labors of Celtic missionaries, both Irish and Cymric, of whom nearly five hundred names still remain on record. The incessant intercommunication of the Irish and Welsh saints at this time in Britain, joined with the paucity of the Welsh records, make it difficult to tell which of them were originally Irish and which Welsh. To the period succeeding the fall of the Roman is ascribed the foundation of many great Celtic monasteries in Wales.

As early as the close of the second century we find Tertullian declaring that "even those parts of the Britannic islands which were unapproached by the Romans were yet subject to Christ." This may be presumed to refer to Ireland and west Britain. Chrysostom, writing in the year 390, provides similar testimony: "Altho thou shouldst go unto the ocean and those Britannic islands . . . . thou shouldst hear all men everywhere discoursing matter of Scripture."

The Acts of the Irish S. Fingar, with his sister Piala, tell of seven hundred and seventy-seven of his countrymen—allowance has to be made for the figures—who carried the faith into south Britain round the fifth century. These Acts bear testimony to the prosperity and progress of Ireland and speak of seven princes, possibly the seven sons of Amalgaidh, king of Connaught, who heard the apostle Patrick on one occasion, but who despised him for the lowliness of his habit and address.

Bangor-Iscoed and St. David's in Wales, as well as the lesser monasteries, were probably as much Irish foundations as Iona or Luxeuil. Keating distinctly declares that Bangor in Wales was founded by Comgall, who founded Bangor in Ulster: "It was he who founded the abbey of Bangor in the aird of Ulster, which was the mother to all the monasteries of Europe (or its order), and who erected another abbey in England beside West Chester, which is called Bangor."[1] Whether founded by Comgall or not, it is highly probable that Bangor was an Irish foundation. It had, as Bede notes, seven parts or churches, like several other Irish foundations. Though the name of Pelagius has been absurdly connected with it, we know that Bangor really dates from the sixth century when Irishmen were founding monasteries all over Ireland, England and continental Europe. We know that Irishmen then were in complete possession of Wales and we know that there was a great revival in Wales at that epoch—"an improvement in their religious and political existence." This improvement was simply a widening of the radius of the intellectual movement then developing in Ireland, that was making itself felt on the borders of Asia and Africa and could hardly have left Wales any more than the rest of Britain out of its powerful sweep.

St. David's of Menevia (Lat. Menapia), no less than Bangor, has all the appearance of being an Irish foundation. It was the nearest Welsh seaport to Ireland and was much frequented by Irish travelers on their way to and

---

[1] Dionbhrollac (trans. by D. Comyn, Introduction to Gaelic History).

from the Continent and south England. S. David (degui, Dewi) is held to have had an Irish mother and may indeed have been wholly Irish. The monastery named after him was established on land given by an Irish noble in Pembrokeshire named Baja, "vocatus Scottus," a pagan and a druid. He was bishop of the Irish colony of Deise.

It is noteworthy that the lives of the Cambro-British saints,[1] which are highly mythical, show that it was considered the correct thing for a British saint to have studied in Ireland.[2]

Glastonbury, the only monastery prominent both under the Britons and the Saxons, probably owed its foundation and certainly owed its renewal to Irishmen. We know that with Malmesbury it formed a chief channel by which Irish influence and teaching entered Britain in the south as they entered across the borders of Cumbria and Northumbria in the north. It is called "Glastonbury of the Irish" in the Leabhar Breac, or Speckled Book of Dun Doighre, as well as in the Martyrology of Marianus Ua Gormain and in the Calendar of Cashel. Cormac, son of Culinan, likewise in his remarkable Glossary, denominates it "Glastonbury of the Gael." Both Lynch in his "Cambrensis Eversus" and Camden in his "Britannia" declare that Glastonbury was founded by Irishmen. Glastonbury, now joined to the mainland, was once an island in the River Brue, or Brent, like so many other Irish foundations, as, for example, Hohenau, Seckingen, Reichenau, and Rheinau, all islands in the River Rhine. The foundation and town did not fall into Saxon hands till 710. It remained then no less a favorite resort of the Irish. The medieval biographer of S. Dunstan writes

1 Edited by Rees.
2 E. g., St. Cadoc (Rees. pp. 35, 36, cf. p. 59); St. Kebi, ib. pp. 184-6; of Chronicle of the Picts and Scots, ed. W. F. Skene, pp. 112-113; Plummer's Bede, 11, 196.

that "numbers of illustrious Irishmen, eminently skilled in sacred and liberal learning, came into England and chose Glastonbury for their place of abode."[1] Eventually Glastonbury Abbey covered sixty acres and is said to have been one of the finest in the world.

The old Latin name, Glastonia, appears to be based on the Gaelic, glas donn, brown river, and inis glais duinn, island of the brown river. On this island at an early date was built a small walled church, which was known as the "old church," ecclesia vetusta, in the time of Ina of Wessex (resigned 728), who built a larger church east of it on the advice of Aldhelm. That the vetusta ecclesia was the church of St. Patrick is shown by two charters.[2] "I, King Ina," says one (c. 704 A. D.), "bestow this freedom on the monks, who in the church of the Blessed Virgin and the Blessed Patrick, serve Almighty God under Abbot Hemgislus, in the ancient town called Glastingaea and place this worth and privilege on the altar." This charter is subscribed by Aldhelm. Previously in 681 Baldred, king of Mercia, granted to Hemgislus, abbot (of Glaston), as an addition to the honored church of the Blessed Mary and St. Patrick (ecclesiae beatae Mariae et Sancti Patricii), the lands of Somerset. In the charter of 725, Ina calls the old church "the first in Britain," but the name of St. Patrick is omitted, the Benedictine having apparently by that time displaced the Irish rule as it did almost everywhere on the Continent later. The lands granted and confirmed by Ina include a parcel called "Boek Ereie" which is frequently mentioned afterwards in grants or otherwise with the addition "little Hibernia" (parva Hibernia). "Boek Ereie" is a phonetic rendering of the Gaelic words "beg Eriu,"

1 Osbern, Vita S. Dunstani.
2 Kemble, "Codex Diplomaticus."

little Ireland, and there was also a famous islet of that
name in Wexford Harbor—it is still known as Begery.
Johannes Glastoniensis (fl. 1400), who wrote the history of Glastonbury, says that there was down to his time
an ancient chapel in honor of S. Brigid on the island of
Beag Erin, and he mentions the ornamentation of the tomb
of St. Patrick.[1] When Cenwealh in 658 captured Glastonbury he found there the Hiberno-British foundation
which since the overthrow of Ambresbury had been a
center of Hiberno-British Christianity. Different from
Ambresbury, it was not destroyed, for Cenwealh had
lately been made a Christian and was under Irish influence.

William of Malmesbury has a great deal about Glastonbury's Irish associations, and quotes a charter of Edgar
(959-975) endowing Glastonbury, in which one of the
parishes is called "Beokery, otherwise little Ireland."
Of the displacement of Irish monks there, Camden says:
"In these early ages men of exemplary piety devoted
themselves here to God, especially the Irish, who were
maintained at the king's expense and instructed youth in
religion and liberal sciences. They had embraced solitude to apply themselves with more leisure to the study
of the Scriptures and by a severe course of life accustom
themselves to bear the cross. At length Dunstan, a man
of domineering and crafty temperament, by underhand
acts and flatteries, wormed himself into an intimacy with
the kings and introduced in their stead the monks of a
newer order, namely, of S. Benedict."[2]

St. Bees Head in Cumberland still speaks of the story
of Begha, or Bee, an accomplished Irish woman, canon-

[1] Ua Clerigh, Ireland to the Norman Conquest.
[2] Britannia.

ized by popular veneration, who in the sixth century established there a convent and school. The promontory looks across the sea directly towards Mona insula Cæsaris, the Isle of Man, which was to remain Irish in speech and population as long as Scotland. Begha's foundation stood in the midst of a strong Celtic state, both Irish and British, that firmly held back the northern Angles beyond the Pennine range. In its mixed population the Irish remained the ruling element and formed a link between their brethren to the north in Caledonia and to the south in Britannia Secunda. A common danger from the English fused Irish and British together and as a sign of the wearing out of old distinctions they took the name of Cymry (Comrades), a name by which the Welsh are known among one another, and which is also preserved in the name of Cumbria, or Cumberland. Cumbria formed part of Strathclyde, where lake-dwellings or crannogs after the Irish model have been discovered.

4. Irish Intellectual Intercourse with Britain

In the early days of Irish Christianity the Irish are usually considered to have turned to Wales for instruction. Not much evidence can be found in support of this view. The Britons were then in a parlous state. Greco-Roman secular knowledge as well as a first acquaintance with Christianity had passed to the Irish through Roman Britain. But when Britain ceased to be Roman the Britons had all they could do to preserve existence in the face of the foes that surrounded them. Neither as soldiers nor as politicians or churchmen did they show initiative.

It was not until the sixth century, when the Irish church

was in its first bloom and strength and was just beginning its great missionary movement, that Wales showed signs of awakening. It is then that the curtain first really lifts on Welsh history—behind that all is gloom, doubt and surmise. Finian of Clonard, Brendan of Clonfert, as well as other Irishmen, had close relations with Wales. The British revival was unquestionably a result of Irish labor.

The British or Welsh church was always a laggard however. Wales did not conform to Roman custom on the Easter question till the year 768, a hundred and thirty-nine years after the south of Ireland, and long even after Iona. Missionary activity abroad it hardly knew. "It is remarkable that while the Scots (Irish) were the missionaries *par excellence* of nearly all Europe north of the Alps, and in particular of all Saxon England north of the Thames," remarks one authority, "not one Cumbrian, Welsh, or Cornish missionary to any non-Celtic nation is mentioned anywhere. The same remark applies to the Armorican Britons."[1] Strange to say, not a single ancient manuscript of any part of the Bible, Latin or Greek, has been preserved that is pronounced to be the work of a Welsh school of copyists.

From the testimony afforded in the treatises of Suadbar, the Irishman, on the art of cryptography published from the text of a Bamberg manuscript, there lived at the court of King Mermin in Wales (d. 844) an Irish scholar named Dubtach, who later on may have been identical with the Dubtach figuring in the Irish literary colonies of Sedulius Scotus at Liège and Milan, on which new light has in recent years been shed. Dubtach must have felt very much at home at this Welsh court, and apparently had assimilated much Welsh national feeling, for

[1] Haddan and Stubbs, i, 154, Councils and Ecclesiastical Documents.

from that vantage-point he issued a challenge to some Irish scholars to compete with him for the palm of learning. The challenge was accepted by Suadbar and his friends and these friends were named, Caunchobrach, Fergus, and Dominnach, all scholars of the famous Colgu of Clonmacnois, master of many Irish scholars well known abroad. The problem put was to find the solution of some difficult matter in cryptography and this the Irish scholars succeeded in doing. Both the names of Fergus and Colgu, as well as that of Dubtach occur on some of the manuscripts dating back to the circle of Sedulius. This Dubtach, it is thought by Ludwig Traube, may be the author of the Leyden Priscian of the year 838.[1]

Apart from the evidences of Irish occupation in the way of Ogham pillars and inscriptions found in the Cornish peninsula, including Somerset, which remained part of the Celtic state till the year 710, when the Saxons under Ina gained the upper hand, the local nomenclature there speaks eloquently of the missionary and colonizing Gaels who dwelt in the region. Thus Buriana, a young Irish noblewoman, is declared to have given her name to St. Burian, near Land's End. Three miles to the southwest again is St. Levan, named, it is said, from the far-famed St. Livinus, an Irish bishop and classical poet, who died in the Low Countries, verses by whom are still left to us written in excellent Latin. St. Piran, known in

---

[1] Traube is also of opinion that Sedulius Scotus, who was the chief figure in the literary colony at Liège in the ninth century, and who knew well how to play the courtier and to cultivate the friendship of royal personages, as his numerous extant Latin compositions show, also had relations with King Ruadri, the successor of Mermin. The name Ruadri occurs on the St. Gall Priscian, which was one of the manuscripts belonging to the circle of Sedulius at Liège, and which is believed to have been brought out by them from Ireland, where it was probably produced, very likely at Clonmacnois. (Kl. Bay. Akad. Abhandl., 1891, O Roma Nobilis; Zeitk. f. deutsches Allthert. XIX, 147.) It is of course certain that many of the Irish schoolmen who became famous on the Continent must have done work in Wales and England, about which we now know nothing.

Ireland as Ciaran, or Kieran of Saigir—it is curious that the Irish "k" or hard "c" always becomes "p" in Cymric—founded a church at Perran Zabuloe on the north coast of Cornwall; while St. Ives, the picturesque port opposite Falmouth, receives its name from St. Ia, one of Piran's missionary companions, who founded both the church and the town. Similarly from Petroc, another missionary Irishman, who labored in Cornwall, is said to be derived the name of Petrockstow, or Radstow. The close similarity of the stone crosses of Cornwall to those of Ireland is a further interesting illustration of the intercourse between the two and an evidence of the Irish settlement.[1] So large was the number of Irish missionaries in Brittany from Ireland or Cornwall that Berger calls Brittany "une colonie spirituelle d'Irlande."[2] But here we are in a region of doubt and will pass on.

5. Ireland's Imperial Status and the Council of Constance

When we realize that the Gaels of Ireland, holding with a strong hand the west of Britain from the Solway Firth to the Channel, were still to conquer Scotland, that Irish navigators were traversing the seas as far north as Iceland and as far south as the tropic of Cancer, that while Cormac the Navigator was exploring the islands of the north, Brendan the Navigator may have reached part of the American continent, that Irish colonists and monks and explorers actually took possession of the Hebrides, the Faroe Islands, the Orkney Islands, and Iceland, as well as the Azores and all the islands between; we seem to be envisaging the spectacle of a great sea-divided

---

[1] Rimner, "Ancient Stone Crosses of England," pp. 10, 11.
[2] Histoire de la Vulgate.

empire in the making. Ireland in those times had unquestionably great fleets of ships and was possest of a naval fighting force that makes more easily comprehensible Roman hesitation in attempting her conquest. When in addition to this immense political colonization we see her moving to the intellectual conquest of Europe, reaching out as far east as the valley of the Dneiper and as far south as Carthage[1] and Egypt, we realize that Scotia and the Scot must have appeared influential figures in the eyes of medieval Europe.

The center of a pulsating life that infused the civilization of the West to its farthest borders, Ireland was also the base of a great political colonization that endured for centuries and to which the term imperium might not unfittingly be applied. The great place that Ireland filled in the medieval eye made the idea of an Irish empire readily acceptable to the medieval mind and we find the idea adumbrated in the records. It was at the Council of Constance, however, held in the fifteenth century that we find indisputable proof of the hold the idea maintained in Europe.

During the proceedings of the council it was solemnly and unanimously affirmed that Europe had contained four empires, or great divisions, and only four—namely, the Greek, the Roman, the Spanish, and the Irish. The discussion on the subject throws light on the international politics of the period. Becchetti,[2] speaking of the council, says that the Cardinal of Cambrai published a document in November, 1416, in which he denied the right of the English to be considered as a nation, or anything more than a German province, and argued that it was in the

[1] Here apparently in 659 the Irish Augustin or Ængus wrote in classic Latin his "De Mirabilibus Sacrae Scripturae."

[2] Istoria degli ultimi quattro Secoli della Chiesa (Vol. III, p. 99.)

interest of the court of France to oppose such English pretensions. This document excited in the minds of the English present the fiercest resentment. It has to be remembered that at that time the governing class of England spoke a French patois, while the mass of the people spoke an English (or as it would have been called in the council, a German) patois, the English language at that time, despite Chaucer, not having been developed as a literary vehicle, most English writers preferring Latin. The representatives of the English crown at the council, themselves probably Francii, or Normans, were eagerly desirous of getting from the entire synod a decree in their favor, while the French wanted to have the question referred to the sacred college. Cardinal Alliaco based an argument on the bull of Benedict XII (d. 1342), in which he enumerates the provinces subject to the Roman pontificate. He divided Europe into four great nations in accordance with the bull, in such a way that several tribes and nations were comprised under the head of Germany, and England was one of these. "Finalmente si rammentano varie divisioni, nelle quali erano gia state partite le provincie della Europa: cibe nei di Roma, di Constantinopoli, d'Irlanda, e di Spagna." Thus it was decreed that Ireland continued to remain one of the four great imperial divisions of Europe. However, as in 1416, when the council was held, the sovereign of England claimed also to be "Lord" of Ireland, by virtue of the bull granted to the French rulers of England by Adrian IV, a document which a church council could not readily disregard, a way was seen out of the difficulty. The king of England's shadowy claim in respect to Ireland, one of the four great divisions mentioned, was allowed, the pretensions of France to the precedency of England was set aside, and the deliberations of the council went on in undisturbed serenity.[1]

[1] Archbishop Ussher has the following in regard to it: "In the year 1417, when the legates of the king of England and the French king's ambassadors fell at variance in the Council of Constance for precedency, the English orators, among other arguments, alleged this also for themselves—it is well known that the whole world is divided into three parts—to wit, Asia, Africa and Europe. Europe is divided into four kingdoms, namely the Roman, for the first; the Constantinopolitan, for the second; the third, the Kingdom of Ireland, which is now translated with the English; and the fourth, the Kingdom of Spain. Whereby it appeareth that the king of England and his kingdom are the more eminent ancient kings and kingdoms of all Europe, which prerogative the kingdom of France is not said to obtain. And this I have inserted the more willingly because it maketh something for the honor of my country to which, I confess, I am very much devoted, and in the printed acts of the Council it is not commonly to be had." (Relig. Ant. Irish. cap. xi, Works, iv, p. 370.) See Ulster J. of Arch., O. S., vii, p. 306.

CHAPTER XV

RECLAIMING THE ENGLISH TRIBES

1. English Ignorance of Debt Owed to Irishmen. 2. Conversion of English Delayed by Neglect. 3. Reputation of English Aborigines among Civilized Peoples. 4. Total Helplessness of the Barbarians.

1. ENGLISH IGNORANCE OF DEBT OWED TO IRISHMEN

LYNCH in his "Cambrensis Eversus"[1] remarks with wonder on the general ignorance in England concerning the debt that country owed to Irishmen, since the story of how they gave Christianity and civilization to the English is so plainly told in Bede. The remark, made in the seventeenth century, might be repeated in the twentieth. It is certainly a matter for enduring wonder that with the pages of Bede lying before their eyes so many English historians should have been tempted to depict ancient Ireland as a barbarian land in comparison with their own. Many English writers indeed have not scrupled to go further and with bland temerity have endeavored to propagate the notion that it was the English who first brought civilization to Irishmen. Of such writers the legion will be forgotten, and with such as are remembered posterity and the facts will deal according to their deserts. Bede was the first as he has remained the decentest of English historians. Nearly a thousand years were to pass after his time before England was able to produce a school of historians writing in their

---

[1] Chapters XVI, XVII and XVIII of this work, first published in Latin in 1662, has a good account of the manner in which the Irish missionaries converted the English natives. The work was republished in three volumes with a translation by Matthew Kelly in 1848.

own English tongue. These historians showed no improvement over Bede. On the contrary they were hopelessly his inferiors in the fundamental virtues of the historian. It would be well if the generality of English writers would study the spirit and the method of the earliest of their historians. He nevertheless told but the beginning of the story of what Irishmen did for the English in the age in which he lived. The present state of our knowledge has permitted us to indicate their work in more extended detail with material drawn from sources as authoritative as the testimony of Bede himself.

Montalembert credits the Irish missionaries with the chief share in the conversion of England: "From the cloisters of Lindisfarne and from the heart of those districts in which the popularity of ascetic pontiffs such as Aidan and martyr kings such as Oswald and Oswin won day by day a deeper root, Northumbrian Christianity spread over the southern kingdoms. . . . . What is distinctly visible is the influence of Celtic priests and missionaries everywhere replacing or seconding the Roman missionaries and reaching districts which their predecessors had never been able to enter. The stream of the Divine Word thus extended itself from north to south, and its slow but certain course reached in succession all the people of the Heptarchy."[1] Again he writes: "Of the eight kingdoms of the Anglo-Saxon confederation, that of Kent alone was exclusively won and retained by the Roman monks, whose first attempts among the East Saxons and Northumbrians ended in failure. In Wessex and East Anglia the Saxons of the West and the Angles of the East were converted by the combined action of continental missionaries and Celtic monks. As to the two

[1] Monks of the West, IV, 88.

Northumbrian kingdoms and those of Essex and Mercia, which comprehended in themselves more than two thirds of the territory occupied by the German (Saxon) conquerors, these four countries owed their final conversion exclusively to the peaceful invasion of the Celtic monks, who not only rivaled the zeal of the Roman monks, but who, the first obstacles once surmounted, showed much more perseverance and gained much more success."[1]

"Augustine was the apostle of Kent, but Aidan was the apostle of England," says Bishop Lightfoot. Aidan was but one of an army of devoted Irishmen, whose unwearying effort slowly lifted the English from savagery to civilization. Very remarkable was the manner in which they performed their work.

2. Conversion of English Delayed by Neglect

When we consider the energy and intrepidity manifested by the Irish monks in so many different places through the long period of their apostolic mission, we are confronted by their singular delay in organizing the conversion of the English. The Saxons, Angles and Jutes began to arrive in England previous to 449 A. D. No organized Irish mission appeared among them till 635 A. D. Thus a period of nearly two centuries was allowed to elapse before the Irish sought to win these new peoples to Christianity. What were the reasons underlying this singular delay? No explanation can be afforded by suggestions as to the inactivity of the Irish themselves. They were indeed far from inactive. Some of the greatest of the Irish schools had by 635 A. D. more than a century of flourishing life behind them. Columcille had been almost forty years in his grave, his laborious and fruitful

[1] Ibid. IV, 125.

life a golden memory to his disciples, who with him had been laboring among the Picts for the greater part of a century. Columbanus and most of his associates too were dead after prolonged labor in France and the borderlands, and a hundred years before Columbanus there had been Irish priests and bishops in Gaul and Italy. In the year 620 A. D. there were Irish missionaries in Bavaria and Helvetia. But they passed the English tribes by. What was at the bottom of this seeming dereliction of duty?

In this attitude of aloofness the Irish were not alone. Gaulish missionaries, whose negligence Pope Gregory later rebuked, showed great reluctance in respect to preaching to the invaders of Britain, for in a letter of introduction which Augustine brought from Gregory to Queen Brunhilda at Orleans we gather that applications from the English for help and conversion had been made in vain to neighboring priests.[1]

"We are informed," wrote the Pope, "that they longingly wish to be converted, but the bishops and the priests of the neighboring region (France) neglect them." The appeals of the English were probably prompted by the presence of Bishop Luidhard, soul friend to Bertha, a Christian Gaulish princess who had married Ethelbert, king of Kent. Bertha was the daughter of Caribert, king of Paris, granddaughter of Brunhilda, the great enemy of Columbanus, and great-granddaughter of Clotilde, wife of Clovis.

Going still further, the clerics of the church of the Britons refused absolutely to have any hand in the conversion of the English, looking on them as being more worthy of eternal reprobation than of the joys of heaven.

[1] Epist. VI, 59. Migne, Pat. Lat. LXXVII, col. 842 seq.

But their hatred is comprehensible. Despoiled and displaced by the newcomers the memory of the wrongs they had suffered was still green. The Irish element in western Britain doubtless shared this sentiment of repulsion. But the inactivity of the Irish in Ireland is less easily comprehensible.

The antipathy of the Britons for the English invader was implacable, and it endured even after the English had become Christians. Bede sorrowfully remarks respecting the intransigeance of the ancient Britons: "Among other most wicked actions, not to be exprest, which their own historian Gildas, mournfully takes notice of, they added this—that they never preached the faith to the Saxons or English who dwelt amongst them."[1]

A letter of Aldhelm to a ruler of Cornwall bears striking witness to the feeling which the dispossest Britons continued to cherish towards the English tribes. "Beyond the mouth of the Severn," he writes, "the priests of Cambria, proud of the purity of their morals, have such a horror of communication with us that they refuse to pray with us in the churches, or to seat themselves at the same table. More than this, what is left of our meals is thrown to dogs and swine, the dishes and bottles we have used have to be rubbed with sand or purified by fire before they will condescend to touch them. The British neither give us the salutation nor the kiss of peace, and if one of us went to live in their country the natives would hold no communication with him until after he had been made to endure a penance of forty days."[2]

Bede tells us further that to his day it was "the custom of the Britons not to pay any respect to the faith and

[1] Historia Ecclesiastica, Bk. I, Ch. XXII.
[2] Epistola 1, Adhelmi ad Geruntium, Migne, Pat. Lat. LXXXIX, col. 87. It was originally found among the letters of Boniface.

religion of the English, nor to correspond with them any more than with Pagans.'"[1]

The English reciprocated the antipathy of the Britons. Thus in the Anglo-Saxon legend of St. Guthlac[2] we find a curious assertion that St. Guthlac, having been among the British, understood the speech of the devils, who used that language.

3. REPUTATION OF ENGLISH ABORIGINES AMONG CIVILIZED PEOPLES

To this sentiment of irreconcilability is it due that of all the barbarian races that descended upon the Roman provinces the Anglo-Jute-Saxons alone found civilization bodily withdrawing as they advanced. In other countries religion, administrative order and the appurtenances of learning were gradually assumed and assimilated by the newcomers. Britain was almost the only province of the empire where Roman civilization disappeared with the people who enshrined and administered it. The antipathy excited in the breast of the Romanized Briton became an insuperable barrier to the blending or association of races, and receding towards Britannia Secunda and Strathclyde before the violence of the new settlers they carried their whole organization of government and society with them. Thus the Anglo-Jute-Saxon invader was condemned to remain as much the primeval savage amid the noble monuments of Roman refinement and power as on the wastes of Sleswick or Jutland.

To this primitive people, capable only of such ratiocination as was needed to maintain a purely animal existence,

1 Hist. Eccl.

2 Contained in the Codex Exoniensis or Exeter Book, a collection of Anglo-Saxon poems given by Bishop Leofric to the library of the cathedral of Exeter, between 1046 and 1073, and published by the London Society of Antiquarians in 1842. The legend concerning Guthlac (c. 673-714) is a metrical paraphrase of the Latin life by Felix, a monk of Croyland Abbey.

Rome was the first to send light and teaching, for tho the Irish Columbanus and Dicuil with companions are said to have been in East Anglia before they were in Gaul, there is little evidence of any work accomplished there by them.[1] Thus it came about that Augustine and his associates appeared in Kent thirty-eight years before the Irish missionaries left Iona for Northumberland. But again in the case of the Roman missionaries we have evidence of the dread and repugnance felt in relation to the English barbarians. Augustine and his company had set out from Rome in June, 596; but the more these representatives of Roman civilization neared their destination the more pronounced became their distaste for the enterprise in hand. At each stopping place accounts reached them concerning the uncouth islanders sufficient to deter the stoutest hearts. The Saxons were more ferocious than wild beasts, it was said; they preferred cruelties to feasting; they thirsted for innocent blood; they held in abhorrence the Christian name; and torture and death were sure to await the emissaries of civilization. At Arles, or Aix-en-Provence, the missionaries, says Bede, "were seized with a sudden fear and began to think of returning home, rather than proceed to a barbarous, fierce and unbelieving nation to whose very speech they were strangers,"[2] finally deputizing Augustine to acquaint Pope Gregory with the facts as they had learned them. Augustine went back to Rome and saw the Pope, while his companions awaited the new word of command. That word, carried back by Augustine, was to go forward on their journey—in the words of the pope, the greater the

[1] Jonas, the biographer of Columbanus, is the chief authority for this sojourn in England. They appear to have "found the hearts of the people in darkness," and despairing of "sowing the seeds of salvation," went to the "nearest nations" (Migne, Pat. Lat., v. 87, col. 1016).
[2] Hist. Eccl., Book I, Ch. XXXII.

suffering the greater would be their reward. So Paris was reached and there the winter months were passed; and finally, after a creeping journey that lasted almost a year, in the spring of 597 Augustine arrived at Thanet and came face to face with the islanders.

What we know of the Angles and Saxons at this period is derived from foreign sources and is expressive chiefly of the vague apprehension and distrust naturally felt by the civilized person towards the remote and little known savage. Their occupation is represented as that of pirates, whom no storm could affright in the pursuit of their prey. They slew their captives, as Freeman notes, with fearful tortures. A contemporary Gallic bishop, Sidonius Apollinaris, describes them as brigands, "the most turbulent of enemies," who made it a point not only of honor but of religion "to torture their captives rather than put them to ransom," whilst they sacrificed the tenth part of them to their gods.[1] Other Roman writers refer to them in similar vein, while Irish writers and speakers of the period habitually allude to them simply as "barbarians," "savages" and "marauders."[2]

What went on after the settlement of the Saxons, Angles and Jutes in Britain we do not know. Cut off almost absolutely from the civilized world, of the very existence of which they could know but little, and utterly unable to make a record of any kind, their history remains a total blank for almost two centuries. Bede, for example, has no word on this period. The glories of Roman art and culture rose up around them, they may even have learnt to use Roman ruins as their dwellings, but tho they must have wondered they were unable to derive further profit from them. Alternating their wars with the Britons by

[1] Epist. VIII, 6.
[2] Adamnan, Vita S. Col.

savage and exterminating assaults on each other, their lives appear to have been a hopeless round of fighting and feasting. At this period the Welsh Triads accuse them of being addicted to the eating of human flesh. Ethelfrith, it is said, encouraged cannibalism at his court, and Georgi, a truant Briton there, is said to have become so enamored of human flesh that he could eat no other. They had also formed the unnatural habit of selling their children into slavery. The traffic in English slaves continued for many centuries and the incorrigible practise was so deeply rooted that even Christianity could not eradicate it. English slavery during these ages had repulsive features absent even from negro slavery at a later date, and the traffic filled Ireland especially with a large population of English fudirs and slaves.[1]

In facts such as these have we to look for the sources of the hesitation manifested by missionaries in endeavoring to carry civilization to the English tribes. The material appeared too menacing even to the self-sacrificing devotion of the missionary. It seems probable that the suicidal ferocity of the invaders tended to spend itself as they became settled in their new home. But their occupation of the country was gradual, and its progressive stages remain very obscure.

4. Total Helplessness of the Barbarians

The pages of Adamnan reveal to us a certain English filtering into or contact with Irish communities even before the official mission of Aidan. There were Saxons among the servants and brethren at Iona in the time of Columcille. One of them named Genere worked as baker at the monastery; another was named Pilu. Columcille is said to have caused the death of a "certain bad frantic

[1] See Appendix A.

man," a Saxon, who smote a monk of his household and cut his girdle with a spear. Aidan, the Irish king in Scotland, fought the English and defeated them at Lethredh, c. 590, losing two of his sons and three hundred men. Adamnan tells us that on the night of the battle Columcille suddenly said to his minister Diarmuid, "Ring the bell." The brethren startled by the sound proceeded quickly to the church with the holy prelate himself at their head. Then he began on bended knees to say to them: "Let us pray now earnestly to the Lord for this people and King Aidan, for they are engaging in battle at this moment." Then after a short time he went out to the oratory and looking up to heaven said: "The barbarians are falling now and to Aidan is given the victory— a sad one tho it be."[1] On another occasion a reference to "marauding savages" (barbari bellatores) indicates the presence of English in the neighborhood.[2]

A century after the reputed landing of Hengist and Horsa had to pass before the Angles colonized Northumbria. Spreading westward and northward the English tribes at last came in contact with the Irish Scots of Caledonia, and some of the native Anglian rulers fleeing from fratricidal strife found refuge with other English aborigines in Iona and Ireland. So Englishman and Irishman began to meet in peaceful intercourse, the one the unredeemed and primeval savage, the other the representative of an immemorial civilization and of the highest culture and purest Christianity of his age.

Such contact with civilization was necessary if the English native was to be raised from his secular degrada-

---

[1] Fordun (Scotichr. iii, 29) identifies this battle, described as the battle of Miathi in Adamnan (I, viii), with the battle of Wodenysburgh, mentioned by the Saxon Chronicle at 591, and places it near Chester. Ussher and Chalmers identify it with the battle of Lethrigh, recorded by Tighnernach in 591 (Reeves' Adamnan, 34).

[2] Adamnan's Vita Columbae (ed., Reeves) I, xxxv.

tion. He himself provided conclusive proof that of himself the barbarian could do nothing, and left to himself was likely to remain a barbarian to the end of time. On this very point some illuminating words have been uttered: "How far human nature is capable by its own efforts of perfecting and developing itself we need not seek far for an example. If such an experiment will satisfy anyone, that experiment was tried here under the most favorable conditions. A century and a half elapsed from their (our Saxon forefathers') first settlement in this island before the first sound of the gospel was heard among them. What is the result? What steps have they taken on the roads of progress and improvement? What advancement in letters; what dawnings of science; what emancipation from the ancient paganism? Have they built up themselves? Have they built up a nation? Is there any improvement of any kind whatsoever at the end of 150 years more than there was at the beginning? None, rather the reverse. Their paganism has grown coarser, deeper, darker; their political confusions and convulsions more hopeless; their tendencies more savage and restless; their culture is an absolute blank. That any nation or any man can by his own efforts erect 'himself above himself,' is the veriest delusion that ever imposed itself on the brain of the thoughtless and unwary. For whatever the Anglo-Saxons have since become they are indebted to an influence external to themselves. Had it not been for Christianity they must have remained forever in this ancient barbarism, making no improvement but sinking deeper into confusion from age to age. It brought them not only higher hopes but literature, arts and science in its train."[1]

[1] Preface to Works of Giraldus Cambrensis, Rolls Series, IV, edited by J. S. Brewer.

CHAPTER XVI

ROMAN AND IRISH MISSIONARIES IN ENGLAND

1. Mission of Augustine a Failure. 2. Irish Work Beginning of English Civilization. 3. Aidan among the English Tribes. 4. Irish Prelate and Anglian King. 5. English Natives and Their Rulers Sheltered and Educated in Ireland.

1. MISSION OF AUGUSTINE A FAILURE

NEVERTHELESS it was not the Irishman but the Roman who was to be the first to attempt to carry Christianity to the English. It is very much to the honor of the great Pope Gregory that, burdened as he was with the cares of a world in travail, he should still concern himself with the rescue of these distant barbarians, before any of their neighbors showed disposition to lend a helping hand to them.

What the Roman missionaries sent by him accomplished is a story that has been often told. Ethelbert, ruler of the Jutes of Kent, was well disposed towards them, for he had obtained in marriage the Christian Frank princess Bertha. The king himself submitted to baptism on Whitsunday and at the following Christmas Augustine was able to cheer Gregory with the news that 10,000 aborigines had followed the example of their king. Evidently the mass of them remained pagans at heart for when the fear of Ethelbert was removed by his death in 616 Essex and part of Kent reverted to heathenism. The associates and successors of Augustine, who died probably in 604, endeavored to carry on and extend his work. They had only indifferent success. Lawrence at Canterbury,

Mellitus at London, Felix in East Anglia, Deacon James in Yorkshire, Ruffinianus at the infant abbey of St. Peter's, Canterbury, worked off and on at their difficult mission amid a population largely indifferent to their ministrations. Their sense of their own inadequacy is revealed by anxious and ineffectual appeals for help to their Brito-Irish coreligionists in western Britain. Paulinus in 627 traveled northwards, and baptized Eadwine of Northumbria, who had married a Kentish Christian princess, and is thought to have founded some churches. Six years later, following the victory of Penda over Eadwine, a pagan reaction swept everything Christian and civilized away and the natives relapsed once more into total savagery and heathenism. Eventually all the associates of Augustine, except Lawrence, fled the country, while Lawrence prepared to flee but was led by a dream to hold his ground.

Such conversion as the Roman missionaries effected amongst the natives was skin deep.[1] When Redwald, king of East Anglia, for example, was ordered by his overlord, Ethelbert, to become Christian, he complied by adding an image of Christ as a god to his heathen deities, later throwing it out and abandoning even the pretense of conversion.

[1] Differences of opinion in regard to Easter, the tonsure, and other matters made cooperation between the Romans and the Irish, as well as the British, difficult. This is made clear by the words of Lawrence himself: "To our very dear Lords and Brothers, the Bishops and the Abbots in all lands of the Irish (Per universam Scotiam),. Laurentius, Mellitus, and Justus, servants of the servants of God. When the Apostolic See, according to the custom of sending missionaries throughout the world, sent us to preach the Gospel to the pagans of the West, we came to Britain without previous knowledge of the inhabitants. But both Britons and Irish we esteemed highly for their sanctity believing that they conformed to the customs of the Church universal. Even when we were made aware that this was not the case with the Britons, yet we hoped better things of the Irish. We have, however, learned from Bishop Dagan, who has lately arrived in the island, and from the Gallican abbot, Columbanus, that the Irish do in no respect differ from the Britons. Bishop Dagan indeed, since he came among us, has not only refused to eat with us, but even to take food in the same house with us." (Bede, Hist. Eccles. II, iv.)

2. IRISH WORK BEGINNING OF ENGLISH CIVILIZATION

It was at this crucial period that the Irish missionaries appeared on the scene and started a more enduring movement of conversion. For it was they who with strong hands put the bit and bridle on the wild English tribes, tamed their savagery, kindled into flame the human spark within them, and led them despite themselves along the paths of Christian civilization. The work was prolonged and suffered many setbacks, from the natural backwardness and brutality inherent in a savage population, from Danish inroads, from unceasing tribal conflicts, and from pestilence and famine. But these great Irishmen persevered and made their work permanent. Where the Roman had signally failed, the Irishman signally succeeded, and wherever he took the work in hand the English never looked back. In the work of these Irishmen English history and English civilization find written their book of Genesis.

William of Malmesbury tells the tale simply when he talks of the faith of the English having been "brought to maturity by the learning of the Irish." Modern writers are more expansive.

"The men who really plowed and harrowed the soil which was lying fallow among the masculine and vigorous peoples of northern and central England, of Northumbria and Mercia, were not Augustine's monks, but, as we have seen, the never-tired, resourceful, and sympathetic spiritual children of St. Columba, St. Aidan and their disciples."[1]

The immediate call that brought the van of the Irish missionaries among the Anglo-Saxon tribes came from Oswald, the native ruler of the Northumbrians. Oswald,

[1] Howorth, Golden Days of the English Church, II, 171.

his brother Eanfrid, his mother, the widow of the savage Ethelfrid, and a large number of his relatives and supporters, had for many years been given shelter and protection in Ireland and Hibernicized Britain.   Oswald was twelve years old at the period of his departure into exile in 617.   He returned in 634 with his companions, all of them enriched by contact with a civilization till then wholly strange to them.   It is easy to imagine the impression made on the minds of these simple barbarians by what they saw in Ireland where Greco-Roman culture blended with ancient Celtic wisdom and splendor mellowed the national life and enriched the channels through which it flowed.   Oswald and his companions returned to England, not only Christianized but also completely Hibernicized, fluent speakers of the Irish tongue, and wholly devoted to Irish ideals.   The returned wanderers were doubtless glad to find themselves once again amid the scenes of their youth, but it is little wonder that the call for help to Iona was speedy.   The brutalities, the indecencies, the horror and the squalor of unchanging barbarism, once so natural to them, could not henceforth be other than unendurable.   To his Irish benefactors Oswald therefore sent hurried appeals, and these, recognizing under the savage manners and exterior of their protégés the elements of a common humanity, and thinking the season opportune, decided to essay their regeneration.

3. AIDAN AMONG THE ENGLISH TRIBES

Bede picturesquely describes the manner in which the Irish missionaries were led into northern England. King Oswald as soon as he ascended the throne sent to the elders of the Irish, among whom he and his followers, when in banishment, had received the sacrament of baptism, desiring they would send him a bishop, by whose instruction and ministry the English nation, which he governed, might be taught the advantages and receive the sacrament of the Christian faith. They were not slow in granting his request and sent him Bishop Aidan, a man of singular meekness, piety and moderation, zealous in the cause of God. On his arrival the bishop fixed his episcopal see in the isle of Lindisfarne. King Oswald also humbly and willingly in all cases gave ear to his admonitions, industriously applying himself to the work of building and extending the church of Christ in his kingdom; wherein when the bishop, who was not skilful in the English tongue, preached the gospel, it was most delightful to see the king himself interpreting the word of God to his commanders and ministers, for Oswald had acquired a perfect mastery of the Irish tongue during his long banishment.[1] Oswald's family and the Northumbrian nobility were in large part fluent Irish speakers and in some degree representatives of the new Irish learning. This learning gradually spread.

The varied labors of the Irishmen are indicated by Bede: "From that time many of the Irish came daily into Britain and with great devotion preached the word to those provinces of the English over which King Oswald reigned, and those among them that had received priests' orders administered to them the grace of baptism. Churches were built in several places; the people joyfully flocked together to hear the word; money and lands were given of the king's bounty to build monasteries; the English, great and small, were by their Irish masters instructed in the rules and observance of regular discipline; for most of them that came to preach were monks."[2]

[1] Hist. Eccl. III, III.
[2] Hist. Eccl. III, III.

Others were, as Bede later tells us, laymen—physicians, scribes, lawyers, goldsmiths and the like—though the monks were working in most of the secular occupations too. Bishop Aidan was himself a monk of the island of Hii or Iona, which monastery was for a long time the chief of almost all those of the northern Irish and all those of the Picts and had the direction of their people. Bede adds: "That island (Iona) belongs to Britannia, being divided from it by a small arm of the sea, but had been long since given by the Picts, who inhabit those parts of Britannia, to the Irish monks, because they had received the faith of Christ through their preaching."[1]

It was from this island and college of monks that Aidan was sent to instruct the English natives, having received the dignity of a bishop at the time when Seginus, abbot and priest, presided over the monastery; whence among other instructions for life Aidan left the clergy a most salutary example of abstinence and continence. "It was the highest commendation of his doctrine with all men," adds Bede, "that he taught no otherwise than he and his followers had lived; for he neither sought nor loved anything of this world, but delighted in distributing immediately among the poor whatsoever was given him by the kings and rich men of the world. He was wont to traverse both town and country on foot, never on horseback, unless compelled by some urgent necessity; and wherever in his way he saw either rich or poor, he invited them, if infidels, to embrace the mystery of the faith; or, if they were believers, to strengthen them in the faith, and to stir them up by words and actions to alms and good works."[2]

Things had become different in England in the days

1 Hist. Eccl. III, III.
2 Hist. Eccl. III, V.

of Bede who wrote nearly a century after the arrival of Aidan: "His course of life was so different from the slothfulness of our times that all those who bore him company, whether monks or laymen, were employed in meditation, that is, either in reading the scriptures, or learning psalms." This was the daily employment of Aidan himself and of all that were with him wheresoever they went. Study, work, and prayer were the main occupations and happiness of their lives, and if it happened, which was but seldom, that Aidan was invited to eat with the king the bishop "went accompanied with one or two clerks, and having taken a small repast, made haste to be gone again with them either to read or write."[1]

In words such as these we sense the consuming passion that flamed in the breast of this great Irish pontiff who, in the course of sixteen years, by unflagging work and planning, effected the regeneration of the English people. His personality singularly affected the English tribes, so that the brightest amongst them thought they could do nothing better than do whatever he did or told them to do, difficult though it might be. "At that time many religious men and women, stirred up by his example, adopted the custom of fasting on Wednesdays and Fridays, till the ninth hour, throughout the year, except during the fifty days after Easter."[2]

Bede goes on to tell us that Aidan never bestowed gifts of money on the powerful men of the world, but only meat, if he happened to entertain them; and, on the contrary, whatsoever gifts of money he received from the rich, he either distributed among the poor, or used in ransoming such as had been wrongfully sold for slaves. Enslaving each other and selling their younger or weaker

[1] Hist. Eccl. III, V.
[2] Ibid. III, V.

relatives into slavery was, as has been said, an habitual practice among the English, and it was against this terrible traffic that Aidan's influence was directed. Many of those ransomed by him he made his disciples, and, after having instructed them, he advanced them in some cases to the order of priesthood. Eata, subsequent bishop of Lindisfarne, and Boisel, prior of Melrose, were among these redeemed protégés of Aidan.[1]

From among the brightest of these young men Aidan formed a school of twelve boys, and the school included Chad and Cedd, who both became distinguished bishops. The tradition was carried through the Irish foundations of the Continent. When St. Anskar, educated at Corbie, began his missionary work in Denmark he also founded a school of twelve boys.

4. IRISH PRELATE AND ANGLIAN KING

Bede tells us that before Aidan the Irish had sent another priest to administer the word of faith to Oswald and his nation, a man of more austere disposition, who, meeting with no success, and being unregarded by the English people, returned home, and in an assembly of the Irish elders reported that he had not been able to do any good to the nation he had been sent to preach to, because they were uncivilized men, and of a stubborn and barbarous disposition.[2] In a great council the Irish authorities seriously debated what was to be done, for they strongly desired that the English nation should receive the salvation it demanded, and grieved that the preacher they had sent had not been received. Then, said Aidan, who was present in the council, "I am of opinion, brother,

[1] Hist. Eccl. III, V.

[2] Ibid. III, V. Bede does not give us the name of this priest, but Hector Boece says he was named Corman.

that you were more severe to your unlearned hearers than you ought to have been and did not at first, conformably to the apostolic rule, give them the milk of more easy doctrine, till being by degrees nourished with the word of God, they should be capable of greater perfection, and be able to practice God's sublimer precepts." Having heard these words of Aidan all present began diligently to weigh what he had said, and presently concluded that he deserved to be made a bishop, and ought to be sent to instruct the incredulous and unlearned; since he was found to be endowed with singular discretion, which is the mother of other virtues. "Accordingly," says Bede, "they sent him to their friend, King Oswald, to preach; and he, as time proved, afterwards appeared to possess all other virtues as well as the discretion for which he was before remarkable."[1]

Bede draws a pleasing picture of the friendship between the Irish prelate and the English king, who under Aidan's influence grew into a beautiful character. Once when sitting at dinner on Easter Sunday with Bishop Aidan a silver dish full of dainties was put before the king and they were just ready to bless the bread, when the servant who had been appointed to relieve the poor came in on a sudden and told the king that a great multitude of needy persons from all parts were sitting in the streets begging some alms of the king; he immediately ordered the meat set before him to be carried to the poor and the dish to be cut in pieces and divided among them. At which sight the bishop, who sat by him, much taken with such an act of piety, laid hold of his right hand and said: "May this hand never perish!" Which fell out according to his prayer, adds Bede, for his arm and hand,

[1] Hist. Eccl. III, V.

being cut from his body when he was slain in battle, remained entire and uncorrupted, being kept in a silver case as revered relics in St. Peter's Church in the royal city of Bamborough. Instructed by the teaching of Aidan, Oswald not only learned to hope for a heavenly kingdom unknown to his progenitors, but also extended his earthly kingdom, and through the king's management the provinces of Deira and Bernicia were peacefully united and their inhabitants molded into one people.[1]

Here we have a picture of Aidan in the character of statesman and prime minister. A man of varied culture and balanced judgment, his influence appears to have been strongly in the direction of union of effort and broader organization in national life. Considering that he was a stranger among a barbarous people, the reverence in which he was held and his undisputed authority speak eloquently for his character and gifts.

Oswald thus, with Aidan's aid, succeeded in uniting Deira and Bernicia and became, after the Irish fashion, a sort of ard righ or high king over most of England. Throughout this area Irish teachers became numerous. Preaching the gospel was their main business, but it was by no means their sole business. As the years went on they trained the natives in agriculture and the breeding of cattle, in carpentry, in building, and the use of the forge, in metal and enamel work, in stonecutting, and in the preparation, transcription and ornamentation of books. In several of these lines their work and that of their English understudies remain in examples that have attracted the attention of archeologists for centuries.

[1] Hist. Eccl. III, VI.

5. English Natives and Their Rulers Sheltered and Educated in Ireland

Considering that Oswald was the son of Ethelfrid, the cannibal king and butcher of the unarmed religious of Bangor in Wales, his transition from the barbarous to the civilized state was a speedy one. The upbringing he received at Iona and in Ireland was effective in eliminating the heritage of savagery which otherwise would have controlled his life. The forced exile imposed on him by Eadwine, who rose to power after his father's death, thus proved a happy circumstance. Oswald was accompanied in his banishment by his brothers and many English chiefs.

The Anglo-Saxon Chronicle says at the year 617: "And he (Eadwine) drove out the ethelings, sons of Ethelfrid; that is to say, first Eanfrid, Oswald and Oswy, Oslar, Oswiedu, Oslaf, and Offa," all of whom were given safe keeping and education in Iona and Ireland.

Oswald's elder brother, Eanfrid, married the daughter of the king of the Picts, and their son, Talorcan (d. 657), presently succeeded to the Pictish throne in right of his mother.

Oswald while in Ireland appears to have married an Irish princess, Fina, mother of Aldfrid later king of Northumbria, who was thus known to the Irish as Flan Fiona. The fact would explain in some degree the growth of Oswald and his brother, and Aldfrid in refinement and culture.

In the "Three Fragments" of Irish Annals, Aldfrid or Flan Fiona is called "the son of Ossa, King of Saxonland, the famous wise man, the pupil of Adamnan" (in t-einaid arma, dalla Adamnain). Here Adamnan, abbot of Iona and Latin biographer of Columcille, is called "Erin's chief sage of learning" (Ardsui Erenn eolusa). This is the King Aldfrid who wrote poetry in Irish and Latin. Adamnan and Aldfrid are dealt with in these respects elsewhere.

Oswald's mother, Acha, sister of King Eadwine, went to Ireland with her sons. Information regarding Oswald's acquirement of the Irish language is given in his life; "linguam Scottorum perfecte didicit et fidei documenta quae prius a matre Christiana perceperunt gentis illius credulae eruditione solidavit, et lavaero sacri baptismatis pureficatus."[1]

Other Irish annalists refer to the brothers. Tighernach, using both Irish and Latin after his manner, speaks of Eanfrid, the elder brother of Oswald, as having fought a regular battle, and says that afterwards he was beheaded; "Cath la (praelium per) Cathlon et Anfraith qui decollatus est."

Adamnan relates a story in reference to the struggle between Oswald and Cadwalla, which his predecessor had heard from the abbot of Iona, who claimed that he had again heard it from the king himself. The night before the battle of Heavenfield while Oswald was sleeping on the ground in his tent St. Columcille appeared to him, radiant with angelic beauty, and his stately height seemed to reach the sky. The saint stood in the midst of the camp, announced himself, and stretched his resplendent robe over the little army of exiles, as if to protect them. He promised to secure them victory over their enemies. At that time there were only twelve of his companions who were Christians, having been baptized with him among the Irish.[2]

[1] Vita Oswaldi, 12 cent., by Reginald of Durham, Simeon of Durham, I, 341.

[2] Vita S. Columbae.

CHAPTER XVII

FIRST STEPS OF THE ENGLISH IN CIVILIZATION

1. King Oswin's Veneration for Irish Prelate. 2. Aidan and His Foundations in England. 3. Finan Succeeds Aidan and Wins Midland England. 4. Re-converts Apostate East Saxons. 5. Rise of the Easter Controversy.

1. KING OSWIN'S VENERATION FOR IRISH PRELATE

THE friendship that united Aidan and Oswald was continued in the case of Oswald's successor, Oswin, whose habitual attitude towards the prelate was one of great veneration. Bede relates an anecdote which illuminates the character both of the bishop and the king. Oswin had given an extraordinarily fine horse to Bishop Aidan, which he might use in crossing rivers or in performing journeys of urgent necessity, tho he was wont to travel on foot. Some short time after, a poor man meeting him asking alms, he immediately dismounted and ordered the horse with all its royal furniture to be given to the beggar; for he was very compassionate, a great friend of the poor, and as it were, the father of the wretched. This being told to the king when they were going to dinner, he said to the bishop: "Why would you, my lord bishop, give the poor man the royal horse, which was necessary for your use? Had not we many other horses of less value and of other sorts, which would have been good enough to the poor and not to give that horse which I had particularly chosen for yourself?" To whom the bishop instantly answered, "What is it you say, O king? Is that foal of a mare more dear to you than the Son of God?" Upon this they went in to dinner and the bishop sat in his place; but the king, who was come from hunting, stood warming himself with his attendants by the fire. Then, on a sudden, while he was warming himself, calling to mind what the bishop had said to him, he ungirt his sword and gave it to a servant, and in a hasty manner fell down at the bishop's feet, beseeching him to forgive him: "For from this time forward," said he, "I will never speak any more of this, nor will I judge of what or how much of our money you shall give to the sons of God." The bishop was much moved at this sight and starting up raised him saying he was entirely reconciled to him, if he would sit down to his meat and lay aside all sorrow. The king, at the bishop's command and request, beginning to be merry, the bishop, on the other hand, grew so melancholy as to shed tears. His priest then asking him in the Irish language, which the king and his servants did not understand, why he wept, "I know," said he, "that the king will not live long; for I never saw so humble a king; whence I conclude that he soon will be snatched out of this life, because his nation was not worthy of such a ruler." Not long after, the bishop's prediction was fulfilled by the king's death. But Bishop Aidan, adds Bede, was also himself taken out of this world twelve days after the king he loved, to receive the eternal reward of his labors from our Lord.[1]

Aidan, Bede tells us, was in the king's country house, not far from Bamborough, at the time of his death; for, having a church and chamber there, he was wont often to go and stay, and to make excursions to preach to the

[1] Hist. Eccl. III, XIV.

country round about, which he likewise did at other of the king's country-seats, having nothing of his own besides his church and a few fields about it. When he was sick they set up a tent for him close to the wall at the west end of the church, by which means it happened that he gave up the ghost leaning against a post that was on the outside to strengthen the wall. He died in the seventeenth year of his episcopate. His body was thence transferred to the isle of Lindisfarne and buried in the churchyard belonging to the brethren. Some time after, when a larger church was built there and dedicated in honor of the blessed prince of the Apostles, continues Bede, his bones were translated thither and deposited on the right side of the altar with the respect due to so great a prelate. When Penda, the pagan king of the Mercians, coming into Northumbria with a hostile army, destroyed all he could with fire and sword, including the village and church in which Aidan died, it fell out in a wonderful manner, says Bede, that the post which he had leaned upon could not be consumed by the flames.[1] He also relates how Aidan, residing in the isle of Farne, by his prayers saved the royal city of Bamborough, when fired by the enemy, this same Penda.[2]

Bede tells us that, like an impartial historian, he has related what was done by or with Bishop Aidan, preserving the memory thereof for the benefit of the readers; viz., his love of peace and charity; his continence and humility; his mind superior to anger and avarice; and despising pride and vainglory; his industry in keeping and teaching the heavenly commandments; his diligence in reading and watching; his authority becoming a priest

[1] Hist. Eccl. III, XVII.

[2] Hist. Eccl. III, XVI.

in reproving the haughty and powerful, and at the same time his tenderness in comforting the afflicted and relieving or defending the poor. "To say all in a few words, as near as I could be informed by those that knew him, he took care to omit none of those things which he found in the apostolic or prophetical writings, but to the utmost of his power endeavored to perform them all."[1]

Bede's eulogy of Aidan has the more value inasmuch as he did not approve of the date of the Celtic observance of Easter, nay, "very much detesting the same," as he clearly indicates by his continued recurrence to a theme which excited great controversy and perturbation of mind in his day. But these aforesaid things he much loved and admired in the bishop. "This difference about the observance of Easter, whilst Aidan lived, was patiently tolerated by all men, as being sensible, that, tho he could not keep Easter contrary to the custom of those who had sent him, yet he industriously labored to practise all works of faith, piety, and love, according to the custom of all holy men; for which reason he was deservedly beloved by all, even by those who differed in opinion concerning Easter, and was held in veneration, not only by indifferent persons, but even by the bishops Honorius of Canterbury and Felix of East Angles."

2. AIDAN AND HIS FOUNDATIONS IN ENGLAND

Aidan, like most of the notable members of other Irish monasteries, was of high birth, a fact which had a good deal to do in endowing him with influence both among the Irish clans and the English tribes. He was a son of Lugair, an Irish saint commemorated on May 11th, and apparently of the same lineage as St. Brigid. He was

[1] Hist. Eccl. III, XVII.

accompanied to Northumbria by several of the brethren of Iona, who increased in number as the work grew.

Bishop Lightfoot writes concerning Aidan: "I know no nobler type of the missionary spirit. His character, as it appears through the haze of antiquity, is almost absolutely faultless. Doubtless the haze may have obscured some imperfections which a clearer atmosphere and a nearer view would have enabled us to detect. But we cannot have been misled as to the main lineaments of the man. Measuring him side by side with other great missionaries of those days, Augustine of Canterbury, or Wilfrid of York, or Cuthbert of his own Lindisfarne, we are struck with the singular sweetness and breadth and sympathy of his character. He had all the virtues of his Celtic race without any of its faults. A comparison with his own spiritual forefather—the eager, headstrong, irascible, affectionate, penitent, patriotic, self-devoted Columba, the most romantic and attractive of all early medieval saints—will justify this sentiment. He was tender, sympathetic, adventurous, self-sacrificing, but he was patient, steadfast, calm, appreciative, discreet before all things."[1]

Aidan, before he became a monk of Iona, had been bishop of Clogher,[2] and had studied under the blessed Senan at Iniscathay (Scattery Island). His arrival in England marked an epoch in its national life. In that hour England may be said to have had its beginning. Where there had been little else but chaos, futility, ignorance and infamy, Aidan placed on the formless mass the first imprint of order, humanity and religion. His work marked the first stage in the transition between savagery and organized culture in English history.

[1] Leaders of the Northern Church, p. 44.
[2] According to Ware and Lynch.

Aidan's chief foundation was that of Lindisfarne, which was to radiate light and healing in the North for generations and eventually to develop into the sees of Durham and Northumberland, and even, tho less directly, into the archbishopric of York. After Lindisfarne he and his missionary countrymen founded Mailros, or Melrose, and Whitby, then known as Streaneshalch. On the isle of Farne he established a hermitage to which he himself was wont to retire—later it became the favorite retreat of St. Cuthbert; and he founded the double monastery of Coldingham, the Urbs Coludi of Bede, which, like Ely and Barking, was modeled on the establishment of Kildare, whose patron was the illustrious Brigid, "Mary of the Gael." In this last foundation Aidan was associated with Aebba, sister of King Oswald, whose name is still enshrined in St. Abb's Head near by. Over Melrose as abbot, Aidan put Boisel, an English youth whom he had ransomed from slavery, master of Sigfrid, who was master of Bede.

Lindisfarne in course of time gathered to itself subsidiary houses or cells, among them St. Balthere's at Tynningham, Craike, Cunceceastre, or Chester-le-Street, Norham and Gainford. The see also came into possession of large lands in York.

The place Lindisfarne held in the veneration of the English is indicated by the emotion of Alcuin on the occasion of its pillaging by the Danes (793): "The most venerable place in Britain, where Christianity first took root among us after Paulinus went away from York, is a prey to heathen men. Who thinks of this calamity and does not cry out to God to spare his country has a heart of stone and not of flesh."[1]

1 Migne., Pat. Lat., C.

In the foundation of other monasteries Aidan was associated with St. Hilda. Bede tells us that Hilda went and lived a whole year in East Anglia with the design of going abroad, but being recalled by Bishop Aidan, she received from him the land of one family on the north side of the River Wear, where for a year she also led a monastic life with very few companions. After this she was made abbess of the monastery called Heruteu, which monastery had been founded not long before by the religious servant of Christ Heiu, whom some identify with Begha, or Begu, an Irishwoman of noble family, whose name is preserved in St. Bees Head in Cumberland. Heiu is said to have been the first woman that in the province of the Northumbrians took upon her the habit and life of a nun, being consecrated by Bishop Aidan; but she soon after she had founded that monastery, went away to the city of Calcacestir, and there fixed her dwelling. Hilda, being sent over to that monastery began immediately to reduce all things to a regular system, according as she had been instructed by learned men; for Bishop Aidan and other religious men that knew and loved her frequently visited and diligently instructed her. Some years later the monastery at Streaneshalch (Whitby) was built and from it came five bishops—Bosa, Hedda, Oftfor, John and Wilfrid (2nd). St. Hilda was the daughter of Hereric, the nepos of King Aedwine. Attracted by the reputation of some of the Irish convents in Gaul, she appears to have made up her mind to join one of them, but if Bede is to be taken literally she did not get out of England, being summoned back by Aidan. She moved to Hartlepool when Heiu went to Tadcaster, and here she appears to have had the help of certain learned Irishmen. In 651 when Finan had succeeded

Aidan, Whitby monastery was established on the Irish double monastery plan, "Mother Hilda" presiding over both.[1]

Several of the Irish foundations in Gaul were double monasteries. Examples were Remiremont, Soissons, Jouarre, Brie, Chelles and Andelys; the last three, as Bede tells us, being especially favored by English female converts. Boniface introduced the feature in Germany, where the establishments were in several cases presided over by nuns trained at Wimborne. It was the example of Hilda's sister Heresuid, mother to Aldwulf, king of the East Angles, who lived at Cale, or Chelles in France, that led her to desire to live there.[2]

From the first these double monasteries flourished in the Irish church, perhaps because they were a feature of the clan system when men and women alike belonged to the same religious community. In Ireland the head of such monasteries was usually a man; but in the Irish monasteries of England, especially in those founded by relatives of the native rulers, and in Columbanus's double monasteries in Gaul and Belgium, the monastery of clerics or priests, which was generally placed at the gates of the convent, was ruled over by the abbess. The singular inversion of the normal relationship was due probably to the fact that in such cases the real center or original foundation was the convent, but that for the spiritual needs of the nuns as well as for the oversight of their lands and estates there grew up a smaller dependent monastery of priests and lay brethren. But in some monasteries the monks were in the majority. Among the double monasteries in England, most of them Irish foundations, Bardney, Barkney, Ely, Whitby, and Cold-

[1] See N. B. Workman, Evolution of Monasticism, pp. 177-8.
[2] Eccl. Hist. IV, XXIII.

ingham are mentioned by Bede. Others existed at Wimborne, Repton, Wenlock, Nuneaton and perhaps Carlisle.[1]

The following churches in England are given as dedicated to St. Aidan: Bamburgh, Benwell, Blackhill, Boston, Gateshead, Hartlepool, Harrington, Leeds, Liverpool, Newbiggin, South Shields, Thorneyburn and Walton-le-dale, with several others in Scotland.

3. FINAN SUCCEEDS AIDAN AND WINS MIDLAND ENGLAND

When Aidan died in 651 the vacancy in the see of Lindisfarne was filled by his fellow countryman Finan, who was likewise a monk from Iona. Bishop Finan speedily revealed himself as a man of action as well as a student. He erected a church at Lindisfarne, larger and stronger than the temporary structure which had served Aidan. Bede says that after the manner of the Irish, he made the church not of stone but of hewn oak and covered it with reeds; and the same was afterwards dedicated in honor of St. Peter the Apostle by the Reverend Archbishop Theodore. Bede's words here have often been taken as evidence that there were no churches or buildings of stone and lime in Ireland in those days. This is an error, as is shown elsewhere in this volume. Numerous stone churches and buildings existed in Ireland in the earliest days of Christianity and some of them are in existence to-day. The oldest stone churches in England, Scotland and Wales are built in the Irish fashion. Eadbert, later bishop of Lindisfarne, took off the thatch at Lindisfarne and covered both roof and walls of the church with plates of lead.

Finan established the monastery of St. Mary's at the mouth of the Tyne and another at Gilling on the spot

[1] See Howorth, Golden Days of the Engl. Church, III, 184.

where Oswin had been murdered. He added to the growth of the abbey of Streaneshalch, or Whitby, which was later the scene of the Paschal controversy. Finan crowded unceasing activity into the ten years of his episcopate. From Iona he brought the ecclesiastical lore and discipline there taught and practised and set up centers for their distribution over the region through which his apostolate carried him. Finan was a man of lionhearted devotion, which the blind ferocities of the paganism amid which he moved could not shake. This element in his character is signally illustrated by his successful missionary work among the wild natives of middle England. By his personality and preaching he won over many of the Mercian tribes with their chiefs, and with Peada, the son of the obdurate Penda, king of the Middle Angles, whom he baptized in 653.[1] His chief associates in this work were the priests Cedd, Adda, Betti, and Diuma. Finan made Diuma, a cultivated Irish Scot, bishop of the Middle Angles and Mercia. He likewise consecrated Chad and appointed him bishop over the East Saxons, whose king, Sigebert, Finan himself baptized. Finan's influence is thus seen to have embraced almost the entire western half of England and he was largely instrumental in the reconquest of the East Saxons who had apostatized. He held strongly to the Irish or Celtic side in the Paschal controversy despite the friendly remonstrance of Ronan, an Irishman who had lived in Gaul and Italy and had learned to conform to the Roman custom.

Bede, relating how the province of the Midland Angles became Christian, tells us that King Peada, son of Penda, was baptized by Bishop Finan, with all his earls and soldiers and their servants that came along with him

[1] Hist. Eccl. III, XXI.

at a noted village belonging to the king called At the
Wall. And having received four priests who for their
erudition and good life were deemed proper to instruct
and baptize his nation, he returned home with much joy.
These priests were Cedd and Adda and Betti and Diuma.
The aforesaid priests, arriving in the province with the
prince, preached the word and were willingly listened to;
and many, as well of the nobility as of the common sort,
renouncing the abominations of idolatry, were baptized
daily.

4. RE-CONVERTS APOSTATE EAST SAXONS

When King Peada was slain and Oswy succeeded him
Diuma was made a bishop of the Midland Angles, as
also of the Mercians, being ordained by Bishop Finan;
for the scarcity of priests, says Bede, was the occasion that
one prelate was set over two nations. Having in a short
time converted many people, Diuma died among the Midland Angles in the country called Feppingum; and Ceollach, also of the Irish nation, succeeded him in the bishopric. This prelate not long after left his bishopric and
returned to the island of Hii or Iona. Ceollach's successor in the bishopric was Trumhere, an Englishman,
taught and ordained bishop by the Irish, being abbot of
the monastery which was called Ingethlingum.[1]

At that time also Sigebert, king of the East Saxons, who
had cast off the faith when they expelled Mellitus their
bishop, continues Bede, was baptized with his friends
by Bishop Finan in the same king's village of At the
Wall. King Sigebert returned to the seat of his kingdom
requesting of King Oswy that he would give some teachers, who might convert his nation. Oswy accordingly,

[1] Leeds, Hist. Eccl. III, XXIV.

sending into the province of the Midland Angles, invited
to him the man of God, Cedd, who with his brothers had
been trained in Ireland, and giving him another priest
for his companion, sent them to preach to the East Saxons.
When these two traveling to all parts of the country had
gathered a numerous church it happened that Cedd
returned home and came to Lindisfarne to confer with
Finan, who, finding how successful he had been in the
work of the gospel, made him bishop of the church of
the East Saxons, calling two other bishops to assist at
the ordination. Cedd, having received the episcopal dignity, returned to his province, and pursuing the work he
had begun with more ample authority built churches in
several places, ordaining priests and deacons to assist him
in the work of faith and the ministry of baptizing, especially in the city of Ithancester as also in what is named
Tilaburg, or Tilbury, where gathering a flock of servants
of Christ he taught them to observe the discipline of
regular life.[1]

Cedd often returned to his own country, Northumbria,
and there built the monastery of Lestingau, or Lastingham,
establishing therein the religious customs of Lindisfarne.
There Cedd died and left the monastery to be governed
after him by his brother Ceadda, or Chad, who was afterwards made bishop first of York and then of Litchfield.
For the four brothers, Cedd and Cynebil, Celin and Chad,
were all celebrated priests, all educated in Ireland and
at Lindisfarne and two of them became bishops.

5. RISE OF THE EASTER CONTROVERSY

Prominent also in England in the time of Finan was
a traveled and scholarly Irishman of the name of Ronan.

[1] Hist. Eccl. III, XXII.

In the controversy which raged around the observance of Easter, Ronan was a zealous defender of the Roman view, which had long before been adopted by people in the southern half of Ireland, but which was strongly opposed by those who clung to the tradition of Columcille. Ronan,[1] Bede tells us, instructed in ecclesiastical truth, either in France or Italy, disputed with Finan, convincing many or at least inducing them to make a more strict inquiry after the truth; yet he could not prevail upon Finan, but on the contrary made him the more inveterate by reproof and a profest opposer of the truth, being, adds Bede, of a hot and violent temper.[2]

Ronan may have been identical with the Romanus, mentioned by Bede, a Kentish priest and chaplain to Queen Banfleda who followed the Roman mode. The different observance created a decided confusion. Thus it happened that Easter was twice kept in one year; when the king, having ended the time of fasting, kept his Easter, according to the Irish fashion, the queen and her followers were still fasting and celebrating Palm Sunday. This difference, says Bede, whilst Aidan lived, was patiently tolerated by all men, for he was deservedly beloved by all, and things were allowed to go on during the episcopacy of Finan, but when he died and Colman, who was also sent out of Ireland, came to be bishop, a great controversy rose. This reached the ears of King Oswy and his son Aldfrid: for Oswy, having been instructed and baptized by the Irish and being very perfectly skilled in their language, thought, says Bede, nothing better than

1 Mabillon argues this Ronan very probably was a certain "Peregrinus ex genere Scottorum," who is called Romanus in a charter reciting the foundation of an ecclesiatical establishment at Mazeroles on the River Vienne in Picardy, of which he and fellow peregrini were the first occupants. (Annal. Ord. S. Bened., i, 474, and J. Stevenson, Bede 426, note; see also Gall. Christ., ii, 1222.)

2 Hist. Eccl. III, XXV.

what they taught. But Aldfrid, instructed by Wilfrid, who had learned the ecclesiastical doctrine in Rome, thought differently, and so the synod of Whitby was held and the Roman observance of Easter adopted. In the controversy Bede tells us that the Abbess Hilda and her followers were for the Irish, who were in the wrong, as was also the venerable Bishop Cedd, who in the council was most careful interpreter for both parties. Agilbert the Frank, bishop of the West Saxons, who had been educated in Ireland, probably in the South, took the Roman side.[1]

The Breviary of Aberdeen says of Finan, who died February 9, 661, that he was "a man of venerable life, a bishop of great sanctity, an eloquent teacher of unbelieving races, remarkable for his training in virtue and his liberal education, surpassing all his equals in every manner of knowledge, as well as in circumspection and prudence, but chiefly devoting himself to good works, and presenting in his life a most apt example of virtue."

[1] Hist. Eccl. III, XXV.

CHAPTER XVIII

FRUITS OF THE IRISH APOSTOLATE IN ENGLAND

1. "Celtic" Usages and the Synod of Whitby. 2. High Birth and Breeding of Irish Founders. 3. Frugality and Devotion of the Irish Clerics. 4. Colman Founds "Mayo of the Saxons."

1. "CELTIC" USAGES AND THE SYNOD OF WHITBY

THE third bishop of Lindisfarne was Colman, the last of the three remarkable Irishmen who established and filled the see. It was during his episcopate that the Paschal controversy culminated in the synod of Whitby, which settled it as far as Northumbria was concerned.

No attempt need be made here to describe in detail the proceedings at the synod. The original account is to be found in Bede and accounts based on that of Bede in almost every English history that has been printed. The result of it is well known. In sorrow but with decision Colman resigned his see and with thirty disciples, including both Irish and English, departed from England.

Irishmen in great number still taught, nevertheless, in England, particularly in the South. The greater part of Ireland had thirty years before conformed to the Roman custom[1] and even in the North and in Scotland what now are called "Celtic" usages—the term was unknown in medieval days—were not in universal vogue. The

[1] As early as 598 A. D., Columbanus writing from France is found expostulating with Pope Gregory on the subject and endeavoring to win the pontiff over to the Irish view. His letter is found among those of St. Gregory's. Epist.) CXXVII, Bk. IX, Registrum Epistolarum.

controversy raged round matters of ritual and did not deal with fundamentals.[1]

The language of Bede, who championed the winning cause in the dispute, has exaggerated the actual extent of the change from the Ionian to the Roman use. The time of keeping Easter was of course altered, as it had already been altered in the greater part of the Irish church. In other matters, such as the tonsure and the special uses in regard to the canonical hours, the old fashions continued largely to prevail. It is not credible that in the Irish monasteries in England there should have been violent changes in matters such as the particular form of the tonsure or of the special psalms or collects used at special times.

While the Irish bishops and missionaries in England did not do everything, they did a great deal, and it is well to acknowledge what they did before dwelling, as some writers do, on what they left undone. Had it not been for the Paschal controversy they doubtless would have gone much farther with their work. To pretend they did not organize dioceses is nonsense. St. Patrick had divided Ireland into dioceses, numerous indeed, and modeled according to clan and territory, and had forbidden one bishop to act in the diocese of another. Aidan, Finan and Colman, as far as they went, followed in England

[1] The most striking literary product of the Easter controversy was the letter addressed by Cummian, writing from Clonfert in 640, to Segenus, abbot of Iona. From it we learn that the Irish government had in 634 sent a commission of representative Irish scholars to Rome to get the full facts on the spot. The report brought back by them won most of Ireland over to the Roman custom. Cummian's work is a marvelous production. "It proves the fact to demonstration that in the first half of the seventh century, there was a wide range of Greek learning, not ecclesiastical merely, but chronological, astronomical and philosophical, away at Durrow in the very centre of the Bog of Allen" (G. Stokes, Roy. I. Acad., Proceedings, 1892, p. 195). The oldest copy of Cummian's work is preserved in a ninth century Irish manuscript at St. Gall. Migne reproduces it (Patrologia Latina, LXXXVII, cols. 969-978), and Healy gives a translated digest of it (Ireland's Ancient Schools and Scholars).

the plan of St. Patrick. Had time been allowed them they and their successors doubtless would have done that Theodore subsequently accomplished in their place. Theodore's work is alleged by historians, the one slavishly echoing the other, to have shown the superior organizing genius of the Roman. The allegation merely betrays the imitative prejudice of the historian. Theodore was not a Roman; Augustine was. Augustine accomplished far less than the Irishmen. Theodore had the work both of Augustine and the Irishmen to build upon. He did a great work, but his work was made possible only by the work of his predecessors. As Stubbs remarks, Theodore could have done very little if the Irish had not prepared the way.

2. HIGH BIRTH AND BREEDING OF IRISH FOUNDERS

An attempt has been made by some English historians to depict Wilfrid, archbishop of York, who appears to have had a kink in his character which prevented sustained cooperation in any work with others, as a sort of grand seigneur and Cardinal Richelieu, a polished and fastidious ecclesiastical statesman and patron of arts and letters, in contrast with the rude but ascetic Irish enthusiasts of Lindisfarne. The attempt is absurd in the last degree. It is true that Wilfrid must have broadened the education he received at Lindisfarne by his travels on the Continent where the chief centers of culture were the numerous Irish foundations. But it is also true that Wilfrid was but one remove from the unwashed savage, while the Irish monks who civilized him, the leaders of them nearly all of high birth, and the greatest travelers of their age, were representatives of the Celtic civilization that was old and mellow even before it was transformed by Christianity. Men like Aidan, Finan and Colman were representative of the highest taste and culture of their time. There were in that age no more cultivated, no better disciplined, no more highly polished, men in the world. The trouble with this type of English writer is that he knows very little of the wonderland represented in Irish literature and the old Irish civilization. In projecting his thought into an earlier age, he carries his modern environment with him and babbles in phrases of hackneyed superciliousness, where a mood of reverential appreciation would be proper to him.

Indeed the more prominent Irish schoolmen and monastic founders were nearly all men of high birth affiliated with the houses of those potent chiefs to whom the annalists give the title of king. The tone of authority which men like Columbanus and Columcille assume in addressing kings and even popes, the facile assurance with which men like Sedulius Scotus and Johannes Scotus Eriugena address the monarchs of their day and mingle in court circles with the highest civil and ecclesiastical dignitaries, the even calmness with which Aidan, Finan and their associates receive the prostrations of English kings and nobles, the directness with which Irishmen on the Continent attain the episcopal or abbatial dignity in days when bishops and abbots were the real rulers of the people, their habitual composure in the presence of demonstrations of popular reverence that might have moved the hearts of kings and potentates— these are the traits of men accustomed to honor from childhood, men whose natural milieu was the association of the great and learned, and in whom an innate pride of birth was so habitual as to be second nature. Iona is indeed one of the palmary instances of the association in Irish civilization of ecclesiastical authority with social dignity. The line of abbots had many of the characteristics of a royal dynasty,[1] so that a genealogical table made out by antiquarians contains fifteen abbots of Iona who, including Columcille, were all related to the reigning families of Ulster, and descendants of the royal Conal Culban, head of the Cinell Conaill.[2]

3. FRUGALITY AND DEVOTION OF THE IRISH CLERICS

Colman was bishop of Lindisfarne three years. Following the synod of Whitby he resigned his see and returned to Ireland, taking with him his Irish and English followers. When Colman was gone back to his own country, says Bede, Tuda was made bishop of the Northumbrians in his place, having also the ecclesiastical tonsure of his crown, according to the custom of that province and observing the Catholic time of Easter. He was a good and religious man but governed his church a very short time; he came out of Ireland whilst Colman was yet bishop, and, both by word and example, diligently taught all persons those things that appertain to the faith and truth. But, continues Bede, Eata, who was abbot of the monastery of Melrose, which Aidan had established, a most reverend and meek man, was appointed abbot over the brethren that stayed in the church of Lindisfarne, when the Irishmen went away. Colman, on his departure, it appears, requested and obtained this of King Oswy, because Eata was one of Aidan's twelve boys of the English nation, whom he received when first made bishop

[1] See "A Genealogical Table of the Early Abbots of Hy, showing Their Affinity to One Another and Their Connections with the Chief Families of Tyrconnell, Constructed from the Naehmseanchus," by Dr. Reeves; "Irish Pedigrees," 2 vols., by John O'Hart, passim; Hill Burton, History of Scotland, I, 247.

[2] Walahfrid Strabo (843) dwells on the high birth of Blaithmac, who belonged to the family of Columcille; Regali de stirpe natus summumque decorem nobilitatis habens florebat regius heres (Poetae Latini A. C. II, 297).

there, to be instructed in Christ; for the king much loved Bishop Colman on account of his singular discretion. This is the same Eata who not long after was made bishop of the same church of Lindisfarne. Colman carried home with him part of the bones of the most reverend father Aidan and left part of them in the church where he presided, ordering them to be interred in the sacristy.[1]

The place which Bishop Colman governed, Bede goes on to say, showed how frugal he and his predecessors were: there were very few houses besides the church found at their departure; indeed no more than was barely sufficient for their daily residence; they had also no money, but cattle; for if they received any money from rich persons they immediately gave it to the poor; there being no need to gather money or provide houses for the entertainment of the great men of the world, for such never resorted to the church, except to pray and to hear the word of God. The king himself, when opportunity offered, came only with five or six servants and, having performed his devotions in the church, departed. But if they happened to take a repast there they were satisfied with only the plain and daily food of the brethren and required no more; for the whole care of those teachers of God was to serve God, not the world, to feed the soul, not the body.

In all which observations of Bede we seem to feel an undercurrent of reflection and reproach on the manners of the times in which he lived as compared to that earlier period when the personal influence of these bishops and teachers was paramount in the land.[2]

[1] Hist. Eccl. III, XXV.
[2] Hist. Eccl. III, XXVI. Bede, like Alcuin, exhibits a chronic pessimism in respect to the English natives. In the commentary on St. Luke, written between 709 and 716, he expresses his fear lest the sins of the natives bring upon them yet sorer punishment (Peiora iamiamque superuentura formidamus —Opp. xi, 253). His letter to Egbert, written in the last year of his life (735), is one long lament over the evils of his time. His works abound in expressions of his gloom in the midst of the aboriginal chaos.

For these reasons, Bede says, the religious habit was at that time in great veneration, so that wheresoever any clergyman or monk happened to come he was joyfully received by all persons as the servant of God; if they should meet him upon the way they ran to him, and, bowing, were glad to be signed with his hand or blessed with his voice. Great attention was also paid to their exhortations; and on Sundays they flocked eagerly to the church or the monasteries, not to feed their bodies, but to hear the word of God; and if any priest happened to come into a village the inhabitants flocked together to hear from him the word of life; for the priests and clergymen went into the village on no other account than to preach, baptize, visit the sick, and to take care of souls; they were so free from worldly avarice that none of them received lands and possessions for building monasteries unless they were compelled to do so by the temporal authorities; which custom was for some time after observed in all the churches of the Northumbrians.[1]

4. Colman Founds "Mayo of the Saxons"

Colman by no means lost his interest in the English after leaving his English see. He dwelt in northern Britain for a couple of years and established some churches there. He then went over to Ireland with the English disciples who had remained faithful to him and settled in 668 at Inisboffin in the principality of northern Hy-Fiachra in the division now called county Mayo. Less than three years later he established in Mayo the abbey exclusively for the accommodation of English students which subsequently attained celebrity as "Mayo of the Saxons."

[1] Hist. Eccl. III, XXVI.

These bald facts Bede invests with an air of picturesqueness and adds certain details. Colman, he says, departing from Britain, took with him all the Irish he had assembled in the isle of Lindisfarne, and also about thirty of the English nation, who had been all instructed in the monastic life; and leaving some brothers in his church, he repaired first to the isle of Hii (Iona) whence he had been sent to preach to the English nation. Afterwards he retired to a small Irish island of Inisboffin or, as Bede calls it, Inisbofinde, the Island of the White Heifer. Arriving there, Bede tells us, he built a monastery and placed in it the monks he had brought of both nations; who, not agreeing among themselves, by reason of the Irish in the summer season, when the harvest was to be brought in, leaving the monastery wandered about through places with which they were acquainted; but returned again the next winter, and would have what the English had provided to be in common. Colman sought to put an end to this dissension and, traveling about far and near, he found a place in the island of Ireland fit to build a monastery, which, says Bede, in the Irish language is called Mageo, and bought a small part of it of the earl to whom it belonged to build his monastery thereon; upon condition that the monks residing there should pray to our Lord for him who had let them have the place. Then building a monastery with the assistance of the earl and all the neighbors, he placed the English there, leaving the Irish in the aforesaid island.

Bede tells us that this monastery continued up to his day possest by the English inhabitants; being the same that, grown up from small beginning to be very large, was generally called Mageo; and as all things had long before been brought under a better method (referring to

Easter controversy) it contained an exemplary society of monks, who were gathered there from the province of the English, and lived by the labor of their hands, after the example of the venerable fathers under a rule and a canonical abbot in much continency and singleness of life.[1]

Meanwhile the good work was going on in other parts of Ireland. At the date of the pestilence of 664, says Bede, "many of the nobility and of the lower ranks of the English nation were there (in Ireland) at that time, who, in the days of Bishops Finan and Colman, forsaking their native isle, retired thither, either for the sake of divine studies or of a more continent life; and some of them presently devoted themselves to the monastic life, others chose rather to apply themselves to study, going about from one master's cell to another. The Irish willingly received them all and took care to supply them with food as also to furnish them with books to read and their teaching gratis."[2]

These words are on many grounds well worthy of meditation by Englishmen.

[1] Hist. Eccl. IV, IV.
[2] Hist. Eccl. III, XXVII, Giles, one of the first translators of Bede, appends the following curious note to this revealing passage. "The reader, who has heard much of the early civilization of Ireland, will remember that the description given in the text applied to a period no earlier than the seventh century" (Bede, Eccl. Hist., p. 163).

CHAPTER XIX

EXTENDING OPERATIONS OVER ALL ENGLAND

1. Sentiment of Idolatry for Ireland and the Irish. 2. Among the East Anglians and West Saxons. 3. Irish Channels of Entry into Britain. 4. Fursa of the Visions. 5. Diuma, Chad, and Ceallach in Mercia.

1. SENTIMENT OF IDOLATRY FOR IRELAND AND THE IRISH

IT is no exaggeration to say that the Anglo-Saxons during all this period looked on the Irish with a feeling akin to idolatry and the sentiment prevailed among all classes, learned and unlearned, rich and poor, from the king and bishop to the meanest churl. To them all Ireland was a land of enchantment in which nothing foul could live, while articles brought out of Ireland carried healing powers with them.

The words of Bede are eloquent on this point. Ireland, he says, was a land "for wholesomeness and serenity of climate far surpassing Britain," a land so benign that "no reptiles are found there and no snake can live there, for tho often carried thither out of Britain, as soon as the ship comes near the shore and the scent of the air reaches them, they die." So wonderful a land was Ireland that all things in the land or brought out of it served as a charm against poison. The island was a land "flowing with milk and honey," full of vines, fish, fowl, deer and goats. The tradition was widespread.[1] To King Aldfrid, who knew Ireland from study and travel, it was "Inisfail, the Fair" too noble and nearly celestial to be honored in

[1] Hist. Eccl. I, I.

239

prose, to which poetry in the meter of the ancients could alone do justice. To William of Malmesbury centuries later the Irish were "a race in genuine simplicity and guiltless of every crime."

We can measure the depth of the veneration then felt by the Englishman for everything Irish by the curious superstitions which the sentiment inspired. Thus even in Bede, much the wisest and best informed of his nation, we find it taking the form of a belief that even the very soil on articles issuing from Ireland had a virtue which made it an antidote against disease: "In short we have known that when some persons have been bitten by serpents the scrapings of leaves of books that were brought out of Ireland being put into water and given them to drink have immediately expelled the spreading poison and assuaged the swelling."[1] Whatever other effect the Synod of Whitby had, it clearly did not diminish the respect entertained by the English for everything Irish. This English sentiment of worship in respect to Ireland did much to keep peace and friendship between the two countries unruffled during the Anglo-Saxon period when the aborigines of the Heptarchy were incessantly assaulting each other. Under Ecgfrid occurred an insignificant raid on the Irish coast, which Bede records with horror and lamentation. Alcuin, in company with Bede, takes note of the fact of Irish benevolence towards the English in that epoch of their feebleness and distraction, which made them an easy prey to all who attacked them.[2]

2. AMONG THE EAST ANGLIANS AND WEST SAXONS

Meanwhile Sigebert, king of the East Angles, who had lived in banishment in France, being desirous of imitating

[1] Hist. Eccl. I, I.
[2] "Scotorum gens Anglis semper amica" (Frobenius edition, II, 250, vers. 839).

the educational institutions he had seen in that country, set up a school for youth to be instructed in literature and was assisted therein by Bishop Felix, who came to him from Kent and who furnished him with masters and teachers after the manner of the country.

The only schools of any account in France at that period were the Irish foundations of Columbanus and his disciples, and it was doubtless in one of these that Sigebert had studied. Bishop Felix, who presided over the see of East Anglia for seventeen years, appears to have been a Burgundian and very probably graduated from one of Columbanus's Burgundian foundations, Luxeuil, Annegray, Remiremont or Fontains. Already the disciples of Columbanus were active in Picardy, establishing monasteries and schools, and doubtless some of them crossed the channel into England. From them the masters and teachers of Felix were very probably drawn. It was while Sigebert governed the kingdom that Fursey and his associates came out of Ireland into East Anglia. His honorable reception by the king and subsequent influence in the province were, it may be inferred, due in part to the king's friendship with his Irish instructors in Gaul. Felixstowe in Suffolk is named after this Felix. After his death his deacon Thomas was consecrated by Honorius as bishop. The West Saxons, formerly called Gewissae, Bede tells us, received the word of God by the preaching of Bishop Birinus, and of his successors Agilbert and Eleutherius. Birinus came into Britain in the reign of Cynegils by the advice of Pope Honorius, having promised in his presence that he would sow the holy faith in the inner parts beyond the dominions of the English where no other preacher had been before him. Hereupon he received the episcopal consecration from

Asterius, bishop of Genoa; but on his arrival in Britain he entered first the nation of the Gewissae and, finding all there most confirmed pagans, he thought it better to preach the word of God there, then to proceed further to seek for others to preach to. Now as he preached in the aforesaid province it happened that the king himself, having been catechized, was baptized together with his people, and Oswald, the most holy and victorious king of the Northumbrians, being present, received him as he came forth from baptism and by an alliance first adopted him thus regenerated for his son, and then took his daughter in marriage. The two kings gave to the bishop the city called Dorcic there to settle his episcopal see; where, having built and consecrated churches and by his labor called many to God, he departed this life and was buried in the same city; but many years after, when Hedda was bishop, he was translated thence to the city of Winchester and laid in the church of the blessed apostles, Peter and Paul.[1]

This Birinus appears to have been an Irishman, who had passed a number of years on the Continent. Birinus would seem to be a Romanized form of the Irish name Brain, which is pronounced and usually Anglicized Byrne, Burn, or Byron.

Birinus may have been associated, as Bishop Forbes of Brechin suggests, with the Irish Scots of the west of North Britain, where the parish of Kilbirnie is suggestive of his name. There is also a Kilbirnie loch in the parish of Beith; there is a parish of Dumbarney in Strathearn, and his name may also be preserved in the spur of the Chilterns, called Berin's Hill.

Birinus was not succeeded by an Irishman, but he was

[1] Hist. Eccl. III, VII.

succeeded, as Bede tells us, by one who had been trained in Ireland. This was the Frank, Agilbert, who figured at Whitby in the Paschal controversy. The son of Cynegils, Cornwalch, had refused Christianity at the hands of Birinus and was banished to East Anglia where he got the faith in due time. Bede says: "But when Cornwalch was to his kingdom there came into that province out of Ireland a certain bishop called Agilbert, by nation a Frank, who had lived a long time in Ireland for the purpose of reading the scriptures. This bishop came of his own accord to serve this king and to preach to him the word of life. The king, observing his erudition and industry, desired him to accept an episcopal see and stay there as his bishop. Agilbert complied with the prince's request and presided over those people many years. At length the king, who understood none but the language of the Saxons, grown weary of the bishop's barbarous tongue, brought to the province another bishop of his own nation, whose name was Wini, who had been ordained in France."[1] Bede's use of the word "barbarous" here is significant and somewhat amusing. We are to assume that he is using it in the sense of "foreign," as on other occasions, or is reproducing the standpoint of some other Latin writer. Even the Frankish speech must at that time have shown greater development than the dialect of the West Saxons, which Agilbert, tho many years in the country, had disdained to learn.

3. IRISH CHANNELS OF ENTRY INTO BRITAIN

While Aidan and his associates were laboring in Northumbria and Mercia, Fursa and his disciples were laying their foundations in East Anglia and Dicuil was

[1] Hist. Eccl. III, VII.

preaching among the Saxons of the South. Only a few years later we find the accomplished Maeldubh, or Maelduf, dispensing lore to the West Saxon youth in an Irish foundation, round which was to rise a cathedral and town which were to carry his name to future ages. Thus during the seventh century in the four corners of England, in the south and in the north, in the west and in the east, Irish missionaries were bringing the blessings of learning and religion to the English heathen. We are not to suppose that the Irish teachers whose names have come down to us were alone in their work. Maelduf was not the only Irish missionary and scholar established at Malmesbury. He was undoubtedly the chief of the learned company or he would not have had the distinction of having his name perpetuated in that of the town which he made the scene of his labors and of which he may be called the founder and apostle. Thus while Wessex was temporarily won by Birinus, its complete conversion as well as the winning of central Britain, the reconquest of Essex, and the first evangelization of the wild South Saxons, were the work of other Irishmen.

Not only through the North did the Irish teachers descend on Britain, they entered it from several directions, some to pass through it as travelers on their way to Rome and Palestine, others to preach and found schools in the island. The journey of Fursa of the Visions, who chose East Anglia as the scene of his labors, appears to have taken the route through what is now South Wales. Fursa was accompanied not only by his brothers Foillan and Ultan, two remarkable men, almost the equals of their brother in celebrity, but by a band of other Irish monks, Gobhan, or Gobain, and Dicuil among them, at least half a dozen of whom later won their laurels and have since been held in veneration in France. Their journey and reception were felicitous. "Landing upon foreign shores," says the old chronicle, "Fursa and his companions are borne through Britain to Saxony (i. e., East Anglia), where, being honorably received by King Sigebert at Burghcastle, he softened the hearts of the barbarians."[1]

Fursa arrived in East Anglia contemporaneously with the arrival of Aidan in Northumbria, and Sigebert, ruler of the Angles of that region, put at the disposal of the distinguished Irishman a tract of land at Cnobheresburg. There Fursa and his associates built a monastery in the Irish fashion within the enclosure of a Roman fort— Burghcastle in Suffolk—surrounded by woods and over-looking the sea. Using this place as headquarters the Irish missionaries labored for years converting and instructing the natives.[2]

Tribal wars then rent the population of East Anglia and left them little leisure or disposition to improve their minds or manners, or to listen to the words of religion. But the indefatigable and lionhearted Irishmen had a way of making most of the least hopeful material. Combining firmness with kindness, they gradually brought the aborigines to reason and put them through their first paces in the direction of ordered living and moral restraint. Sigebert was renewed in his fervor by Fursa. The devoted Irishman labored without pause except for the interval of one year of retirement and did not abandon his task till tribal warfare growing ever more widespread made it impossible to continue, obliging him to transfer the theater of his operations to Gaul, after an apostolate in England of about fifteen years.[3]

[1] Vita S. Fursae.
[2] Hist. Eccl. III, XIX.
[3] Hist. Eccl. III, XIX.

4. FURSA OF THE VISIONS

Bede describes Fursa as a holy man, renowned both for his words and actions, and remarkable for singular virtues, being desirous of living a stranger for our Lord wherever an opportunity should offer. Among the East Angles he performed his usual employment of preaching the gospel and by the example of his virtue and the efficiency of his discourse he converted many unbelievers to Christ and confirmed in his faith and love those that already believed.

Here he fell into some infirmity of body and was thought worthy, continues Bede, to see a vision of God; in which he was admonished diligently to proceed in the ministry of the word he had undertaken and indefatigably to continue his usual watching and prayers; inasmuch as his end was certain but the hour of it would be uncertain. Being confirmed by this vision, Fursa applied himself with all speed to build a monastery on the ground which had been given him by King Sigebert and to establish regular discipline therein. This monastery was pleasantly situated in the woods and with the sea not far off; afterwards Anna, king of that province, and the nobility embellished it with more stately buildings and donations.

Fursa was of noble Irish blood, says Bede, but much more noble in mind than in birth. From his boyish years he had particularly applied himself to reading sacred books and following monastic discipline, and he carefully practised all he learned was to be done. In short he built himself a monastery wherein he might with more freedom indulge in his heavenly studies. There falling sick, as the book about his life informs us, says Bede, he fell into a trance and, quitting his body from the evening till the cock crew, he was found worthy to behold the choir of angels and to hear the praises which are sung in heaven. Bede then goes on to tell us concerning what Fursa saw and heard in the vision, the accounts of which later became so celebrated.

We are told that Fursa, after building his monastery in East Anglia and preaching with much success, became desirous of ridding himself of all business of the world, and even of the monastery itself, and forthwith left the same and the care of souls to his brother Foillan and the priests Cobham and Dicuil and, being himself free from all that was worldly, resolved to end his life as a hermit. He had another brother called Ultan, who, after a long monastical probation, had also adopted the life of an anchorite. Repairing all alone to him, he lived a whole year with him in continence and prayer and labored daily with his hands. Afterwards seeing the province of East Anglia in confusion by the irruption of the pagan Mercians under Penda, who slew King Sigebert and slaughtered his army, and presaging that the monasteries would be also in danger, Fursa left all things in order and sailed over to France, and, being there honorably entertained by Clovis, king of the Franks, accomplished a great work. The facts related concerning Fursa, his work and visions, Bede tells us, he found in a little book about his life, a book he advises everybody to read believing that much spiritual profit would be thereby derived.[1]

When Fursa arrived in East Anglia, Algeis, with Corbican, and his servant Rodalgus, went on to Corbei and thence to Laon, while Foillan, Ultan, Gobain, Decuil, Etto and Madelgisilus remained behind with Fursa. They all appear in France later on, and two of them gave their names to French localities, St. Algise and St. Gobain

[1] Hist. Eccl. III, XIX. The life of Fursa to which Bede refers is extant.

—the forest figured much in despatches during the recent great war. Fursa left his girdle at Burghcastle and this the people afterwards lovingly covered with gold and jealously preserved.

5. DIUMA, CHAD, AND CEALLACH IN MERCIA

Meanwhile in Mercia and among the Mid-Angles Diuma, Chad, Ceadda, Ceallach and their associates were duplicating the work of Aidan, Finan and Colman in the North and Fursa and Dicuil in the South and East. Diuma was the Irish priest who was made bishop of the Mid-Angles by Finan. His associates were either Irish or had been educated in Ireland. The nationality of Chad and his three brothers Ceada, Cynebil and Caelin, has been the subject of dispute. Bede describes them as Northumbrian; other writers declare them to have been Irish. They had all however been educated in Ireland; they may have been among the twelve boys of Aidan; and they showed their training in strenuous emulation of their great Irish examplar. Diuma, who was bishop both of Mercia and the Middle Angles, was succeeded, as has been noted, by his countryman, Ceallach, who was in turn succeeded by Trumhere, an Angle or Saxon educated by the Irish. Trumhere founded a monastery in Gethlingen (Gilling) near Richmond.

Chad, says Bede, "was one of the disciples of Aidan and endeavored to instruct his people by the same actions and behavior according to his and his brother Cedd's example. Wilfrid also being made a bishop came into Britain and in like manner by his doctrine brought into the English church many rules of Catholic observance. Whence it followed that the Catholic institutions daily gained strength and all the Irish that dwelt in England either conformed to these or returned into their own country."[1]

Ceadda built a monastery at Talburgh, or Tilbury, at the mouth of the Thames. Chad founded Lestingham near Whitby and Itanchester, now Froshwell, in Essex. His celebrity is founded on his work as bishop of the extensive diocese of Mercia of which Finan fixed the see at Lichfield, so called in one view from the number of martyrs buried there under Maximinanus Herudeus, and, in another, from the marshy nature of the surrounding country. Bede assures us that Chad zealously devoted himself to the laborious functions of his charge, visiting his diocese on foot, preaching the gospel, seeking out the poorest and most abandoned natives in the meanest hovels that he might instruct them. Like many of the Irish saints his name became associated with wells and he became in England the patron saint of medieval springs. Around his resting place arose the cathedral and city of Lichfield.

[1] Hist. Eccl. III, XXVIII.

CHAPTER XX

CENTERS OF IRISH INFLUENCE IN ENGLAND

1. Maelduf, Founder of Malmesbury, and Other Irishmen in Wessex. 2. Founders of Abingdon, Chichester, and Lincoln. 3. Aldhelm and English Students in Ireland. 4. Correspondence between Aldhelm and Cellan.

1. MAELDUF, FOUNDER OF MALMESBURY, AND OTHER IRISHMEN IN WESSEX

IN the meantime among the West Saxons, Maeldubh, or Maelduf, "eruditione philosophus, professione monachus," as he is described by William of Malmesbury—had established the monastery and school of which Aldhelm, later Bishop of Sherborne, was to be the chief ornament. It was probably after the battle of Bradford-on-Avon in 652 that Maelduf, whom Camden describes as an Irish Scot, settled in the forest tract that had been torn from the Britons and that had borne the name of Ingelborne before it bore his own. Dependencies in course of time branched forth at Wareham, on the south coast near Poole, Bradford-on-Avon, Frome, on the banks of the little river of that name, and Sherborne. The churches raised at these spots were the first instances of building in Wessex. At Bradford-on-Avon a replica of one of the little stone Irish churches, dating from the earliest days of Christianity, is still to be seen incorporated as chancel in one of larger plans, the oldest ecclesiastical edifice in England. William of Malmesbury, Roger de Hoveden and others refer to Maelduf's work and call Malmesbury "the city of Maidulph."

William of Malmesbury quotes a deed, dated 672, by which (Bishop) Leutherius gave "that portion of land called Maidulfesburgh" to Aldhelm, the priest. Aldhelm, the deed says, "from his earliest infancy and first initiation in the study of learning, has been instructed in the liberal arts and passed his days nurtured in the bosom of holy mother church." This refers to his upbringing by Maelduf and his companions. Maelduf was a figure in the continual stream of Irish teachers pouring through Bristol, Malmesbury and Glastonbury, and spreading throughout South Britain parallel to those other streams that found their way through Chester, Cumberland, and over the Tweed, into northern and midland England.

Exeter, or Eaxeceaster, where Boniface was educated, was probably an Irish foundation. It could not very well have been a West Saxon foundation—the West Saxons were not then sufficiently advanced—and it was in what had long been distinctly Brito-Irish territory. Hardly anything is known of it beyond the fact that it was the seminary in which Boniface spent his youth. Elsewhere evidence is given in support of the view that Boniface was born of Irish parents in the Irish colony of Britain.

Daniel, or Danihel, bishop of Winchester, who corresponded with Boniface when the latter was in Germany, appears from his name to have been an Irishman and, like Boniface, probably belonged to the Brito-Irish colony into which the West Saxons had driven a wedge. The practice of giving children Hebrew names like Daniel did not come into vogue in Saxon England or elsewhere till long after this period. Thus in the Domesday Book only two Johns—the name is derived from the Hebrew Jehohannen, "God is gracious"—are listed and one of them is a Dane. Yet John became the commonest of all names under later usage in England as elsewhere. The bishop's name was probably Domhnaill, or Donnell, as it is written in its Anglicized form, a name which in modern times is also usually corrupted, in Ireland, when a Christian name, into Daniel.

Daniel was one of the persons with whom Boniface had entered into a contract for mutual intercessory prayer. In the records his name appears as Danihel, which resembles the Irish spelling. He was an intimate friend not only of Boniface, but of Aldhelm at Sherborne and Bede at Jarrow. Daniel like Aldhelm had been educated under the Irish scholar Maeldubh or Mailduf at Malmesbury and it was to Malmesbury that he retired in his old age (he died in 745) when loss of sight compelled him to resign the bishopric. He supplied Bede with the information regarding the church history of the south and west of Britain.[1] But he is best remembered for his intimate connection with Boniface. It was from Daniel that Boniface received commendatory letters when he started for Rome and to Daniel he continually turned for counsel during his work in Germany. Two letters of the bishop to Boniface are preserved and give an admirable impression of his piety and good sense.[2] In the second of these epistles, which was written after his loss of sight, Daniel takes a touching farewell of his correspondent: "Farewell, farewell, thou hundred-fold dearest one!" Daniel made pilgrimages to Rome in 721 and 731 and assisted at the consecration of Archbishop Tatwine. A vision recorded in the "Monumenta Moguntina" No. 112 perhaps implies that he was considered lacking in energy; nevertheless it would follow from William of Malmes-

[1] See Bede, Hist. Eccl. Praef.
[2] See Haddan and Stubbs, "Councils," III, 304, 343.

bury's reference to a certain stream in which Daniel stood all night that he was of remarkable austerity.[1] Florence of Worcester and others have references to him.

The Irish continued the ruling element in the Devonian peninsula and in what is now Wales to the seventh and eighth centuries. Exeter was probably the scene of the labors of some of the Irish teachers who poured through what is now Bristol. There appear to have been many such and had there been a West Saxon Bede doubtless we would be in possession of a story of their work in the south similar to that told of Aidan, Finan, Colman and their associates and successors in Northumbria.

2. FOUNDERS OF ABINGDON, CHICHESTER, AND LINCOLN

Abingdon, in Berkshire, originally Abban-dun or Dun Abban, has its name derived from that of Abban, an Irish scholar, who founded a monastery there and converted many. He was a hermit, and authorities are cited concerning his connection with the place by Camden who says that "in course of time that monastery rose to such magnificence that in wealth and extent it was hardly second to any in England."

There is a difference of opinion between Colgan and Lanigan in regard to Abban's work in England. Colgan agrees with Camden and considers that Abban labored at Abingdon and lived to a great age. Lanigan[2] throws doubt on the account on the ground that in Abban's lifetime the district continued in possession of the pagan Saxons. Kelly,[3] rejects the objections of Lanigan and propounds the view, now generally accepted, that Abban was actually the foster-father of the town and the original

1 Gest. Pont. I, 357.
2 Ecclesiastical History of Ireland.
3 Translator of Lynch's "Cambrensis Eversus."

founder of the monastic establishment. The town, which is near Oxford on the Thames, lay well within the orbit of influence of the southern stream of Irish missionary teachers, travelers and merchants that flowed in and out of the trading port of Bristol and South Wales. In modern times Irish fibulæ have been found around Abingdon.

According to the Chronicle of Abingdon, the famous abbey was founded in the first year of the reign of Centwine, who was the leading figure in Wessex during the period when, says Bede, "for ten years after the death of Coinwalch there was anarchy in the kingdom." We read in the Chronicle that during the reign of Centwine, who is thought by some to have been the father of Aldhelm and Bugga, there was a petty prince called Cissa, who ruled over Wiltshire and the greater part of Berkshire. He had a local bishop with a see at Malmesbury, but his own capital city was Bedeeuwinde (i. e., Bedwyn, in Wilts). In the southern part of the town he built a castle which from him was called Cyssebui. He had a nephew called Hean, a rich, powerful and religious man who had a pious sister called Cilla. When Hean one day heard the preacher say in church that it was easier for a camel to pass through the eye of a needle than for a rich man to enter the kingdom of heaven he began to despise his own wealth and to turn his thoughts to heavenly things. Thereupon his sister Cilla went to her uncle and asked him to make him a grant of land where he could build a monastery. To this Cissa assented and discovered in the south of Oxfordshire a place called Abba's Hill, where it was reported there had previously been a small religious establishment and, as it was a woody district (the Bagley Wood of that period), he proceeded to build a monastery there. This was in the year 685. The new foundation was endowed with much land and money by Cissa, while Hean made over to it his own hereditary property. The founder of the abbey was succeeded as abbot of the monastery by Conan, a distinctly Irish name, as is also that of Hean.[1] The small religious establishment referred to was possibly that of Abban.

Dicuil—the name appears to have been a prevalent one among the learned Irish of that age—founded the monastery of Bosham in Sussex, whence issued the see of Chichester. Dicuil had with him five or six brothers, but for some reason they did not show the enterprising spirit that was characteristic of other missionary Irishmen. Bede says the native South Saxons paid little attention to them. "There was among them," he writes, "a certain monk of the Irish nation, whose name was Dicuil, who had a very small monastery at the place called Bosanham, encompassed with the sea and woods, and in it five or six brothers, who served our Lord in poverty and humility; but none of the natives cared either to follow their course of life or to hear their preaching."[2]

The founder of the see of Lincolnshire was Æthelwine, brother of Alduini, abbot of Partney, and of the abbess Ædilhilda. He fixed his seat in 679 at Sidnaceaster, a few miles from Lincoln, now called Stow, where in later Saxon times a stately minster arose which still remains, the finest building extant of Saxon date and with many Irish features. Æthelwine and his brother Æthelhun were of noble birth and were educated in Ireland. Bede says that Æthelwine having been well instructed returned from Ireland into his own country and being appointed

---

[1] Chronicle of Abingdon, II, 268, 273.

[2] Hist. Eccl. IV, XIII.

bishop governed the province of Lindissi most worthily for a long time.[1]

3. ALDHELM AND ENGLISH STUDENTS IN IRELAND

Evidence has already been given of the extent to which the English, in common with other foreigners, went to Ireland for purposes of education. By the time of Aldhelm the habit had become something of a passion and his remarks on the subject are curious. In a letter to Eadfrid, later bishop of Lindisfarne (698-721), just returned from Ireland where he spent six years, he says in his flowery way: "We have heard from newsmongers that you have arrived safely at the ambrosial shores of the British territory, having left the wintry climes and storms of the island of Ireland, where for a triple two years' period you have drawn nourishment from the udder of wisdom (uber sophiae). . . . . Our ears have been tingled by assertions beyond the bounds of mere rumor of those who dwell on Irish soil with whom you yourself have lived, assertions like peals of thunder from the crashing clouds, and through many and wide stadia of the land, the opinion spreads and grows in force." He then goes on to remark on the stream of scholars crossing and recrossing the sea to and from Ireland: "The coming and going of those who pass by the ship's track, the whirlpools of the sea, hence and thence, hither and thither, is so frequent that it resembles some brotherhood of bees, busily storing the nectar in the comb."[2]

Strange bombast this, yet Aldhelm was the first Englishman to cultivate classical letters with any success. His luxuriance of speech is the evident result of an almost boyish delight in his new found knowledge and in its

[1] Hist. Eccl. III, XXVII.
[2] Migne, LXXXIX, Epistola III, col. 94.

display. The chief value of these passages is the light they throw on Ireland's preeminence as the school of the West in that period. He remarks that in Ireland English students learned not only the arts of grammar and geometry but also physics and allegorical and tropological interpretations of scripture.

In another letter to his protégé, Winfrid or Wilfrid, the companion of Æthelwald with whom he went to Ireland Aldhelm, like some later people on the Continent, gives evidence of apprehension respecting the danger in the philosophy and classical learning taught in Ireland as well as in the vagaries of living in the university towns of that country. In this he says that he had heard of the intended voyage of Winfrid to Ireland in pursuit of knowledge and he warns him against the perils of pagan philosophy to the faith and especially of mythology. What benefit, he asks, can orthodox truth derive from the studies of a man who spends his strength in examining into the incests of the impure Proserpine, the adventures of the petulant Hermione, the bacchanals of Lupercus, or the parasites of Priapus. These things have passed away and become as nothing before the cross victorious over death. He also counsels him against keeping loose company and wearing extravagant dress.[1]

Aldhelm himself claims to have been the first Englishman to practise the art of Latin composition in prose and verse. "No one," he says, "sprung from our stock, and born of German blood, has before our mediocre work done this kind of thing."[2] And thus he applies to himself Virgil's own lines:

> Primus ego in patriam mecum (modo vita supersit)
> Aonio rediens deducam vertice Musas
> Primus Idumaeus referam tibi, mantua palmas.

[1] Giles, Aldhelmi Opera, p. 377.
[2] Epist. ad Aircium, ed., Giles, 327.

"His language," says Haddan, "for enigmatic erudition, and artificial rhetoric rivals Armada, and Holophernes or Euphues."[1] Taine calls him a Latinized Skald.

Roger has noted the fact that the inflation and grandiloquence of Aldhelm's style became still more pronounced when he was writing either to Irishmen or to men educated in Ireland. In view of Aldhelm's naive envy of the fame of the Irish schools to which English and continental students continued to stream despite the presence of Theodore and Hadrian at Canterbury, his motive would seem very evident. It would appear that he wanted to demonstrate, as Roger notes, that one was quite capable of being in possession of a beautiful style without having to go to Ireland to acquire it. Perhaps also he considered the school which produced such compositions as Hisperica Famina a fine model and wanted to give satisfaction to those who were among its admirers. On the other hand, "English magnificence" is the quality of Aldhelm's Latin prose and verse in the opinion of William of Malmesbury.[2]

4. Correspondence Between Aldhelm and Cellan

There is in existence a letter written to Aldhelm by Cellan, the Irish abbot of Perrone, the successor in the monastery to Ultan, the brother of the famed Fursa. The mere correspondence gives us a pleasant picture of the brotherhood of letters then existing, in which the intercommunication over a wide area was conducted by such Irish scholars as attended Hadrian's school at Canterbury, as well as the Englishmen who went to Ireland, and the Irishmen who traveled from one country to another. One of Cellan's letters, which is signed with his name, is

1 Remains, 267.
2 Gesta Pontificum, V, 189.

addrest to "My Lord Aldhelm, the Archimandrite (i. e., the Abbot), enriched in the study of letters, adorned by honey-bearing work by night, who in a marvelous manner has acquired in the land of the Saxons that which some in foreign parts hardly obtain by dint of toilsome labor. Cellanus, born in the island of Ireland, dwelling obscurely in an extreme corner of the land of the Franks, near those of a famous colony of Christ, greeting in the whole and sure Trinity." Cellanus then proceeds to pay Aldhelm some compliments and inter alia tells him that though they were not worthy to hear him at home, they read his finely composed works painted with the attractions of various flowers. He reports how he had heard praises of his Latin and goes on to say: "If you would refresh the sad heart of a pilgrim, send him some small discourses (sermunculos) from your sweet lips, the rills derived from which pure fountain may refresh the minds of many in the place where rest the holy remains of the Lord Fursa."[1]

William of Malmesbury, to whom we are indebted for the letter of Cellan gives us only one clause from Aldhelm's reply, which is not illuminating. "I wonder," he says, "that from the renowned and flower bearing fields of the Franks, the activity of your fraternity addresses such a poor little creature (tantillum homunculum) as myself, sprung from the Saxon race and cradled in my tender years under a northern sky (sub Arctos axe)."

Another letter to Aldhelm, which as it has been preserved to us is anonymous, is with great probability identified as written by Cellan. In this letter the writer describes himself as "an Irishman of unknown name," and at that time he had probably not yet become abbot

---

[1] Giles, Aldhelmi Opera, 331; Bonif. Ep. 4 (Mayor's Bede, p. 298).

of Perrone. Giles,[1] and Hole,[2] both identify this Irishman with Cellan, and Ludwig Traube, who found a number of Cellan's Latin verses at Florence, makes the authorship almost certain.[3] The letter is addrest "To the Lord Aldhelm, holy and most wise, to Christ most dear; an Irishman of name unknown sends greeting in the eternal God." It then continues:

"Knowing how you excel in intellect, in Roman excellence, and in the varied flowers of letters after the manner of the Greeks, I would rather learn from your mouth, the purest fount of knowledge, than drink from any other spring, especially from the turbid master (turbulento magistro praesertim, to whom Cellan refers is not apparent). I beseech you to take me and teach me, because the brightness of wisdom shines in you beyond many lecturers, and you understand the minds of foreigners who desire to acquire knowledge, for you have been to Rome, and besides you were yourself taught by a certain holy man of our race. Let this serve as a summary of reasons . . . ." the upshot being that the writer wanted to borrow a certain book, the letter ending with a sacred poem of twenty-one lines.

The "holy man of our race" who taught Aldhelm was of course Maelduf of Malmesbury. Another teacher of Aldhelm was Hadrian at Canterbury, but Aldhelm was between forty and fifty before he met Hadrian, and even at Canterbury was in the society of Irish scholars, as he himself tells us. The Irishmen had little to learn either from Theodore or Hadrian and they appear there more in the character of controversialists and logicians, already wielding the dialectical method for which they were to

---

[1] Aldhelmi Opera, 331.
[2] D. C. B. i, 434.
[3] Perrona Scotorum, Abhandlungen der Bay. Akad (1900) 469-538.

become famous on the Continent, than as meek learners. Doubtless the chief attraction to the Irishmen in Canterbury was the opportunity of extending their knowledge of Greek of which they were almost the sole representatives in western Europe.[1]

[1] William of Malmesbury has preserved for us also a letter written by a young Irish prince named Artuil (he is called Artwilius in the manuscript) and directed to Aldhelm, in which he requests the Englishman to polish for him his first literary efforts, "ut perfecti ingenii lima eraderetur scabredo Scottica."

CHAPTER XXI

IRISH TUTELAGE OF ENGLAND

1. Irish Influence, More than Roman, Potent Among English. 2. Theodore and "Molossian Hounds" at Canterbury. 3. Irish Plant Arts and Industries in England. 4. By the Time of Bede and Alcuin. 5. Irish Scholars and King Alfrid. 6. Irish Literati Before and After Dunstan.

1. Irish Influence, More than Roman, Potent Among English

TO some it has appeared that the Irish tutelage of England came to an end with the Synod of Whitby and the withdrawal of Colman and his associates. The truth is that Irish preceptors continued their work in England and English students continued to go to school in Ireland almost without let-up until after the French conquest. The Irish foundations in England, swallowed up one after another by the engulfing barbarism with its reiteration of sporadic outbreaks, in the intermittent periods of calm saw new founders amid the ruins carrying on in the face of heavy discouragement the work of regeneration. The influence of the Irish missionaries over the aborigines of the country continued as powerful almost as that of the native rulers. The Easter question had only a fraction of the importance that has been attached to it. Ireland outside of Columcille's country, as Bede observes and as the Paschal letter of Cummian[1] bears evidence, yielding to the admonition of the Apostolic See, had already conformed to the Roman usage and canonical

[1] Migne LXXXVII, cols. 969, 978, Epistola de controversia paschali.

262

custom in 634 A. D., thirty years before the Synod of Whitby. Iona, which was the last to hold out, relinquished its intransigeant attitude in 715. Such differences of view as existed moderated but little the amenability of the English natives to Irish exhortation. Irishmen following the so-called "Celtic" usages and Irishmen following the Roman usages continued therefore to carry on their work before and after uniformity had been established between the two islands.

It thus becomes evident that whatever of civilization the English made their own from the period of the fifth century invasions to the French conquest of 1066 was acquired by them from Irishmen and Irish schools outside of the small territory which was the orbit of Augustine and his successors. Even in the small kingdom of Kent the harvest was more apparent than real. There has been much exaggeration, as has been before remarked, about the schools supposed to have been introduced by Augustine and his monks. There is no reason to suppose that they had any other ideals than those of their master, Pope Gregory, who, we know, greatly undervalued secular learning and entirely disapproved of the clergy teaching it. His extraordinary letter to the Bishop of Vienne is eloquent of his views on the subject and even better proof of his prejudice is to be found in the fact that, despite his sojourn at Constantinople, the great pope never took the trouble to learn Greek, in which the best thought of the Old World was enshrined and in which nearly all the theology of the earlier centuries of the Church had been written. We may be sure that Gregory's influence in these matters, at all events in Italy, was widespread and that his monks from St. Andrew's monastery were deeply imbued with his views. There is no reason to believe, as a modern writer remarks, that they were in any sense learned men. All that the pope demanded from his pupils and protégés was sufficient learning from them to be able to read the Scriptures, service books, lives of the saints, and to explain the elementary dogmas; and, secondly, to be able to chant the psalter. There is no evidence anywhere of his patronage of libraries and schools, except choir schools. The only teaching traditionally associated with Augustine and his colleagues was that preparatory to a clerical life and the schools founded by them were, as far as the evidence goes, seminary schools and schools for the teaching of choir boys and men through the medium of no language but Latin. "It was very different with the Irish missionaries who presently lighted a great lamp in Northumbria and who came from a country then all aflame with zeal for learning as well as religion."[1] Not even to Augustine can be rightly attributed the introduction of the Benedictine rule into England. That was the work of Benet Biscop, Wilfrid and Ceolfrid, and to the time of Dunstan it was only a fragmentary introduction, a blend of the Irish and Benedictine rule, as in the majority of the foundations in Gaul before the time of St. Benedict of Aniane.

2. THEODORE AND "MOLOSSIAN HOUNDS" AT CANTERBURY

The influence of Theodore and Adrian, who established a school with a wider curriculum at Canterbury, has been similarly exaggerated. Theodore was an old man, sixty-nine years of age, when he arrived in England in 668. Neither he nor Adrian knew anything of the Anglo-Saxon tongue and it is very doubtful whether either of them ever attempted to learn a word of what was to them

[1] Howorth, Golden Days of the English Church, III, 359.

the mere brutal jargon of uncouth savages. On the face of it it taxes our credulity to invite us to believe, as is uniformly done, that such development as is discernible in England at that time was mainly due to their labor. There is no real evidence even that Theodore did any actual teaching outside of his preaching. The Roman tradition, plainly voiced by Gregory the Great in respect to the impropriety of a bishop teaching secular subjects, could not have but influenced Theodore. It is true that Bede praises both of them highly. It is true that from Theodore and Adrian some of the natives actually learned Latin and Greek. It is likewise true that such knowledge speedily died out, as the very passage of Bede relating to it indicates. But a mere consideration of indubitable facts makes it clear that we must look elsewhere for the real source of such civilized progress as the English tribes were then making. That source lay in the impassioned efforts of strenuous, accomplished Irishmen in every corner of England. Wherever real progress was evident, wherever books were being written, wherever scholars of note appeared, wherever a school showed real results, wherever the arts were being cultivated, there Irishmen were in the midst of it. Count the number of scholars in England during the Anglo-Saxon period who left anything behind them. Almost without exception they were Irish-trained. Canterbury has hardly a single scholar worth mentioning to show. Aldhelm, Bede, Alcuin, Fredegis, Egbert, Caedmon, Cynewulf, Dunstan, were everyone of them associated with Irish teachers and Irish foundations. Up to the period of the Conquest Anglo-Saxon manuscripts were written entirely, as has been said, in the Irish script. Not a single document exists in the Roman script with the dubious exception of a small chart, half Roman, half Irish, belonging to the eleventh century. And so through all the visible evidences that have been preserved to us of that period—books, metal work, sculpture, architecture and other products of the allied arts. The portable specimens might have been made in Ireland, and are believed, many of them, to have been made in Ireland, so manifestly are they examples of Irish craft.[1]

In the school founded by Theodore, the Cilician archbishop had the cooperation of Irish scholars. Even then that love of dialectical controversy, of probing into the ratio of things, which was later to make the Irish schoolmen the stormy petrels of the continental church, and which already had found its illustrations in the Paschal disputations and in the correspondence between Columbanus and the Frank bishops and between Columbanus and Popes Gregory and Boniface, had become habitual to them. Aldhelm, who was stationed at Canterbury at the time, in one of his letters indicates that in the Greek from Tarsus the Irishmen discovered a doughty antagonist. The archbishop, he says, was "densely surrounded by a crowd of Irish students, who grievously badgered him (globo discipulorum stipetur) as the truculent boar was hemmed in by a snarling pack of Molossian hounds. He tore them with the tusks of grammar and pierced them with the deep and sharp syllogisms of chronography till they cast away their weapons and hurriedly fled to the recesses of their dens."[2] The point to be noted here is that even at Canterbury and in Kent, with which Irish influence is seldom associated, Irish scholars were active,

[1] "It is now well ascertained that all the sacred books so highly venerated by the Anglo-Saxon Church and left by her early bishops as heirlooms to their respective sees were obtained from Ireland or written by Irish scribes." (Rev. J. H. Todd, Proc. Roy. I. Acad., Vol. I, 41.)

[2] Giles, Aldhelmi Opera, p. 94; Brown, Aldhelm, 263-4. Compare Aldhelm's description with Gregory Nazienzen's account of the encounter of Basil with the Armenian students in Athens (Oration XLIII).

and had probably been familiar figures since Dagan had refused the hospitality of Lawrence, successor of Augustine.

Bede furnishes us with little detail respecting the kind of teaching fostered by Adrian and his master Theodore, but he gives us a goodly list of their scholars. The really important new element introduced by Adrian into the Canterbury school was the teaching of Greek. Beyond that the great Irish schools had little to learn and it was doubtless in pursuit of a more advanced knowledge of Greek that those Irish scholars were present at Canterbury who were not merely sojourning there in their journey to the Continent. They alone appear to have been able to take permanent advantage of the opportunity thus afforded, and to this source we may look for at least one tributary to that Hellenic knowledge which they display in subsequent ages when such knowledge was elsewhere dead in the West. To the brighter spirits among the English natives the fame of the African and the Greek, with all the prestige of the Roman empire behind them, could not compete with the fame of Irish scholars and the Irish schools, then rising to the meridian of their influence and development. Instead of flocking to Canterbury, they continued to flock in the direction of Ireland. The letter of Aldhelm to Eahfrid exhibits in turgid Latin his naive irritation over the superior attraction of the Irish schools: "I, a wretched small man, have revolved these things as I wrote them down and have been tortured with the anxious question: Why should Ireland, whither students ship-borne flock together in summer, why should Ireland be exalted by some ineffable privilege as though here on this fertile turf of Britain teachers of Latin and Greek (didacaii Argivi Romanive Quirites) cannot be found, who, solving the seven problems of the celestial library are able to unlock them to untutored smatterers. The fields of Ireland are as rich in learners and in the exuberant number (pascuosa numerositate) of students as the pivots of the pole quiver with vibrations of the glittering constellations, and yet Britain (if you like to say so) placed almost at the extreme verge of the world, possesses a glowing sun and a lustrous moon, that is to say, Theodore, the archbishop of the island, who has grown old in acquiring the flowers of the philosophic art, and Adrian, his companion in the brotherhood of learning, and ineffably endowed with pure urbanity."[1]

While it is sometimes asserted that Adrian founded other schools in England besides that at Canterbury there has been found only one charter, accepted as genuine by Kemble, containing grants to him. This is dated 686 and is a conveyance of land in Kent, being a part of his own demesne (terrae juris mei) made with the consent of his elders by King Eadric to St. Augustine's abbey.

3. Irish Plant Arts and Industries in England

No missionary from Italy had ever, till the installation of Theodore of Tarsus, dwelt outside the boundaries of Kent. Their hold even on Kent was a feeble hold, for reversion to heathensim was the order of the day and the graces of civilized life were not even coveted or imparted. Of themselves the English could do nothing. As a result of their almost absolute barbarism they showed from the beginning an incapacity for initiating or originating anything. Thus while Britain was everywhere encumbered with Roman buildings of stone, intact or in ruins, Benet

[1] Giles, Adhelmi Opera, p. 94; Migne Pat. Lat., LXXXIX, col. 94. Stubbs suggests that Eahfrid, to whom Aldhelm's letter is addrest, may have been either Echfrith, abbot of Glastonbury, or Eadfrid, bishop of Lindisfarne. Raine definitely identifies him with this latter.

Biscop had late in the seventh century to import artizans from Gaul to build the simple houses he desired to erect at Wearmouth and Jarrow. Among the native population he could find nobody capable of the simplest work of carpentry, quarrying and construction, though the models of the vanished empire were ever before their eyes.

Everywhere throughout England on the other hand where the arts and works of civilized life were superseding the futile monotony and disorder of barbarism, Irishmen were themselves accomplishing the work or instructing the reclaimed English how to do it. In the region spreading out like a fan from Malmesbury they dotted the land with edifices that rivaled the Roman models in design and durability. The church erected at Bradford-on-Avon, whether the work of Aldhelm's time or a renovation of the ninth century, shows the influence of Irish hands and endures to this day. At Frome, Sherborne, and Wareham on the south coast, where the first buildings known to Wessex were raised, they must have worked in goodly numbers. The monastic life they introduced into the country was fruitful in good work. As Green puts it: "It broke the dreary line of the northern coast with settlements which proved the forerunner of some of the busiest English ports. It broke the silence of waste and moor by homes like that of Ripon and Lastingham. It set agricultural colonies in the depths of vast woodlands, as at Evesham and Malmesbury, while by a chain of religious houses it made its way step by step into the heart of the Fens."[1]

It was of course chiefly in the north that Irish activity directed its first energies. But soon the Irish missionary, artist, and craftsman was exercising his humanizing

[1] Hist. of England.

influence in every corner of the island. Fursa in East Anglia, Dicuil in Sussex, Finan in Essex, and Diuma and his associates in Mercia were but representative of a great apostolate, embracing industry and art as well as religion and learning, that elevated and organized the land. Wherever the Irishmen concentrated their energies the result was seen in a general speeding up of effort in every department of national or provincial life. Under their tutelage Northumbria became the first of the English states in influence and the first in the department of letters. Its kings were educated in Iona and Ireland, and there they learned to speak and write the Irish tongue and become acquainted with the graces of Irish literature, then already embodied in the literary shape in which its splendid fragments have come down to us.

There can be little doubt that there were other English records akin to Bede's telling among other things of the work of Irishmen in England. Simeon of Durham's chronicles[1] appear to be based on a Northumbrian history now lost. Had Bede's history been destroyed we would know very little concerning what Irishmen did in England, yet Bede wrote only a century after Irishmen began their work. Of their later work there is no connected narrative and we have to assemble our information from scattered sources. The fact appears to be that the Irish records in England were destroyed by the Danes, who devastated the very provinces where their influence was strongest. We know that Irish influence was the strongest leaven in Anglo-Saxon life, but had we the full, instead of only the partial facts concerning that influence, doubtless the origin of much that is obscure would be revealed.

1 Historia de Gestis Regum Anglorum.

4. BY THE TIME OF BEDE AND ALCUIN

By the time of Bede and Alcuin, the north of England was covered with Irish schools. Bede himself was trained at Jarrow and had as masters there, as he himself tells us, Trumhere, or Trumbert, the disciple of St. Chad and Sigfrid, who had been the fellow pupil of Cuthbert at the Irish foundation of Melrose under Boisil and Eata, whom Aidan had rescued from slavery, educated and ordained. From these Bede "derived the Irish knowledge of Scripture and discipline."[1] Another of those who influenced him was John of Beverly, the pupil of Theodore and of the Irish foundation of Whitby. Trumbert was brought up among the Irish-trained monks of Lestingham, founded by Chad. Sigfrid was living at Jarrow an aged invalid when Bede was writing his history and the methods and all-consuming passion for teaching and learning derived from his Irish masters are movingly portrayed by Bede in the scenes preceding his death.[2] Ceolfrid,[3] the patron and teacher of Bede, had always been subject to Irish influences, having assumed the habit and entered the monastery of Ingetlingum (i. e., Collingham), where his elder brother, Abbot Cynefrid, then ruled. He committed him for instruction to his relative Tunberht, who afterward became bishop of Hexham. Cynefrid himself, as the "Anonymous History of the Abbots" tells us, had been to Ireland for the purpose of studying the Scriptures and "of seeing the Lord more frequently in tears and prayers." Benet Biscop, who founded Jarrow and Monkwearmouth, received like Wilfrid his education among the Irish monks of Lindisfarne and its dependent foundations, who cooperated in the new

[1] Stubbs, Dict. of Chr. Biog., sub voce Bede.
[2] De Abbatibus.
[3] Migne, Patrol. Lat., LXXXIX.

creations on the banks of the Tyne and Wear. Bede's
history seems to have been modeled on Irish historical
works like those of Adamnan, who wrote his life of
Columcille when Bede was a young man, and who is
said to have written also in Latin a history of the Irish
people down to his own times.[1]

There was evidently a very close connection between
Northumbria and Clonmacnois, for Tighernach, abbot
of that great seat of learning, in his Annals, gives the dates
of Bede's works as they are written, evidently copied from
contemporary records, and notices the date of the founding of Lindisfarne and the changing of Easter at Iona.
The letters of Alcuin reveal the intimate intercourse
between Clonmacnois and the school of York as well as
Tours and the court of Charlemagne.[2] In the Annals of
Ulster under the year 730, and in the Annals of Tighernach in 731, we read, "Echdach (i. e., Eochaid), the son
of Cuidin (i. e., Cuthwene), King of the Saxons, was
tonsured (clericatus) and imprisoned (constringitur)."
The Eochaid here referred to was Ceolwulf, King of
Northumbria, to whom Bede dedicates his history. Ceolwulf, like Aldfrid, had apparently an alternative Irish
name, but there is no other indication, beyond the fact
that he was an ardent student, that he had lived in Ireland.
He lived for the last twenty-three years of his life at
Lindisfarne. During the central years of Bede's life the
reigning king of Northumbria was Aldfrid, whose affilia-
tions with Ireland were so intimate and enduring.[3]

---

[1] Ward, Vita Rumoldi, p. 218, Lovan., 1662.

[2] From Tours he addresses Colgu, Fer-leiginn or Rector of Clonmacnois, as
"master and father" and discusses its affairs with him. He gives the gossip
of Clonmacnois to Josephus Scotus, who was student under Colgu at Clonmacnois and instructor at York (Migne, Pat. Lat. C, cols. 128, 142, 143, 445).
His learning made him appear an Irishman to his contemporaries. Thus the
Chronicon Turonense at 791: "Erat autem Alcuinus Scotus, ingenio clarus,"
etc. (Migne C, col. 128).

[3] See Dublin Review, XXI, 519.

There were Irish monks and Irish trained monks at York, at Jarrow, at Monkwearmouth, at Melrose, at Hexham, at Whitby, and other foundations. The later English schools, brief and fitful in their career, were often but the piecing together again, on the site or in the neighborhood, of the older Irish foundations, broken up in the periodic homicidal welter of internecine conflict that succeeded the passing of one petty king or another through Anglo-Saxon history. At York, an offshoot of Lindisfarne, Alcuin appears to have acquired from Irish Hellenists there resident such knowledge of Greek[1] as he possest, tho the knowledge may likewise have been acquired at Clonmacnois, if he actually studied under Colgu in that great seat of learning.[2] The master who influenced Alcuin most in company with Ælbert had been brought into the monastery by Eata, the protégé of Aidan and one of the earliest representatives of Irish learning among the English.[3] The Irish scholars and craftsmen all over England put no curb on the liberality with which they dispensed their learning and skill. That the pupils should lag behind the masters is only in the nature of things. The slough of an age-long barbarism was not easily shed; but if a mere film of mediocrity and dulness in contrast to the depth of brutality and despair underneath is what is represented by progress in the Anglo-Saxon epoch, it is well to remember that in one or two directions and in one or two examples Anglo-Saxon skill rivaled its Irish

1 This is the opinion of Gardthausen, the German authority on Greek paleography.

2 As to whether Alcuin studied at Clonmacnois: cf. Monnier, Alcuin et Charlemagne, Paris, 1854. Alcuin's admiration for the culture of Irishmen as well as his dread of their "Egyptian" philosophy break out frequently in his correspondence and other works (Frobenius edition, I, 185, 285, 284, 286 note; II, 185, 246, vers. 458).

3 At York under Alcuin was Liudger, later archbishop of the Frisians, apparently the only continental student that ever went to England for education.

archetype. The singularity of the Book of Lindisfarne as a work produced in England by the natives themselves, instructed by Irish artists, is manifest in the contrast between its finished beauty and the other memorials of its school. Its ascription to Eadfrid, a student in Ireland, may be correct. But, if genuinely Anglo-Saxon, it is no less manifestly a creation of Irish art, indistinguishable in its characteristics from other works of the period produced in Ireland. A succession of paleographers have labored in the pursuit of some distinguishing mark which would enable them to differentiate Irish from Anglo-Saxon manuscripts, illuminated and non-illuminated. Their labor has been in vain. The strong tutelary Irish hand kept its grasp on England, guiding the hands and feet of the aborigines of the country, recording their first lispings of the syllables of civilization, nursing the promise of individuality in custom and speech, imposing the bridle of Christian principle on the gaping ferocities of barbaric appetite and passion, and impressing everywhere the Irish form and imprint, so that the work of their hands was as the copy to the prototype, differing only as the voice of the neophyte reproduced in halting but faithful words the meaning of his instructor.[1]

5. IRISH SCHOLARS AND KING ALFRED

Missionary Irishmen labored to restore learning in England during the prolonged period when the Danes

[1] Symeon of Durham has preserved a poem by Æthelwulf "de Abbatibus" which was dedicated to Egberht, then living in Ireland. In this poem he has a chapter devoted to an Irishman, named Ultan, who was a priest and skilled in the ornamentation of books.
"Comtis qui potuit notis ornare libellos
Atque apicum speciem viritim sic reddit amoenam,
Hac arte ut nullus possit se acquare modernus
Scriptor."
(Æthelwulf's poem, Appendix, Sym. of Durham, ed., Arnold, p. 274.)
Ultan was also a zealous teacher and lived to be an old man. We are told moreover of a brother, named Cuicin, also apparently Irish, who was a skilful smith and a very holy man, mingling the singing of psalms with his noisy occupation.

assisted in ruining it. The early chroniclers are unanimous almost in associating Irishmen with King Alfred's reforms and some of them bring in the celebrated Johannes Scotus Eriugena as leader of an intellectual revival, confounding him, as Huber notes, with John from German Saxony. Alfred himself supplies us with the names of three Irishmen who acted as his co-workers and a recital of the extraordinary manner of their arrival. In the Chronicle, the origin of which is attributed to him, at the year 891, occurs the passage: "In this year three Irishmen came to Alfred king on a boat without oars or rudder. They had stolen away from Ireland because they would be for God's love on pilgrimage, they recked not where. The boat on which they fared was wrought of two and a half hides and they took with them meats for seven nights. And at the end of the seventh night they came to land in Cornwall and straightway fared to Alfred king. Thus were they named, Dubslane, and Macbeth and Maelinmain." The story is redolent of the spirit of Irish history and saga, and reproduces preeminently the spirit of the Irish pilgrim. In the Book of Leinster is a story how three young Irish clerics set out on a pilgrimage; they took as provision on the sea only three loaves. "In the name of Christ," said they, "let us throw our oars into the sea and let us commend ourselves to the Lord."

According to the chronicle of Fabius Ethelwerd, the three Irishmen, after leaving Alfred, "who with his senate rejoiced at their coming," went to Rome and Jerusalem "as is customary with teachers of Christianity." He describes the three respectively as "flourishing in the arts, skilled in letters and a distinguished master of the Scots."[1]

[1] Bk. IV, Ch. III, A. D. 891.

Asser, Alfred's minister and biographer, speaks of ambassadors from Ireland to Alfred, writing of "the daily embassies sent to him by foreign nations from the Tyrrhenian Sea to the furthest end of Ireland."[1] He talks of Alfred making gifts to Irish churches and of numbers of Irishmen among those who came voluntarily into his domain. Concerning John the Saxon, whom William of Malmesbury and other English chroniclers confound with Johannes Scotus Eriugena, little is known. But he came from Corbie in Saxony, a branch of the Irish foundation of Corbie on the Somme. Asser himself came to Alfred from Menevia, or St. Davids, a great Brito-Irish center and the point in Wales nearest Ireland. He may have been wholly or partially Irish. The mere fact of his culture in that age, when Wales was far from conspicuous in culture, would tend to show that he had Irish connections.[2]

6. Irish Literati Before and After Dunstan

We are informed concerning Dunstan, archbishop of Canterbury (d. 988), who became notable for many reforms, including the restoration of the Benedictine monasteries, that "he received his education under certain Irish monks who were excellent masters of the sciences and at that time resided in Glastonbury, which the wars had left in a most ruinous condition."[3]

Dunstan, the first Englishman meriting the name of statesman, came from the half-Celtic region of Somerset

1 Giles, Six Old English Chronicles, p. 78.
2 The apparently authentic Asser is preserved almost intact in only one edition, that of 1722, which was printed from a tenth century Cottonian MS. (Otho, A. xii), destroyed by fire in 1731. Thomas Wright (Biogr. Brit. Lit. and "Archaeologia," xxix) questioned the authenticity of any part of the work attributed to Asser. The question is thoroughly discussed by Pauli in the introduction to his "Life of Alfred the Great," and by T. D. Healy in the introduction to Petrie's Monumenta.
3 Vita S. Dunstani, auctore Osberno, Migne, CXXXVII, 417-8.

on the borderland of the Brito-Irish colony and a good deal of the Celtic temper ran probably with the blood in his veins. Under Dunstan's administration Celtic Britain revived again. He was himself first an abbot of the old Brito-Irish monastery of Glastonbury; he promoted men from that region to the principal posts of the kingdom; and he had Eadgar hallowed king at the ancient West Welsh royal city of Bath, married to a Devonshire lady and buried at Glastonbury. Indeed that establishment was under Dunstan what Westminster was under the later kings. Florence uses the strange expression that Eadgar was chosen "by the Anglo-Britons"; and the meeting with the Welsh and Scotch princes in the semi-Welsh town of Chester conveys a like implication.[1] Dunstan showed the versatility characteristic of so many products of Irish training. He was musician, painter and scholar and it was he who really ruled England.

It has been shown elsewhere that Glastonbury owed its renewal and probably its actual foundation to devoted Irishmen. King Eadgar in his charter endowing Glastonbury in Dunstan's time says of one of its parish churches, Beokery, that it is "called otherwise little Ireland." Osbern[2] of Canterbury tells us that many Irishmen—"men of great renown, nobly preeminent in liberal and sacred learning"—made pilgrimages through England at that period and promoted the revival there. Thus in the tenth century we see the identical work going on which Aidan, Finan, and Colman undertook in the seventh. And the need was almost as great in the tenth as in the seventh.

Irish scholar-monks appear to have been active at Can-

---

[1] See Allen, Anglo-Saxon Britain, 147.
[2] Migne, Pat. Lat., CXXXVII, 417-8; Wharton, Anglia Sacra II, 91.

terbury in the time of Ethelred II. One of them, abbot 992-994, is considered to have been the author of the so-called Anglo-Saxon Cottoniana map of the world, intended to illustrate a scriptural subject, but still very much superior to most other medieval maps even up to the end of the thirteenth century. The map was found bound up with the Peregesius of Priscian, both of them written in Irish characters and by the same hand. Unlike the later maps of Dulcert and Pizigani St. Brendan the Navigator does not figure in it, but Ireland—called not Scotia but Hibernia—is correctly and prominently portrayed, with Armagh as the capital. This Irish geographer is supposed to have been a coadjutor of Archbishop Sigeric, with whose itinerary, relating to his pilgrimage to Rome, his map probably had connection. The study of geography degenerated after the destruction of the Roman Empire, but Irishmen remained foremost in it as in other sciences, tho the world of Strabo had become distorted by the partial acceptance as facts of the stories of heathen mythology and medieval romance. The maker of the Cottoniana showed knowledge unusual in his day. He places in the north and east of Europe the Scrittofinns (in Iceland), the Huns, the Turks, the Slavs, the Goths in Dacia, and the Bulgarians. The Dneiper is mentioned, strange to say, by its native name, Naper fluvius. A curious entry is Sud Bryttas, and seven principal cities in Italy are given.

Apart from the Irish missionaries, literati, and craftsmen, to whom reference is made in the scanty English records, it is plain that there could hardly have been a time when numbers of other Irishmen, concerning whom there is no record whatever, must have been in England. The Irish schoolmen who in the Carolingian era were found in their thousands in cathedral, monastery and school on the Continent must nearly all of them have journeyed or resided for a time in England. Some sailed directly from Irish ports to French ports; that we know, but these must have formed a minority. The vast majority must have taken the more easy route through England, except in the frequent periods when the natives were on the warpath and the journey was impossible, as on the occasions to which Alcuin in his letter to Colgu of Clonmacnois[1] alludes. Columbanus and his company traveled by way of England, made an effort at missionary work there, and only passed on because of the hopelessness of the undertaking. Probably by that way went also Dungal, Dicuil, Clement, Ferghil of Salzburg, Johannes Scotus Eriugena, Sedulius Scotus, Marianus Scotus, and those other Irishmen who attained fame abroad. The presence of men such as these in England, whether transitory or prolonged, could not have been without results. Some of them probably lived and taught in England for years and only sought the Continent, when, as in the case of Fursa and his company, the internecine conflicts among the English tribes eddied in their direction and undid their work. In these Irish colonies will be found the key to much that is dark in English history as well as the roots of that fugitive blooming of the arts showing itself here and there on the rank soil of English barbarism.

[1] Migne, Pat. Lat. C, 142, Ad Colcum Lectorem in Scotia (anno 790), Epistola III.

CHAPTER XXII

CURRENT OF IRISH CIVILIZATION IN ENGLAND

1. Whole Art of England Transplanted Irish Art. 2. Seed of Irish Law and Opinion. 3. Anglo-Saxon Mediocre Imitation of Irish Civilization. 4. Incorrigible Brutality of English Aborigines. 5. Killing English Learning at its Birth. 6. Irish Authority Gives Way to French.

1. WHOLE ART OF ENGLAND TRANSPLANTED IRISH ART

IT was the method of the Irish teachers, as Zimmer notes, so to train the natives of whatever country that these in course of time might be able to go forward of their own accord. With that end in view they took what was already good among them and built from that foundation. As the English, when the representatives of Irish culture first went among them, were in a condition of total savagery, they had to build from the bottom up. They taught the natives how to read and spell and write, and this they did through the medium of the Irish characters used from that time forward in England till its conquest by the French, when that other style of the Caroline hand, which continental Irish scribes had been instrumental also in developing on the basis of the old Merovingian, was introduced from the Continent. And so in the other departments of art and knowledge. Thus it came about that the products of Anglo-Saxon life have the universal Irish imprint, as the conception of the teacher is reproduced in the laborious essay of the scholar.

The whole art of England, during the Anglo-Saxon period, was thus a transplanted Irish art, and the extant

280

remains among other things show this very clearly. The Bewcastle Cross, the crosses of Ampney Crusis, near Cirencester, Bag Enderly; the Anglo-Saxon stone carvings from Jedburgh Castle, the Ruthwell Cross and other stone carvings; the Alfred Jewell, the St. Cuthbert's Cross and the like in metal work; the oratories at Hexham and Bradford-on-Avon in architecture, and similar examples of the art of the period that remain, are eloquent on this point. Clearer even is the Irish hand in the work of those illuminated masterpieces which were long labeled as examples of "Anglo-Saxon" or "Franco-Saxon" or "Hiberno-Saxon" art.

Roman influences competed with Irish in the English architecture of the period. That the Irish were great builders the famous round towers, having their origin in a period from which date very few structures of value in Europe, are alone sufficient witness. Earlier than these are the vast military strongholds of Dun Aenghus, Staigue Fort, Aileach of the Kings or Grianan Ely, and Emain Macha, the vast incised tumuli of New Grange, Knowth and Dowth, which rank almost after the Pyramids of Egypt in the stupendous labor that must have been expended in their erection.[1]

"Most small English churches were built on a plan" says Micklethwaite, "which is purely 'Scottish' (that is, Irish) all through the Saxon time and beyond it. There are scores of them all over the country." The church of Deerhurst, which dates from the eleventh century; Kirkdale, near Kirby Moorside in Yorkshire (tenth century); Corhampton, in Hampshire; St. Martin's, Wareham; Wittering in Northamptonshire; and many others show the same plan almost complete. "I believe," adds

[1] See "Irish Archæological Remains," by Benedict Fitzpatrick. Encyclopædia Americana, 1919, Vol. 15.

Micklethwaite, "that the same is true of most of the very many churches with Saxon west towers, but nothing else so old is to be seen in them." In spite of the prestige of Roman and Italian architecture the Irish or Scotic type "continued all through Saxon times and was passed on to those that came after."[1]

Old memorial crosses are found in the north and west of England, Northumbria and North Mercia, where Irish influence was strongest. They are unmistakably of Irish origin, ornamented with Irish interlaced patterns, and the inscriptions, on such as have them, are in Irish minuscules. The number of them must run into thousands, for there are more than five hundred in Yorkshire alone. The Bewcastle Cross, the Ruthwell Cross, Trumwine's Cross, Acca's Cross (formerly at Hexham now at Durham) are among the chief. The Normans destroyed many of the Irish and Anglo-Saxon crosses and sepulchral monuments and used them as wall stones.

There is in existence still what is probably the shaft of the cross erected to the memory of Bishop Trumbert, whom Cuthbert succeeded in the see of Hexham. The stone was discovered at Yarm a few years ago and was then used as a weight for a mangle. It is now preserved at Durham. It bears an Anglian inscription in several lines, six of which are clear enough, written in Irish minuscules and adorned with Irish interlaced ornament. Another example is the cross of St. Oswin at Collingham with Irish interlaced ornament. It bears Oswin's name and was discovered in 1841.

2. Seed of Irish Law and Opinion

In other departments of knowledge and activity a similar tale has to be told. It would have been strange

[1] Archæological Journal, vol. XXXIX.

if, with Irish influence so powerful in Britain, there had been no reflex in the larger isle of that wonderful development reaching to the remote past out of which had come the old Irish laws. It has been the habit to ascribe the similarities between the brehon laws of Ireland and the old Saxon laws to their common origin in Aryan custom. Calculations have been made as to how much of ancient British custom survived the Anglo-Saxon conquest and became incorporated in English law. The coincidence of particulars in early bodies of law has been held to prove nothing beyond the resemblance of all institutions in certain stages. The existence of a real organic connection between what is called Celtic and English law is not denied, but the source of such affinity has been looked for in the general stock of tradition antecedent to the distinction of race and tongue between German and Celt.

This is looking for recondite explanations where more natural and plausible explanations are ready at hand. It is like ignoring a man's parents and going back to more remote ancestors for family resemblances. Irish influence and example appear a much more reasonable answer to questions as to the origin of certain English laws than learned discussions on Aryan traditions or references to Welsh laws. The English rulers, who, as we know from the words of Bede, looked up to the Irishmen of their age as their great exemplars and could find nothing better than what was the custom among them, were not likely to borrow from almost every other department of Irish life and ignore the highly developed Irish laws. The coincidences that exist between early Irish laws and institutions and early English laws and institutions may well be taken as coincidences arising from simple borrowing, imitation and transplantation.

The fashions, the ideas, the methods, the points of view, the motive, spirit, law and rule that formed the current of Irish civilization found its way into channels of English life more numerous than it is possible to trace. But Irish influence is easily followed in many other directions. Nearly all the monasteries of northern and central England had been founded by Irish monks and were tenanted by them and their disciples. They adopted the rules and usages of the Irish even in critical matters, like the practise of having double monasteries, so that monks were often placed under the rule of an abbess. These and other points of rule and ritual survived long after the Synod of Whitby and greatly distinguished the larger part of the English monasteries from those that had adopted the rule of St. Benedict. Thus there continued a twofold character and divergence in matters of discipline, usage and ritual in the English monasteries. The churches over which Irish influence prevailed were easily distinguished from those in which continental custom had been introduced. This does not mean that there were actual divergences of doctrine; rather was it a variety of rite and custom.

In the English monasteries the Irish rule continued to be followed long after Colman turned his back on the country and went to Ireland. Thus it is noted concerning Ceolwulf, to whom Bede dedicated his Historia Ecclesiatica and who died in retirement in 760, that "when this king became a monk license was given to the brethren to drink wine and beer; for down to that time water and milk alone had been permitted them, according to the rule of St. Aidan."[1]

[1] Simeon of Durham, II, 102.

3. Anglo-Saxon Mediocre Imitation of Irish Civilization

Anglo-Saxon civilization, such as it became, was thus in a large measure a transplanted Irish civilization, and it partook of the mediocrity in comparison with the original that is the fate of all reproductions. Its scholars were not numerous. Bede and Alcuin, the greatest of them, were collectors and distributors rather than thinkers and originators. For that "philosophy" and speculative activity for which the Irish schools were famous no English scholar showed an aptitude. No English school attained to the fame of even the lesser establishments in Ireland. In truth the career of such English schools as came into existence was brief and their end violent. No English scholar arose to challenge comparison in originality and strength of intellect with Eriugena, or Dungal or Sedulius Scotus. None of them in anything they have left to us have shown real knowledge of Greek literature or philosophy despite Theodore and Adrian and despite their close association with Irishmen. Though the literary works of medieval Irishmen have been systematically destroyed, though we know the titles of many Irish works of which nothing but the titles have been preserved, the fragments that remain brilliantly prove the actuality and permanence of Irish intellectual supremacy, everlastingly helping others, but always keeping itself in the lead. Reference is made here mainly to Irish literary remains in Latin. Irish medieval literature in the Irish tongue is an isolated phenomenon of another class, a world in itself and a luminous link between the ancient and the modern age, of which here the treatment can be only indirect.

All this converges in the same direction. Civilization

in England traces its genealogy not to the work of Theodore and Adrian but to that of Aidan and his countrymen. An Englishman wedded to conventional views and desirous of cleaving to the conventional account may choose to put faith in legends that look to a different origin. He will find himself justified in doing so by distinguished examples. Cardinal Newman, for instance, gave credence to the imaginary story, often quoted, of a school in Wiltshire called for its classical learning "Greeklade," since corrupted into Cricklade, and transferred afterwards to Oxford as one of the first elements of its university. It is true the name Greeklade occurs in Drayton's "Polyolbion." But Cricklade or Greeklade, so called from the beginning in the Saxon Chronicle, owes its nomenclature to its position on the Thames at a creek or inlet, like several places similarly situated and with the same prefix. Cricklade had no school founded by Theodore or Adrian and had such a school existed it would have gone the way of the other schools centuries before Oxford had even a beginning. But this legend is given as typical of others which might be cited, showing how men are led in the absence and sometimes in the face of fact to build a thesis agreeable to their prepossessions.

Metaphors are deceptive. To picture Theodore and Adrian as sowing and planting the new civilization that was to come sounds plausible as long as we do not stop to consider how slowly civilization develops and how laboriously the powers of the mind are to be cultivated by individual effort alone. The teachers and preachers from the Continent had little permanent influence on England. We have seen that in whatever regions the Roman and Gallic missionaries preached their influence proved transitory and the natives fell back into heathen-

286

ism. Within a few years of Adrian's death hardly a soul in England knew Greek. In other departments of knowledge we find the same tale. Benet Biscop had brought glassmakers into England to build and adorn churches at Jarrow and Monkwearmouth. But fifty years later we find a pupil of Bede writing to a French bishop imploring him to send somebody capable of making glass, as the English did not possess the art.

During the intervals in which the guiding hands of the Irish directors were taken from England, the political incapacity and general degradation of the English were nearly always asserted. The barbarism of the people was apparently too recent to permit it to be self-sustaining in the face of the sore trials of that epoch. The general slackness is indicated in the fact that for two centuries after the death of Alfred, no writer or thinker of note appeared among his countrymen. But there were of course graver evils. "A tendency to swinish self-indulgence, and the sins of the flesh in some of their most degraded forms, had marred the national character."[1] Thus much of the work of reformation and education which devoted Irishmen with so much patience had accomplished was largely undone.[2]

4. Incorrigible Brutality of English Aborigines

To transform a conglomeration of savage tribes into a civilized people was a herculean task and it is little

[1] Hodgkin, Political History of England, p. 491.

[2] The English imitated the Irish habit of making pilgrimages to Rome, with dire results, particularly in the case of the female pilgrims, to their less vigorous morality. Thus Boniface in his letter to Cuthbert, archbishop of Canterbury, observes: "It would be some mitigation of the disgrace which is reflected upon your church if you in a synod and your princes cooperating with you, would make some regulation with respect to female pilgrimages to Rome. Among your women, even your nuns, who go in crowds to Rome, scarcely any return home unpolluted, almost all are ruined. There is scarcely a city in Lombardy, France or Gaul, in which some English prostitute or adventuress may not be found. This is a scandal, a disgrace to your whole church." (Epp., Boniface, 105.)

wonder that the Irish missionaries should have won only partial success. The obstacles they encountered could not well have been greater. The history of the Heptarchy was like a history of kites and crows.[1] Not only were the English everlastingly fighting among themselves undoing the work of regeneration which Irish missionaries with immense difficulty had set up among them, but the conquest of England was almost continuous from the time of Hengest and Horsa to the time of the Conqueror. The Anglo-Saxons slew the British, reducing some to slavery, fought the Irish colonies in the west and the Irish and Pict colonies in the north, massacred each other, and were then hewn down and cut to pieces by the Danes till the French conquerors arrived and laid both Danes and English by the heels. In a hundred years, out of fourteen kings of Northumbria, seven were slain and six deposed. Within two hundred years thirty kings and queens cast away their crowns and took refuge in monasteries like Lindisfarne, where Irish missionaries had established oases of peace in the wilderness of disorder. Penda of Mercia killed five kings and at Bamborough heaped the ruins of all the surrounding villages into an enormous pile on which he projected the burning and extermination of all the English in Northumbria.

In the tenth and eleventh centuries things showed little improvement over the seventh. Observe the manners of the highest ranks in the family of the last king. At a feast in the king's hall Harold was serving Edward the Confessor with wine, when Tostig, his brother, moved by envy, seized him by the hair. They were separated. Tostig went to Hereford, where Harold had ordered a

[1] "War was waged daily and everywhere; the aim of life was not to be slain, ransomed, mutilated, pillaged, hanged, and, of course, if it was a woman, violated." (Taine, Hist. of Eng. Lit., 37; Turner, Hist. of the Anglo-Saxons, II, 440, Laws of Ina.)

royal banquet to be prepared. There he seized his brother's attendants and cutting off their heads and limbs placed them in vessels of wine, ale, mead, and cider, and sent a message to the king: "If you go to your farm you will find there plenty of salt meat, but you will do well to carry some more with you."

King Edwy having chosen as concubine Elgiva, his relation within the prohibited degrees, quitted the hall where he was drinking on the very day of his coronation to be with her. The nobles thought themselves insulted and immediately Abbot Dunstan went himself to seek the young man. "He found the adulteress, her mother and the king together on the bed of debauch. He dragged the king thence violently and setting the crown upon his head, brought him back to the nobles."[1] Afterwards Elgiva sent men to put out Dunstan's eyes, and in the tumults that followed saved herself and the king by hiding in the country, where they lived as brigands, but the men of the north having seized her "hamstrung her and then subjected her to the death she deserved."[2] "When we regard their deeds of violence, their ferocity, their cannibal jests, we see that they are not far removed from the sea kings or from the followers of Odin, who ate raw flesh, hung men as victims on the sacred trees of Upsala, and killed themselves to make sure of dying, as they had lived, in blood."[3]

5. KILLING ENGLISH LEARNING AT ITS BIRTH

"In vain the great spirits of this age endeavor to link themselves to the relics of the fine ancient civilization and

[1] Vita S. Dustani, by the Monk Osbern, Anglia Sacra, II.
[2] See Turner, Hist. of the Anglo-Saxons, II, 216.
[3] Taine, Hist. of English Lit., I, 39. Tantae saevitiae erant fratres illi (the last king) quod, cum alicujus nitidem villam conspicerem, dominatorem de nocte interfici uberent, totamque progeniem illius possessionemque defunct obtinerent. Henry of Huntingdon, VI, 367. Turner, III, 27.

to raise themselves above the chaotic and muddy ignorance in which the others flounder. They are almost alone, and on their death the others sink again into the mire."[1] They feel their impotence and decrepitude, and are filled with gloom and foreboding for their country and countrymen. The Synod of Pincanhalth, held in 790, recalls, as in an epitaph, the "days when we had righteous kings and dukes and bishops, of whose wisdom Northumbria still smells sweetly." Bede, dividing the history of the world into six periods, says that the fifth, which stretches from the return of Babylon to the birth of Christ, is the senile period; the sixth is the present "aetas decrepita, totius morte saeculi consummanda." The last paragraph of Bede's history ends in a note of doubt concerning times "so filled with commotions that it cannot yet be known what is to be said concerning them or what end they will have." His pessimism was well founded. Wars and dissensions were in a fair way to kill English learning but little after its birth and the work of destruction begun by the English themselves was almost carried to completion by the Danes. Outside the work of Alcuin and Alfred there is almost a literary waste from the eighth century to the revival of Anglo-Latin literature in the twelfth, and this among the French conquerors. No historian of like mold with Bede was to arise in the succeeding centuries and though the book of Simeon of Durham preserves the remnants of a lost Northumbrian history the period from the death of Bede to 870 is difficult and dark of comprehension in English history. There are periods in English history, as during the century and a half that preceded the coming of Augustine, and the century and a half that followed the French conquest, when the

1 Taine, I, 68.

English people appear to sink out of sight and History with mute eloquence draws a curtain over the indescribable scene, and this period, including part of the eighth and part of the ninth century, constitutes one of these historical blanks.[1] The words of King Alfred give us some indication of the demoralization that had been proceeding.

Referring to the decay of learning, especially among the religious orders, he observes: "So clean it (learning) was ruined among the English people that there were very few on this side of the Humber who could understand their service in English or declare forth an epistle out of Latin into English; and I think there were not many beyond the Humber. So few such there were that I cannot think of a single one to the south of the Thames when I began to reign. To God Almighty be thanks that we have any teacher in stall." Alfred's efforts to educate his people, related by himself and Asser, were pathetic. With the help of the foreign scholars around him he sought to translate into Saxon parts of the Bible, and of the works of Boethius, Orosius,[2] and Pope Gregory. But the translations bear witness chiefly to the barbarism of those for whom they were intended. The language is infantile. "He adapts the text to bring it down to their intelligence, the pretty verses of Boethius, somewhat pretentious, labored, elegant, crowded with classical allusions of a refined and compact style worthy of Seneca, became an artless, long-drawn-out and yet desultory prose

[1] The scantiness and imperfection of early English authorities have led to much imaginative writing on the part of historians. Thus Green begins a part of his history with the observation: "Of the temper and life of the folk in this older England we know little," and then proceeds to give minute details regarding political and social organizations, covering several pages. He has given birth to a school of historians who write in the same high falsetto.

[2] The Anglo-Saxon version has this reference to Ireland:—"Igbernia baet we Scotland hatad"—"Hibernia which we call Scotland."

like a nurse's fairy-tale, explaining everything, recommencing and breaking off its phrases, making ten turns about a simple detail, so low was it necessary to stoop to the level of this new intelligence, which had never thought or known anything."[1] And the ignorance is such that the teacher himself needs correction.

The arrival of the Danes merely accentuated a condition that had arisen from internal causes and that left the English almost as putty in their hands. The demoralization wrought by the terror of the Danish sword never left the natives till the time came when they fell an easy prey to a handful of Frenchmen from Normandy and Angevin. The picture painted by Wulfstan, bishop of Worcester, of the aborigines of the country is painful in the pitifulness of the degradation it depicts and the total loss of manhood that had fallen on the once fierce Saxons. The Danes, whom Irish power wielded by King Brian had crushed, were able nevertheless to turn England into a compound, and its inhabitants into a slave population. Progress and learning under such conditions were ludicrous dreams, and beneath the deep of ignorance which Alfred had depicted there were other and crueler deeps into which the unresisting English were thrust by their oppressors. It is hard to conceive of the forms of cruelty which Danish brutality could have employed so to subdue the English to moods meeker than that of lambs led to the slaughter. "For a long time now," says Wulfstan in his sermon Ad Anglos, still extant in Anglo-Saxon, "there has been no goodness among us either at home or abroad, but there has been ravaging and onset on every side again and again. The English have now for a long time been always beaten in battle and made great

[1] Taine, Hist. of Eng. Lit., I. 64.

cowards, through God's wrath; and the sea robbers so strong, by God's allowance, that often in a fight one of them will put to flight ten of the English, sometimes less, sometimes more, all for our sins. A thrall often binds fast the thegn who was his lord and makes him a thrall, through the wrath of God. Wala for the wretchedness, and Wala for the world-shame which now the English have, all through God's wrath. Often two or three pirates drive a drove of Christian men huddled together from sea to sea, out through the people, to the world-shame of us all, if we could a sooth know any shame at all, if we would ever understand it aright. But all the disgrace we are always bearing we dutifully pay for to those who shame us. We are for ever paying them and they ill use us daily. They harry and they burn, they plunder and rob and they carry off to ships; and lo, what is there any other in all these happenings save the wrath of God clear and plain upon this people."

6. IRISH AUTHORITY GIVES WAY TO FRENCH

It was amid conditions such as these that the Irish missionaries and schoolmen, many of them belonging to the bluest Milesian blood, impelled solely by supernatural motives, worked for the reclamation of the English. It is astonishing that most of them did not lose their lives surrounded as they were with the barbarian lust of murder. On the Continent, particularly in Germany, many of the Irish missionaries met violent deaths. In England no such fate awaited them. The sentiment of adoration which medieval Englishmen cherished for the authoritative Irishmen who walked among them stayed their homicidal hands and quelled their savage yells even when thirsting for their kinsmen's blood. A rebuke from an Irish bishop was often potent enough to bring even the

English kings prostrate at his feet. Such was the magic which the prestige of an immemorial civilization, typified in its nobler representatives, worked on a national mind slowly shedding the barbarism of ages. To this spell which the Irish will cast over a stolid, superstitious and undeveloped people, in whom a powerful war hysteria flowed as a perpetual undercurrent, are we to look for the root of the surprising results achieved by them, results which under like conditions could have been achieved by no other race under Heaven.

The so-called Norman[1] Conquest marked the passing of Irish authority and influence over the English and the substitution in an infinitely harsher and more strongly organized form of French influence and authority. The guide, cicerone and friend gave way to the military conqueror and master. The hand that held the cross, the pilgrim's staff, and the illuminated manuscript was followed by the hand that wielded the sword and the thonged whip. The apostles of law and order, humanity and learning, were followed by the apostles of the thumb screw and crucet house, of Tenserie and the Sachentege. Human annals contain little that exceeds in inhumanity the retributions which the French conquerors of the English laid on the people they thenceforth trod beneath their feet.[2]

[1] The men who, under William the Conqueror, took England from the English, called themselves and were called not Normans, but Francii or Frenchmen, which was what they were. They came from every province in France—Maine, Anjou, Poitou, Brittany, Ile-de-France, Aquitaine, Burgundy, Flanders—and even from beyond the Alps and Pyrenees. Among those who belonged to Normandy, the Northman strain had been merged by intermarriage, and Northman speech and custom had totally disappeared. The French conquerors of England repudiated all kinship with any Northern or German people. They could be called Normans chiefly in the sense that the expedition set out from Normandy under the Duke of that province.

[2] Consult the Anglo-Saxon Chronicle in the reign of Stephen, Anno 1137. Maddened by cruelty, the hapless natives sometimes waylaid their French masters and cut their throats, stripping the corpse and mutilating the features and members so that it would be impossible to tell whether it was French or English, the object being to escape the fines and punishments laid on all the inhabitants of the neighborhood. It was then enacted that the corpse should be deemed French unless a jury found it was only an Englishman. This law, called the presentment of "Englischerie," with its attendant cruelties, lasted to the reign of Edward III.

From that time on the English nation was represented by a slave population of terror-stricken boors and hinds, looking up to their foreign masters with the awe with which the savage regards his idol. Little wonder that from that time on all that was French was regarded as sacrosanct and anointed, and all that was Anglo-Saxon was regarded as mean and base. To be English was to be a churl and a villein, a natural-born clod and criminal, taxable and floggable at will, so that "it was considered a disgrace to be called an Englishman."[1] Time deepened rather than mitigated the national degradation till an abasement under the Tudors was reached lower than that ever touched by any other European people.

Culture in England thenceforth was simply French culture and even in a more modern age when the Englishman had gained a little freedom his chief method of improving himself was to play the sedulous ape to the Frenchman as he had before played the sedulous ape to the Irishman. The university of Oxford was simply a branch, established by Frenchmen, of the university of Paris, which gave it its organization and its professors.[2] The English legal system and national organization were in reality a transplanted French system and transplanted

[1] Ut Anglum vocari foret opprobrio (Matthew of Paris, Bk. I, c. 12). The native English of both sexes for quite trivial offenses had their noses and ears cut off or were stript naked and brutally whipt through the public streets or at the cart's tail, without regard to tender or advanced age. This continued for centuries. In 1597, a new law, passed in 22 Henry VIII, was slightly mitigated, the victims being stript only "from the middle upwards, and whipt till the body should be bloody." Lists of persons whipt, some of them aged women and young children, were kept in parish books and church registers (See Burn's Justice, Vol. V, 501; Notes and Queries, Vol. XVII, 327, 425, 568; Book of Days, I, 598-601). Brutalities of this degrading character were totally unknown in Irish law.

[2] It is remarkable that students from the four provinces of Ireland were at Oxford at a date almost as early as that of the admission of the English, forming one of the most important "Southern Nations." From out of their ranks appeared the most powerful mind ever known at Oxford, Duns Scotus, who dying at thirty-four, left behind a record of work, only once or twice exceeded in human history. (See Rashdall, University II, 362; Macleane, Pembroke College, 45; Mrs. Green, Making of Ireland and Its Undoing, 266-7, 289; Milman, History of Latin Christianity, VI, 466-7.)

French organization, which gave both nine tenths of their phraseology. It was the French who added Romance elements of refinement to the English tongue, to them for three centuries an alien speech, and raised what had remained for a thousand years the gross dialect of clod-hoppers and scullions to the dignity of a literary vehicle.[1] The architects and artizans who built the castles and fortresses, the cathedrals, abbeys and parish churches of England were French, as they had formerly been Irish. For the immediate centuries that followed the conquest the history of England was the history of the French population of England and had hardly any reference to the submerged English. The French kings of England showed little disposition to live there. Henry II spent most of his life in France. Richard Cœur de Lion, during a reign of ten years, spent only a month or two in England. Magna Carta is usually represented as a preeminently English document, and Parliament as a preeminently English institution. The truth is the English had about as much to do with the winning of Magna Carta[2] and the establishment of Parliament, as the negroes and red men of America had in the writing of the Constitution of the United States and the establishment of Congress. The movement among the French in France that issued in the local parlements of Champagne, Provence, Brittany and Languedoc, and in the national Parlement or Estates General, was precisely the movement among the French in England that issued in the Parlement or assembly of the estates in England. The thing

1 Chaucer, for example, was wholly French in blood. He lived much abroad and his works are translations and adaptations of Latin, French and Italian models. Piers the Plowman represented the highest flight to which the native muse attained.

2 The rights thus won by the French were completely surrendered without a fight to Henry VIII by the English three centuries later.

as well as the name was entirely French. And so through the whole national life of England. It is only by the accident of a defeated sovereign's fear that his English province might go the way of Normandy and Guienne that England is not to-day a French province, as it long was, instead of an English kingdom.

In 1169, Diarmuid, King of Leinster, a bad character who had been driven out of Ireland, after promises of vassalage to Henry II in France if he would help him to recover his kingdom, brought over from Wales to Ireland some Cambro-French[1] knights and men-at-arms led by Richard de Clare, earl of Striguil.[2] King Diarmuid with their help won a number of battles and by way of rewarding his foreign auxiliaries bestowed the hand of his daughter Eva on Richard and lands and dignities on others of his followers. Henry II crossed to Ireland in 1171 and entertained and was entertained by a number of Irish princes. There was no battle and the entire proceedings appear to have been amicable. Yet these events have been described as a Norman conquest[3] of Ireland and even as an "English conquest."[4] The position in the country attained by this first wave of Cambro-French emigrés represented the high water-mark of foreign influence in Ireland during the next 400 years. Once settled

1 The Norman-French, who would as soon have married into a negro as into a native Anglo-Saxon family, married freely with the Welsh. Thus the FitzHenrys, FitzGeralds, de Barries, de Cogans and FitzStephens, who emigrated to Ireland were a mixture of French and Welsh, being descended from Nesta, daughter of Rhys Ap Tudor, Prince of South Wales. (Giraldus Cambrensis, p. 183, genealogical table.) For a remarkable Norman comparative estimate of the Welsh and English see p. 86 note. See also Macaulay, History of England, I, 15.

2 This man who couldn't speak a sentence in English has been absurdly given the English name of "Strongbow," never heard of till four centuries after his death and then in an annotation of Camden—dictus Strongbow, fortis arcus.

3 Giraldus, who was the first to use the term "conquest" (expugnatio) repeats a prophecy to the effect that Ireland would never be really conquered till just before the Day of Judgment. (Opera, V, p. 385.)

4 This is one of the numerous inanities in D'Alton's History of Ireland.

in Ireland the foreigner began to lose his foreignness[1] and became merged in the brilliant life around him. The first settlers married the daughters of Irishmen of equal station, and the generation that followed were born Irishmen with kinsmen over all Ireland. They abandoned the French for the Irish tongue, took to Irish apparel and custom, appealed from the meannesses of the feudal to the fairness and equity of Irish law, and entered battle as Irish clansmen and followers of Irish kings with Irish battle-cries on their lips. The destruction of Irish records has given the records of the foreign colony or pale in Ireland a value out of all proportion to their importance. There was not a period during these 400 years when that foreign colony might not have been extirpated or expelled. But the truth is that Ireland had nothing but welcome for the foreigners—Norman, French, Cambro-French, and Flemish, attended at times by their English serfs—who sought a home on her soil, tolerating even their local courts and "parliaments"—really obscure meetings of foreign officials—where at a later date immigrant "English Hobbes" as the older settlers called them—buddagh Sassenach ("Saxon clowns or yokels") was the Irish sobriquet—passed "Statutes of Kilkenny" against the Irish enemy, whose lands they coveted and whose free tenure they envied. This Irish hospitality was true wisdom, for before the sixteenth century the foreign pale or colony in Ireland had almost ceased to be.[2]

[1] The "foreigners had given up their foreignness for a pure mind, their surliness for good manners, and their stubbornness for sweet mildness, and who had given up their perverseness for hospitality" (Tribes and Customs of Hy Many, ed., O'Donovan, 1843, p. 136), c. 1315.

[2] The futile expedition of Richard II (1399) was the only one ever attempted by the English against the Irish people before the sixteenth century. Art MacMurrough, King of Leinster, told Richard that he (King Art) "would not submit, that he was the rightful King of Leinster and would never cease from war and the defense of his country until his death, and that the wish to deprive him of it by conquest, was unlawful" (Gilbert's Viceroys, p. 281). Leinster alone proved more than a match for Richard, whose expedition was a disastrous failure and indeed proved a prime factor in depriving him of the English crown.

Current of Irish Civilization in England

The idea of conquering Ireland—and indeed Wales and Scotland as well—first took practical shape in the bloody-minded brain of Henry VIII, a crowned megalomaniac brute and savage, the strangler, hangman, disemboweler, mutilator and burner, amid unending shrieks to Heaven, of tens of thousands of the unresisting English,[1] the first to assume the style of "Your Majesty" and the title of King of Ireland, and the first English imperialist, whose diversion it was to set one half of his panic-stricken subjects spying upon, torturing and killing the other half, his reign reading like a monstrous tragedy of Œdipodean incests and Thyestean feasts. The war of conquest set on foot by the Tudor despot was inconclusively concluded by William of Orange at Aughrim over a century and a half later.[2] The sixteenth century opened in calm for Ireland. The Irish and the English had lived side by side for over a thousand years. Fortune up to that time had greatly favored the smaller island, in which despotism appeared to be unable to breathe, and in the sixteenth century the difference between Ireland and England in population and resources any more than in area was not great. Almost as many people spoke Irish as spoke English. In the opening calm of that century there was nothing to forecast the unparalleled tragedy that was to fall on the one, or the unparalleled territorial loot that was to fall to the other. The words "empire" and "imperial" had an uncanny fascination for Henry VIII,[3] who lived the first

1 Henry is computed to have put 72,000 persons to death. There was only one step from the lash and the branding iron to the gallows and disembowelment, and he even enacted a Boiling Act under which people were boiled alive at Smithfield.

2 The physical conquest of Ireland, begun in 1534, the combined forces of England, Scotland and Wales failed to bring to an end before 1691, a period of 157 years. This is an illuminating commentary on talk about a conquest by Henry II, in which no battle was fought.

3 He wanted to begin by uniting Wales and Scotland with England and calling himself Emperor (and Pope) of Great Britain.

part of his life in gaiety and arrogance, and the latter part swollen to a dreadful bulk of corpulency with running and loathsomely smelling sores, and who died horribly the death of persecutors, such as Lactantius describes. A future historian of empires may have cause to read a moral and draw an analogy from the course and end of persecuting empires and the careers and fate of the persecutors who first conceived them and endowed them with their spirit.

Forcubus caichduini imbia arrath inlebran colli aratardda bendact forainmain in truagain rodscribai.—Colophon from the Book of Deir, ninth century.

APPENDICES

APPENDIX A

THE ENGLISH SLAVE POPULATION IN IRELAND

THE relative positions of the Irish and English peoples in respect to education, commerce, wealth and civilized development, are indicated more clearly than through any other criterion by the large English slave population in Ireland. Slaves were numerous in medieval Ireland and—the subject is worth dwelling upon, for English historians have shrouded the facts in a disguise of specious phrases—most of these slaves were English men and women, English boys and girls, traded for export to slave dealers in English ports by their own degraded fathers and mothers and other more powerful relatives.

There is little testimony more conclusive of Ireland's national and social prestige in those ages than the fact that while foreign slaves, and particularly English slaves, were so plentiful in the island, there is no record of Irishmen being traded as slaves either in Britain or on the Continent. That Irishmen should always have been the purchasers and never the purchased in this traffic of human merchandise, which naturally represented then as in other ages the most valuable of personal property, reveals to us in convincing fashion the enormous width of the gulf, indicated in many other directions, that separated the immemorial Irish nation from the welter of tribes on the other side of the channel.

The non-free population in Ireland was divided into three classes: Bothach, Sencleithe, and Fudir. The individuals belonging to the first two divisions were herdsmen, laborers, squatters on waste lands, horseboys, hangers-on, and jobbers of various kinds—all poor and dependent. But they enjoyed the great advantage of belonging to the clan tho debarred from most of its privileges.

The third class—the Fudirs—constituted the lowest of the three. They were not members of the clan and consequently had no right of residence, tho they were permitted by the chief to live within the territory from which they might be expelled at any moment. The Fudirs themselves were again divided into two classes, a higher and a lower, called saer-fudir and daer-fudirs (free and bond). The daer-fudirs, the lowest and most dependent of all, consisted of escaped criminals, captives taken in battle or raids, convicts respited from death, and purchased slaves. The fudirs were nearly all strangers or foreigners, and it was to this class that the English slaves in Ireland belonged.[1]

The Anglo-Saxons were a leading slave race of the Middle Ages and in respect to the civilized world of Ireland, Gaul and Italy, occupied a position akin to that of the colored aborigines of Africa in respect to the civilized nations of Europe in recent times. Traffic in English slaves was as prevalent throughout Europe in the Middle Ages as negro slavery became in Africa and America at a later epoch, but in no land were English slaves more numerous than in Ireland. The traffic continued till at least the thirteenth century and probably dated back to the fifth, for references to widespread Anglo-Saxon slav-

[1] Joyce, Social History, I, 162-166.

ery are numerous in the sixth.[1] In Irish medieval literature there are numerous references to slaves brought from
beyond the sea to Ireland, most of whom must have been
English. In the sixth century Jewish slave dealers were
in the habit of selling in Gaul, Italy and other countries
slaves obtained in England. The story is well known of
the English slaves in the market place at Rome whose fair
hair and complexion, differing from those of the South,
drew Gregory's attention. The Pope also in 595 wrote
to Candidus, a priest in Gaul, enjoining him to redeem
English slaves who might be trained as monks and sent
to Rome,[2] and some commentators believe that it was this
letter of Gregory's that gave rise to the obviously
apocryphal angel-story of the slave boys in Rome. St.
Eligius of France is recorded as buying and ransoming
English slaves. St. Aidan, the apostle of Northumbria,
as we have seen, used most of his superfluous wealth in
the redemption of Anglo-Saxon males and made some of
them auxiliaries in the regeneration of the aborigines of
the island.

Slaves began to be exported from England almost from
the period of its settlement by tribes from Germany.
There had been a certain amount of traffic in British
slaves during the Roman period, as the biographies of
Irishmen bearing on that period bear witness, but this
earlier traffic was on a scale very much smaller than that
which the English traffic attained. Selling men beyond the
seas is mentioned in the Kentish laws as an alternative to

[1] William of Malmesbury talks of the practice (morem) as "vetustis-
simum" "inveteratum," and handed down from ancestors to their descendants (a proavis in nepotes transfusum) (Anglia Sacra II, p. 258).

[2] "We desire thy Love to procure with the money thou mayst receive
clothing for the poor or English boys of about seventeen or eighteen years
of age, who may profit by being given to God in monasteries" (Epistles of
St. Gregory, Book VI, Ep. VII, Nicene and Post Nicene Fathers, Vol. XII, p.
190).

capital punishment. The dooms of Ina forbade the men of Wessex to sell a countryman beyond the seas, even if he were really a slave or justly condemned to slavery: "If anyone sell his own countryman, bond or free, tho he be guilty, overseas, let him pay for them according to his wer."[1] The place overseas from Wessex was manifestly Ireland. The prohibitions are repeated down to Ethelred's "that Christian men and condemned be not sold out of the country, especially into a heathen nation; and be it jealously guarded against that those souls perish not that Christ bought with his own life"—in which we sense the admonition of Irish clerics against a traffic dishonoring alike to the principals and the victim. They are more forcibly exprest in the canons and penitentials of the English Church. Archbishop Theodore prohibited the selling of children into slavery by parents after the age of seven. Ecgberht of York threatened with excommunication on the sale of a child or of kinsfolk.

The Danes, after they had defeated the English, herded them together, and attached them to themselves as body slaves and personal property. A great many of them they sent over the sea and delivered to continental dealers. William of Malmesbury says of Canute's sister, the wife of Godwin, that "she was in the habit of purchasing companies of slaves in England and sending them into Denmark; more especially girls whose good looks and age made them of greater value that she might accumulate money by this horrible traffic."[2] The invading French from Normandy and the other French provinces, following the Danes, took advantage of the general degradation of the country and the wealth of Franco-Nor-

1 Stubbs, Select Charters, p. 61.

2 De Gestis Regum, Lib. II, c. 13 (Giles edition, p. 222).

man nobles was said sometimes to spring from the breeding of Anglo-Saxon slaves for the market.[1]

The testimony bearing on the traffic points to an indescribable demoralization among the English and brings home some of the herculean difficulties with which the Irish missionaries had to contend in a milieu where brutal and suicidal excess had resulted in dissolving the foundations of even natural virtue and decency. Thus William of Malmesbury, describing conditions in England, remarks: "Unnatural as was such conduct it was often the fact that heads of families, after seducing the women of their household, either sold them to other men or to houses of bad repute."[2] In the Latin life of Wulstan, bishop of Worcester (d. 1022) founded on the Anglo-Saxon life of Coleman, we are told that it was a common sight all over England to see long trains of young men and women of the English chained together and marched by slave dealers to the neighboring ports to be shipt to Ireland as slaves.[3] The unfortunates were purchased by slavedrivers from their own families and were treated with a cruelty that made them, as the biography tells us, an object of pity even to the barbarous West Saxons through whose villages they were marched on their way to the sea.[4] The native vendors of the girls were in the habit of putting them in a condition of

[1] The Irish Scots in North Britain, in line with their compatriots in Ireland, were large owners of English slaves. Thus Symeon of Durham (Historia Regum, II, 192) observes: "Scotland was filled with slaves and handmaids of the English race so that even to this day cannot be found, I do not say a hamlet, but even a hut, without them." Symeon explains this large slave population by the captures of prisoners after the Battle of Carman (1018) in the course of which the Irish forces in Scotland inflicted a terrible defeat on the English; but the explanation is obviously insufficient. The greater number of the slaves must have come from trading between the Irish in Scotland and the English.

[2] De Gestis Regum, Lib. III (Giles, ed., p. 279).

[3] Videres et gemeres concatenatos sunibus miserorum ordines et utriusque sexus adolescentes (Anglia Sacra II, p. 258).

[4] Barbaris miserationi essent (Ibid.).

pregnancy in the hope that they might thus fetch a higher price from the Irish merchants and owners of estates to whom they were to be consigned.[1] The commerce was brisk—"day after day they were exposed for sale, and day after day they were sold."[2]

Writers like William of Malmesbury make it clear that there were numerous slave-markets throughout England, and numerous ports whence the slaves were shipt, but Bristol, being directly opposite Ireland where families were habituated to the use and ownership of English slaves, and being convenient to the aborigines of the English hinterland who served as merchandise in the traffic, was the chief port of embarkation.[3] It appears that the Irish and continental merchants were able to pay three or four times the rate that ruled in England where the native chattel was cheap and where poverty was rife. The traffic appeared quite the natural thing to the English themselves, who knew no better and who resented the efforts to rid them of a vice which brought them profit. Franco-Norman writers are however unmeasured in their protests and in their expressions of horror over it, and particularly over the depravity involving so many unnatural forms of vice.[4]

The canker had eaten its way into the national life at an early date so that even church dignitaries thought themselves justified in enslaving their compatriots. Thus

1 Ancillasque prius ludibrio lecti habitas jamque praegnantes venum proponebant (Ibid.).

2 Cotidie prostitui, cotidie venitari (Ibid.).

3 Vicus est maritimus Brichstou dictus, a quo rector cursu in Hiberniam transmittitur, ideoque illius terrae barbariei accomodus. Hujus indigenae cum caeteris ex Anglia cause mercimontii saepae in Hiberniam annavigant. . . Homines enim ex omni Anglia coemptos majoris spe quaestus in Hiberniam distrahebant. (Anglia Sacra II, p. 258.)

4 Facinus execrandum, dedecus miserabile, nec belluini affectus memores homines, necessitudines suas, ipsum postremo sanguinem suam servituti addicere. (Anglia Sacra II, p. 258.)

we find Boniface writing to Fortheri, bishop of Sherborne, supporting the request of a man named Eppa for the release of the latter's sister who had been kept in bondage (captivae puellae) by Beorwald, abbot of Glastonbury, and offering a ransom of thirty solidi for her emancipation in order that she might spend the rest of her life among her own people instead of in slavery.[1]

The contemporary Irish literature bearing on the traffic is copious and it supplements and illustrates the testimony from outside sources. Thus the Leabar na g-Ceart, a remarkable tenth century Irish work containing elements very much older and throwing a flood of light on medieval forms of revenue in Ireland, has repeated references to slaves brought into Ireland from over the sea, describing them for the most part as "foreigners without Gaelic," that is, foreigners who could not speak Irish. From one reference it would appear that the ancestors of the family of Ua Dubhlaighe, Anglicized O'Dooley, were large owners of English slaves:

> Entitled is the stout king of Fera Tulach
> To six steeds from the middle of boats,
> Six swords, six red shields
> And six foreigners without Gaedhealga [2] (Irish).

Fera Tulach has the meaning of "men of the hills" and is the name now applied to the barony of Feartullagh, in Westmeath. After the establishment of surnames the chief family in this territory took the surname of Ua Dubhlaighe.[3]

Another reference shows that English slaves figured in

---

[1] Jaffe, Mon. Mag. 7. In another letter to Cuthbert, archbishop of Canterbury, Boniface severely animadverts on the practice of English pilgrimages to Rome and the frailty of the females taking part in them, declaring that as a result there was hardly a city in Lombardy or France that had not an English prostitute. (Haddan and Stubbs, iii, 381.)

[2] Leabar na g-Ceart, or Book of Rights, translated by O'Donovan, p. 181.

[3] See also O'Hart, Irish Pedigrees, under Ua Dubhlaighe or Dooley.

the stipends presented by the monarch of Ireland to the provincial and subsidiary kings:

> The stipend of the king of Brugh-righ
> From the King of Eire (Ireland) without sorrow
> Ten tunics, brown red
> And ten foreigners without Gaedhealga. [1]

Again among the stipends of the king of Cashel to the kings of his territories we have:

> Eight bondmen, eight brown-haired women
> To the of the Deise, and ten ships,
> Eight shields, eight swords for wounding,
> And eight horses (brought) across the green sea. [2]

Among the payments and stipends of the king of Aileach to his chieftainries and tribes for refection and escort enumerated in the Leabhar na g-Ceart are given:

> Entitled is the king of Cineal Aedha
> To five shields, five slender swords,
> Five bondmen (brought) over the bristling surface of the sea
> Five fair-haired, truly fine women. [3]

Other stipends for the king of Aileach are mentioned:

> Entitled is the king of Inis Eoghain
> To six bondmen—no great gratuity,
> Seven steeds, six women (brought) over the great sea,
> Seven beautiful horns for drinking. [4]

In view of the evidence given by English chroniclers there can be hardly any doubt that these foreign slaves "without Gaelic" were all or nearly all English, and the numerous references to them, which could be greatly added to, give us an idea of the volume of the traffic. Irish missionaries in England and occasional decent Englishmen did what they could to restrain the evil, which

1 Leabar na g-Ceart, translated by O'Donovan, p. 87.
2 Leabar na g-Ceart, p. 73.
3 Page 131.
4 Page 133.

attained dimensions so notorious that even the distant pope had to take a hand in denouncing it. Thus the lesson of the feast of St. Wulstan tells us that he was able, shortly before the conquest, to "bring the citizens of Bristol to a better mind, who in spite of king and pope, had persisted in the nefarious practise of selling their own children into slavery."[1]

The truth is that Wulstan did not cure them and the traffic continued long after his death. Anselm, the Piedmontese archbishop of Canterbury, and successor to his countryman, Lanfranc, likewise worked in vain to cure the evil, tho doubtless they all helped to abate it.

One obstacle to the extinction of the traffic was that the taxes on it brought money into the royal exchequer. With respect to its supposed cessation William of Malmesbury says:[2] "The credit for this transaction I do not know whether to attribute to Lanfranc or to Wulstan, who would scarcely have induced the king, reluctant from the profit it produced him, to this measure, had not Lanfranc commended it, and Wulstan, powerful through the sanctity of his character, commended it by episcopal authority."[3]

According to the tract on Ui Maine, the patrimony in Connaught of the Ua Ceallaigh, or O'Kelly family, preserved in the Book of Leacan,[4] the king of Ui Maine was entitled to ten steeds, ten foreigners (slaves), ten standards, and ten mantles (mantals) to be paid by the

---

1 The lesson is taken from the Coleman and Malmesbury life, reproduced in Anglia Sacra II, 241-270.

2 De Gestis Regum, Lib. III.

3 The same author elsewhere informs us that the kings of Ireland bestowed many favors on Wulstan, probably because of his efforts against the slave trade and its accompanying evils, for the Irish princes on other occasions gave evidence of their feeling that the traffic was dishonoring to those who bought and owned slaves apart from the degradation to the unfortunates themselves. (Anglia Sacra II, 249.)

4 See Tribes and Customs of Hy-Many, pp. 92, 93.

King of Connaught. As this differs from the subsidy mentioned by the Leabhar na g-Ceart[1] O'Donovan concludes that it belongs to a later period and was modeled on the exactions of the Norman invaders.[2] So that it would appear that the Ua Ceallaigh or O'Kelly family of Ui Maine continued owners of English slaves even after the twelfth century and the decree of the Synod of Armagh.

The Synod of Armagh, after the appearance of the Norman and Angevin French in Ireland under Henry II, attributed this foreign intrusion to the sin of slave dealing and counseled that all the English slaves throughout the country the ownership of whom was claimed by the Norman French should be emancipated. This event occurred in the year 1172 and is noteworthy as one of the first recorded emancipations of slaves in modern history. At this synod "the poets and bishops of Ireland were gathered to Armagh, and there they considered what was the cause of the plague of outlanders upon them." This referred to the interference of the Norman French two years before. "This they all understood, that it was because of buying children from the English, for the English, when they were in want of wealth, used to sell their children to the Irish (as slaves). And God does not inflict more punishment on him who sells his children than on him who buys them. They therefore counseled that all the English they held in bondage should be let go free. And thus it was done."[3]

The evidence is that English slaves in Ireland were humanely treated. The number of English slaves in

1 Page 115.
2 Preface, Leabar na g-Ceart, XVIII.
3 Irish Abridgment of Expugnatio Hibernica, ed., Stokes. See English Hist. Review, 1905, p. 87; Mrs. Green, Making of Ireland and Its Undoing, p. 249.

Ireland appears to have been one of the reproaches leveled against Ireland by Henry II and other Normans, but consider how the French themselves handled the English in England. "They greatly opprest the wretched people by making them work at these castles and when the castles were finished they filled them with devils and evil men. Then they took those whom they suspected to have any goods, by night and by day, seizing both men and women, and they put them in prison for their gold and silver, and tortured them with pains unspeakable, for never were any martyrs tormented as these were. They hung some up by their feet and smoked them with foul smoke; some by their thumbs, or by the head, and they hung burning things on their feet. They put a knotted string about their heads and twisted it till it went into the brain. They put them into dungeons wherein were adders and snakes and toads, and thus wore them out. Some they put into a crucet-house, that is, into a chest that was short and narrow and not deep, and they put sharp stones in it and crushed the man therein so that they broke all his limbs." And so on.[1] This was in the twelfth century. In the sixteenth century the average Englishman was no better off from the point of view of the punishments which might be inflicted upon him. He was a serf in the twelfth century; he continued to be a slave in the sixteenth. The chief difference was that while he was the slave of his immediate master in the twelfth century, both he and his master were in the sixteenth century also slaves of the king. Under the laws of Henry VIII for small offenses and often for no offense at all the Englishman was liable to be stript naked and brutally whipt, on all fours or tied to the end of a cart in the public market place. The

1 Anglo-Saxon Chronicle, anno 1137.

English "gentleman of leisure" likes to think he is representative of a very ancient type, but it is certain that his type was rare in the time of Henry VIII. Idleness—at least other people's—was in the view of Henry the "mother and root of all vices." It was punished by repeated public whippings "till the body be bloody by reason of such whipping."[1] A second offense was punished by further whipping, exposure in the pillory, and the cutting-off of the ears, and the third offense was followed by "pains and execution of death as a felon and as an enemy of the commonwealth."[2] Social position counted for nothing. The scholars of the universities of Oxford and Cambridge, proctors, pardoners, prophesiers, leisured travelers, tourists, pedlers, lecturers, professors in "physick, physnamye, and palmistry, or other crafty science," and sturdy vagabonds, all looked alike to Henry, whose sovereign cure for every shortcoming and not a few virtues was the bathing of the body in blood with the universal cat-o'-nine tails.[3] The Englishman could not leave his job, he could not change from one job to another, he could not go from one place to another, he could not take a holiday, he could not have an independent opinion of his own about anything, without facing the prospect of a public flogging or the pillory, of losing his ears, or of death or torture in some horrible form. Now the old

1 Acts of Henry VIII, 12th of the 22nd; Amended Statute, 27 Henry VIII, cap. 25. By an Act of 1547 idle Englishmen were also adjudged to honest neighbors as "slaves" and had to wear rings of iron on their arms, necks or legs.

2 For the offense of idleness or unemployment, often repeated, repeated whippings were provided by the earlier act. Apparently to be stript naked and publicly whipt was regarded as less disagreeable than work by large classes of Englishmen. Henry, accordingly, with characteristic savagery, five years later made another law establishing capital punishment for the third offense.

3 Nearly all these Acts were Henry's own. Parliament existed merely to obey, and when the king's name was mentioned in debate its members groveled in the direction of his empty chair, in token of their complete submission.

Appendices

Irish laws[1] are singularly free from these brutalizing punishments, degrading man below the level of brute beasts, and are indeed characterized by a humaneness such as that to which modern sentiment tends. It is not too much to say that the English slave under his highly civilized Irish masters was better off under certain circumstances than the average Englishman of the twelfth or sixteenth century, when not even his thoughts were his own and when mutilation and death under the law lurked round every corner.

[1] They may be consulted in "Ancient Laws and Institutes of Ireland," Dublin, 1865-1891, 6 vols. See also Joyce's "Social History," I, pp. 198-216 (Administration of Justice).

APPENDIX B

THE IRISH PROVINCE OF SCOTLAND

IN the effort to propagate the notion that the Gael formed but a small minority of the population of Scotland and that the great majority are of Teutonic descent, a theory has been built up to the effect that, despite the fact that Scotland was at one time peopled by an Irish-speaking people sprung in the main from the Irish settlers in the country, that condition of things endured only during the earlier centuries of Scottish history, at the end of which period these Celts or Gaels or Irish were expelled from what is now called the "lowlands" and confined to what is now called the "highlands" where they live at this day. The supposed expulsion of the Gael is generally ascribed to some undefined period between the opening of the eleventh and the close of the twelfth century, following the French conquest of England, which is credited with sending many English over the Scottish border. This theory, tho without a leg to stand upon, is the theory that holds the ground in many minds to-day. It has been shown to be utterly opposed to all the facts of history, and has time out of mind been decently buried, only to be resurrected to walk the earth again. More than a century ago Chalmers showed its absurdity in his well known work, "Caledonia." Sixty years ago E. W. Robertson, in his appendix to "Scotland under her Early Kings," demolished the Theory of Displacement, as he termed it. Still more recently Professor Rait has pointed out that the theory is quite untenable. But it is a theory useful for political purposes in

314

Great Britain and as such has shown itself possest of more than the proverbial nine lives.

All available evidence is opposed to any notion that Scotland, in the highlands or in the lowlands, has ever been peopled by other than Irish Gaels, since they first gave the name to the country. Thus long after the period when the Celt is supposed in the imagination of some historians to have been prest back by an English or Teuton population from the lowlands we find the Irish language spoken all over the country as far as the south and east, we find men with Irish names figuring plentifully in legal documents, we find the survival of Irish laws and customs and Irish officialdom both in the Church and in the State, and we find Irish place-names outnumbering other place-names even to the English border.

THE IRISH TONGUE IN SCOTLAND.—Irish remained the literary language of Scotland till after the middle of the eighteenth century. It remained the spoken language of Scotland till the sixteenth century. "Most of us spoke Irish a short time ago," says John Mair, or Major, who wrote a history during the reign of James IV of Scotland, who died in 1513. "Those who live on the borders of England," says his contemporary, Hector Boece, "have forsaken our own tongue (Irish) and learned English, being driven thereto by wars and commerce. But the Highlanders remain just as they were in the time of Malcolm Canmore, in whose days we began to adopt English manners." Sir Thomas Craig, writing in the reign of James VI (1625), says: "I myself remember the time when the inhabitants of the shires of Stirling and Dumbarton spoke pure Gaelic."[1] Stirling and Dumbarton are in what has come to be called the "lowlands" of Scotland.

[1] De Unione Regnorum Britanniae, Scott. Hist. Soc., trs. Terry, pp. 418-9.

Both Wallace (c. 1270-1305) and Bruce (1274-1329) are credited with having been fluent Gaelic speakers. In Ayrshire and Galloway, as Professor Mackinnon notes, Gaelic was spoken for centuries after Wallace's time, and Wallace himself was also in the habit of wearing Gaelic dress. In 1434 an Englishman of the name of Hendry visited the lowlands of Moray and Aberdeen and found the Irish language still commonly spoken there. About 1505 Dunbar wrote his Flyting of Dunbar and Kennedie. Walter Kennedy was the third son of the first Lord Kennedy, heritable bailie of Carrick. He was well acquainted with Irish, then common in Carrick, on which account Dunbar abuses him as an "Irische bryour baird" and an "Ersch katherane with thy polk breik and rilling," from which it may be inferred Kennedy wore Irish dress. To Dunbar's abuse of the Irish language, Kennedy replies with dignity and good sense:

> "Bot it suld be all trew Scottis mennis lede (i. e., speech);
> It was the gud langage of this land,
> And Scota it causit to multiply and sprede."[1]

Between the years 1563 and 1566 an English official drew up a military report on the districts of Cunningham, Kyle, and Carrick, with reference to the possibility of their occupation by an invading English army. He described Carrick as follows: "Inhabited by therle of Cassils and his frendes, a barrant cuntree but for bestiall; the people for the moste part spaketht erishe."[2] In another description of Carrick and other parts of Scotland in 1577 it was remarked that "the people's speech is mingled with the English and Irish, not far from Carrickfergus."[3] The same writer noted that the people of the

[1] Dunbar's Poems, ii, 11-29.
[2] Archæological and Historical Collections of Ayr and Wigton, IV, 17.
[3] Calendar of Scottish Papers, V, 257.

Earl of Atholl and of "Camel," Earl of Argyle, also spoke Irish. In 1618, John Taylor, the "Water Poet," visited Scotland, and afterwards recorded his impressions in the Pennyles Pilgrimage. He says: "I did go through a country called Glaneske. At night I came to a lodging house in the Lard of Eggels Land (i. e., Edzell) where I lay at an Irish house, the folkes not being able to speak scarce any English." (P. 134, edition of 1630.) Later he refers to the "Highlandmen, who for the most part speak nothing but Irish." According to the Rev. James Fraser, the minister of Wardlaw, Gaelic was held "in esteem" at the court of Charles II. Comparing that court with Malcolm Canmore's, he says: "Formerly Latin and Irish was the language spoken at our Scots court, now a nursery of all languages, arts and sciences . . . . and yet the Irish still in esteem at court. Franciscus Fraiser was master of the languages at the court; the Scots who spoke only Irish called him Frishalach Francach."[1]

In the eighteenth century Irish was the language of the people in the Ochil hills. Again about 1792 the minister of Drom wrote as follows in the Old Statistical Account: "Gaelic . . . . is said to have been the common language not only here . . . but even through the whole country of Fife not above two or three generations back." About 1730, Edward Burt, wrote: "The Irish tongue was, I may say, lately almost universal even in many parts of the Lowlands, and I have heard it from several in Edinburgh that before the Union it was the language of the shire of Fife—and as a proof they told me, after that event (the Union) it become one condition of an indenture when a youth of either sex was to be bound on

[1] Wardlaw MS., p. 38.

the Edinburgh side of the water, that the apprentice should be taught the English tongue."[1]

Thus Irish survived as a spoken tongue in southern Scotland, particularly in Galloway and Carrick, after the middle of the eighteenth century. It is a fact of great significance that the early Scottish writers, whether they knew Gaelic or not, invariably referred to that tongue as the "Scottish" and to the Teutonic dialect of Lothian as English. For example an early record of benefactions to Loch Leven was abridged from an older book written in Gaelic, which is referred to as the idiom of the Scots (vetus volumen antiquo Scotorum idiomate conscriptum).[2] A charter of William the Lion mentions a certain will, "qui Scottice tobari nuncupatur," an evident reference to the Irish word tobar. In 1221 certain land is mentioned, "que Scotice dicitur Abthan."[3] Fordun in his description of Alexander III's coronation refers to Irish as the Scottish language, and elsewhere in his history (Book II, chap. 9) he alludes to the two languages spoken in Scotland, the Scottish and the Teutonic as he termed them (Scotica et Theuthonica), that is Irish and English. A mid-thirteenth century perambulation of the bounds of Kingoldrum refers to the two languages as Scottish and English, for it describes two places, "Hachethunethouer quod Anglice dicitur Midefeld" and also "Marresiam quamdam quae Scotice dicitur Moynebuch."[4] Barbour, Wyntoun, Blind Harry and Dunbar all referred to the language which they spoke and wrote as "Inglis," or "Inglisch," etc. Wyntoun, altho he wrote

1 Letters, I, 158-9, 5th edition.
2 Registrum Prioratus S. Andreae, p. 113.
3 Charters of Inchaffray Abbey, p. 44.
4 Registrum Vetus de Aberbrothoc, p. 228.

in English, yet referred to Gaelic as "Scote" or "Scottis."[1]
We find the General Assembly of the Church of Scotland in 1570 referring to Gaelic as the Scottish language. The Assembly was informed that a certain Donald Munro, the commissioner of Ross, had but an imperfect acquaintance with his own language. Accordingly the Assembly commanded that assistance should be given him, because he was not "prompt in the Scottish tongue." Much later occasional reference is made to Gaelic as the Scottish language. Thus James MacPherson, of pseudo-Ossianic fame, writing in 1773 a dissertation to his poems, says: "A Scotchman tolerably conversant in his own language, understands Irish composition."

Gavin Douglas was the first native Scottish writer to refer to the Teutonic speech of Lothian and Northumberland as "Scottish." In 1513 in the prolog to his Aeneis he wrote: "This buik I dedicate writing in the language of Scottis natioun." Before the close of the sixteenth century this use of the word "Scottish" became fairly general, owing, it would appear, to the national susceptibilities of the English-speaking Scots, who not knowing the old language of Scotland sought to save their faces by a little word jugglery. Dunbar even went so far as to use the phrase, "oure Inglische."[2]

Irish continued the classic and literary tongue in Scotland, the peasantry using a colloquial dialect, known to speakers of English as Earse (Irish), a broad-Scots term which is translated into proper English now as Scotch-Gaelic. This provincial dialect was never written or printed until Mr. MacFarlane, minister of Killinvir, in Argyleshire, published in 1754 a Scotch-Gaelic translation of "Baxter's Call to the Unconverted." This printed

1 Orygynale Cronykil, II, 112-3.
2 Goldyn Targe, line 259.

Scotch-Gaelic is in the main Irish written phonetically according to the rules of English orthography. So Mr. MacFarlane of Killinvir may be regarded as the somewhat recent Homer or Andronicus of Scotch-Gaelic literature.

Dr. Johnson's dictum that "there are not in the language five hundred lines that can be proved to be a hundred years old" was strictly true as applied to Scotch-Gaelic. Scotch-Gaelic in his day had no more literary value than the Yorks or Northumbrian dialect of English. The vast and valuable literature of the Gaels both of Ireland and Scotland was enshrined in the classical Irish tongue.

Hume says that the name of Earse, or Irish, given by the low country Scots to the language of the Scottish Highlanders, is a certain proof of the traditional opinion, delivered from father to son, that the latter people came originally from Ireland. Bedell's Irish version of the Scriptures was circulated in Scotland with a glossary from 1690 to 1767, and Bishop Carswell's version of Knox's Prayer-book (1567) is pure Irish.

FRENCH SPEECH AND INFLUENCE.—There are those among the historians of Scotland who profess to note the birth of English influence in that land following the marriage of Malcolm Canmore (1057-93) with Margaret, the expelled Anglo-Saxon princess. In this case the eyes see what they want to see. Such English influence as the welcome given to Margaret precipitated was a tenuous influence and it died a speedy death. In truth English influence at that time was a thing that was almost non-existent. England as a nation had been almost blotted out by the Danes. Danes and English went down in common ruin under the French heel. In the centuries that

followed the influence of Anglo-Saxon civilization, if
such a civilization may be said to have existed, would
find its fittest comparison with the influence of negro
civilization under the slave-owners of the southern parts
of the United States. It is absolutely no exaggeration to
say that the English people living in England under
French rule occupied a lower status during the eleventh,
twelfth and thirteenth centuries, than the negro slave
population in the southern states of America occupied
during the seventeenth and eighteenth and nineteenth centuries.   .

As Macaulay puts it: "So strong an association is established in most minds between the greatness of a sovereign
and the greatness of the nation which he rules, that
almost every historian of England has expatiated with a
sentiment of exultation on the power and splendor of her
foreign masters (the French kings of England) and has
lamented the decay of that power and splendor as a
calamity to our country. This is, in truth, as absurd as
it would be in a Haytian negro of our time to dwell
with national pride on the greatness of Lewis the Fourteenth, and to speak of Blenheim and Ramilies with
patriotic regret and shame. The Conqueror and his
descendants to the fourth generation were not Englishmen; most of them were born in France; they spent the
greater part of their lives in France; their ordinary speech
was French; almost every high place in their gift was
filled by a Frenchman; every acquisition which they made
on the Continent estranged them more and more from
the population of our island. One of the ablest among
them indeed attempted to win the hearts of his English
subjects by espousing an English princess. But by many
of his barons this marriage was regarded as a marriage

between a white planter and a quadroon girl would now be regarded in Virginia."[1]

During almost the two centuries which followed the Conqueror, there is very little that can be called English history. Those centuries are almost as much a blank as the two centuries following the arrival of the Saxons in England. History in England in that period was simply the history of the French conquerors.

French, not English, moreover, was the language to which Irish first gave place in the Scottish court. Most of the Gaelic nobility were probably bilingual, understanding, if not speaking, French, as well as their ancestral Gaelic. French was in use in David's court (1124-53) as it certainly was also in that of Alexander III (1249-86). An English chronicler, Walter of Coventry, referring to the events of the year 1212, says that the more recent kings of Scotland, i. e., William and his immediate predecessors, profess to be Frenchmen in race, manners, language, and culture, and that they admit only Frenchmen to their friendship and service.[2] At a later period French died out as the language of the court, being replaced by the speech of the Lothians.

There is no record of English writing in Scotland before John Barbour, who died in 1395, and Andrew Wyntoun, who died after 1420, wrote their compositions. Since then English has gradually displaced Gaelic, tho even to-day the old Irish tongue is in full vigor over a large part of Scotland. Nor is there the slightest evidence that the defeated English entered Scotland at this time in any considerable numbers. Such English as lived in the country lived there merely as hinds and slaves, as Symeon of Durham testifies, and being absolutely ignorant and unlet-

1 History of England, I, 15.
2 Memoriale, II, 206.

tered they could have no influence whatever. "Norman" knights did later arrive, and these occupied positions of influence, acquired land, and even ascended the throne of Scotland. But these "Normans" did not speak English. Like their brethren in England they spoke French and they wrote both French and Latin, and in the Scottish documents of the period they are called Frenchmen or Francii. They married into the families of equal status of the Irish Scots of Scotland just as they married into the families of the Irish Scots of Ireland. In Scotland as in Ireland they became *ipsis Hibernis Hiberniores*. They dropt French and learned to speak Irish in Scotland just as they dropped French and learned to speak Irish in Ireland. The prestige and influence of Irish civilization, which conquered and absorbed the Danes, who had defeated and enslaved the English, likewise conquered and absorbed the more powerful Normans in Scotland as in Ireland. Till that period Irish civilization and the Irish language had been a growing and prevailing civilization and language both in Ireland and Scotland, while English had been stagnant and receding.

IRISH NAMES AND SURNAMES IN SCOTLAND.—The evidence provided by the survival of the Irish language in Scotland even in the South is supplemented by the testimony supplied by Irish names which have outlived the language in the same region. Thus Malcolm IV (1153-65) and William the Lion (1165-1214) both addrest charters to the inhabitants of the lowland diocese of Glasgow concerning the payment of tithes. These charters make mention not only of French and English, but also of Scots, Galwegians and Strathclyde British (Scoti, Galwejenses et Walenses). We have an even later reference to the Strathclyde British, for Edward I, the English king, attempted to abolish the laws of the Brets and Scots. Again in 1263 an inquisition was held concerning the lands of Stephen Blantyre in Renfrewshire. The jurors who decided that his son Patrick was the heir must have been the social equals of the claimant. They all bear Irish names like Patrick de Blantyre himself: Gille Michel Mac Edolf, Malcolmus filius Galle, Donecanus Mac Edolf, Anegous de Auchenros, Dougal Mac Malcolm, Gillemor Mac Mohan, Patricius clericus, Patricius Pylche, Johannes Mac Galle, Gillecrist Mac Kessan, Dogal Mac Houtre.[1] Andrew Lang, who in his history shows the habitual itch of the lowland Scot to make himself out an Englishman, has this to say concerning the people of Renfrew: "Where Anglo-Normans obtained lands in Moray, or Renfrewshire, there seems to have been no displacement of the population; tho a Fitz-Alan was dominant in Renfrewshire the 'goodmen,' or gentry, still bore Gaelic names, till territorial names—'of' this or that place—came into use."

Similarly an inquisition was held in 1260 at Girvan. The jury was formed of three knights with territorial surnames and nine others, all bearing Irish names.[2] Mr. Bain also printed lists of Galwegian prisoners and others concerned in the War of Independence.[3] Nearly all the names are Irish. Lists of Dumfries names, belonging to people living close to the English border, have been printed in the Register of the Privy Council, and many of them are obviously Irish.[4]

The lists of names of those who were appointed to perambulate boundaries also demonstrate that the popu-

1 Acts Parl. Scot, I, 92.
2 Bain's Calendar of Documents, I, 553.
3 Ibid., II, 253, 301.
4 Vols. IV, VI, etc.

lation of the lowlands continued as Irish or Celtic or Gaelic or Scottish—whatever the term preferred—as it had ever been. Twelve of the names in a perambulation, c. 1200, of the lands of Stobo in Peebleshire, are Irish, such as Gylmihhel, Gillamor, and Gylcolm. Again in 1246 the following persons conducted an inquiry into the marches of Westere Fedale, apparently near Auchterarder: Patrick Ker, Simon of Fedale, Gillemury son of said Simon; Simon Derech, Gillebride, Gillefalyn, son of said Gillebride, Gillecrist Mac Hatheny, Gille crist Mac Moreherthach, Gill Ethueny, Gillecostentyn.[1] In the year 1219 a perambulation was made between certain lands of the monastery of Aberbrothoc (Arbroath). The perambulators all bore Irish names, while several bearing French or Norman names were present, showing that the members of both the Gaelic and the Franco-Norman aristocracy met on equal terms. The evidence derived from royal charters show an equal predominance of Irish names long after the Teuton was supposed to have driven the Gael into the highlands. So far from there having been any expulsion of the Celt from the lowlands at the period indicated the only expulsions of which we have authentic record were of foreign intruders at court and elsewhere, both English and Norman.

Thus English courtiers were expelled from Scotland on two occasions shortly after the death of Margaret, two English chroniclers, Symeon of Durham, and the writer of the Anglo-Saxon Chronicle, even going so far as to state that all the English were driven out of Scotland. William of Newburgh relates that after the capture of William the Lion in 1174, the Scots fell upon those English burghers who were in the Scottish army, that

[1] Chartulary of Lindores, p. 26.

some of these burghers were killed, and that the rest fled to the royal castles.[1] This points to the numerical inferiority of the English element. One of the consequences of the battle of Carham (1018) was the reintroduction of Irish speech and Irish rule into Lothian. Indeed Irish even spread into the county of Northumberland. Moreover the lists of burgal names illustrate a movement of the Gaelic country population into towns like Aberdeen, which admittedly had a large foreign element. This movement is an ever persistent phenomenon, as marked to-day as it was in those days.

The lowland personal names of even the present day are predominantly Irish, not English. The late Sheriff Ferguson of Kinmundy, in commenting on the Registrar-General's report in 1864, pointed out that one half of the fifty commonest Scottish surnames were either recognized clan names, or else were names the form of which indicated their Celtic origin. The remaining half included six formed by the addition of "son" and several, such as Smith, which might possibly be translations from the Gaelic. Common lowland names are Bain, Dow, Ferguson, Glass, Allison, Anderson, Smith, Gow, Grierson, Kennedy, Kerr, Orr, Scott, and Wallace—nearly all these being the altered forms of Irish originals. Concerning the penultimate name, Robertson remarks that the "first ancestor must have stood out among the Saxons of the Lothians as Scotus, the Gael." Allison and Ellison were Mac Alistair; Smith was MacGowan; Ferguson was Mac Fergus; Anderson, MacAndrai; and so on.

Other common lowland names, outwardly English, such as Black and Whyte, are in most cases merely translations of the corresponding adjectives in Irish speech—names such as Domhnull Dubh for example.

[1] Chronicles of Stephen, etc., I, 186.

Even surnames that cannot be shown to have any but an English origin are no proof of English ancestry. They merely show that the name was established after the English language had displaced the Irish language in that part of Scotland in which the name originated.

Nothing is more certain than that the lowlands of Scotland, whatever the change in speech and habit that later came, remained in population as permanently Irish or Gaelic or Scot or Celtic—whatever the term preferred—as the highland portion of the country. In truth as time passed the northern parts of England, such as Cumbria and Northumbria, acquired a considerable infusion of Gaelic blood as well, for the path of emigration has always been in a southerly direction, and the family names prevalent in the northern parts of England are largely Gaelic to-day. But in course of time English speech spread slowly northward and we are able to point almost to the very earliest circumstances that induced a population, Gaelic in the mass, gradually to submit to processes that were eventually to wean them from allegiance to their ancient motherland. Thus Grant Allen observes, speaking of Archbishop Dunstan:

"One act of Dunstan's policy, however, had far-reaching results of a kind which he himself could never have anticipated. He handed over all Northumbria beyond the Tweed—the region now known as the Lothians—as a fief to Kenneth, king of the Scots. This accession of territory wholly changed the character of the Scottish kingdom and largely promoted the Teutonization of the Celtic north. The Scottish princes took up their residence in the English (sic) town of Edinburgh and learned to speak the English language as their mother tongue."[1]

[1] Anglo-Saxon Britain, p. 147.

The same writer goes on to remind us how Eadmund had already ceded Strathclyde, or Cumberland, to Malcolm so that the Scottish kings ruled over all Scotland, except the Scandinavian jarldoms of Caithness, Sutherland, and the Isles, and how Fife also was Anglicized as well as the whole region south of the Highland line. "Thus a new and powerful kingdom," he continues, "arose in the North and at the same time the cession of an English district to the Scottish kings had the curious result of thoroughly Anglicizing two large and important Celtic regions, which had hitherto resisted every effort of the Northumbrian or West Saxon overlords." Grant Allen is here on the right track, but he exaggerates. The Anglicization of which he speaks was a much slower process than he supposes. The Anglicization described took place very much later than the period he assigns to it, and it was preceded by a Gallicization. Gaelic was spoken in Fife in the seventeenth century, and Gaelic was spoken in the Scottish parliament in the days of Bruce, and long after. But he is correct in so far as he indicates that the Anglicization of Scotland has come about not through English immigration but by the discarding on the part of the Gaels of Scotland of the ancient Irish tongue inherited from their ancestors.

Even in the four counties of Lothian, often confounded by non-Scotch people with the so-called "Lowlands," the population was mixed. The passages in Bede, which seem to refer to Anglian colonization immediately south of the Forth, can only have been based on temporary overlordship. The seaboard from the southern wall to the Lammermuir Hills fell into the uncertain possession of the Angles. But the tract, looking seaward from that range to where the Avon empties itself into the Forth or thereabouts, and commonly known as the Lothians, was occupied by a considerable mixture of races, as may be gathered from the place-names there.[1] The district north of the Lammermoors forming the peninsula over against what is now the county of Fife would thus seem to have been Celtic.

The real boundaries of the English colony in Scotland are indicated by Symeon of Durham in his description of the boundaries of the ancient diocese of Lindisfarne, a diocese of which the province of Lothian formed the northern part. Symeon says that the boundaries of the northern part of the diocese of Lindisfarne were marked by the (White) Adder, the Leader and the Esk. He also mentions that Melrose, Jedburgh, Yetholm, and other places east of Roxburghshire pertained to the diocese of Lindisfarne.[2] Thus the Esk in Dumfriesshire near the English border marked the real northern limit of the English province. Beyond that river the Angles had only isolated settlements, such as Abercorn.

IRISH PLACE-NAMES.—The assertions as to English settlement and suzerainty between the Tweed and the Forth are based largely on the false etymology of the name Edinburgh, meaning the "forehead" or "brow" (aodann) of a "hill" (bruch), Aodann-bruch. Most English historians, being ignorant of the Irish language, have been unaware of this. One after the other they have echoed the mistaken notion that the city derived its name from Edwin, king of Northumbria, and they have proceeded to magnify his character and exploits in grandiose words on account of it. Thus Green says concerning Edwin: "Northward his frontier reached the Forth and was guarded by a city which bore his name, Edinburgh, Eadwine's burgh, the

[1] Rhys, Early Britain.
[2] Historia, I, 197-9; II, 101.

city of Eadwine." Plausibility is given to the derivation
by the error of a copyist or interpolator of Symeon of
Durham, but Aodann, or edin, occurs as a prefix in more
than a hundred places in Ireland and Scotland and there
is no doubt of the Irish character of the name. Similarly
Auld Reekie is derived from the Irish alt (high place)
ruighe (slope); Arthur's Seat, from the Irish ard-thir
suidhe, a place on high ground, and so on.[1]

Irish place-names in Scotland outnumber all others by
ten to one, while such of them as are or appear to be
English have in cases like those just mentioned been translated or corrupted from their Irish form. Thus Edderon,
near Tain, is Eadar duin, "the town between the hillocks";
Falkirk is a translation of Eaglais breac, "the speckled
church" (Varia Capella); Earlston is Ercheldon or
Ercildun; Almond is a corruption of Amhuinn, a river;
and Glen Howl is Gleann-a-ghabail, "the glen of the
fork."[2] In a similar way Strathclyde has become Clydes-
dale; Strathnith has become Nithsdale; Strathannan has
become Annansdale; and so on. In some cases the Irish
prefix "kil-" has been supplanted by the Saxon "kirk-," as
Kirkpatrick for Kilpatrick. But "Kil-" is still the more
common prefix, as Kilmarnock, signifying the "chapel
of Marnock," a famous Irish saint. In Galloway alone,
almost the most southerly part of Scotland, Sir Herbert
Maxwell found 220 "Knocks" (Irish Cnoc, "a Hill").[3]
There are Irish place-names even in Berwickshire on the
English border and they increase as we go north and west
in the rest of the Lothians. The subject of place-names
however needs no laboring. A glance at any large scale-

[1] See Milne, Gaelic Place-Names in the Lothians; Joyce, Irish Names of Places.
[2] Johnston, Place-Names in Scotland, p. XVII.
[3] Studies in the Topography of Galloway, 1885.

map of Ireland and Scotland even by a person who knows next to nothing of the Irish tongue is sufficient to make it clear that the vast majority of place-names in the two countries have a common and an Irish origin.

HIGHLANDERS AND LOWLANDERS BOTH GAELS.—The supposed racial differences between "highlanders" and "lowlanders" moreover find no support in the pages of early Irish, Scottish, and English historians. These last had not then discovered that the two-nation theory would be a valuable political asset to England in its dealing with its northern neighbor. John of Fordun remarks that the speakers of the Scottish language inhabit the hill country and the outer isles and that the speakers of the Teutonic language dwell in the maritime regions and the plains.[1] Gaelic continued to exist in the south of Scotland long after Fordun's time, even in some of the more low-lying districts. He says the Scottish-speaking hillmen are hostile to the English, and even to their own nation, on account of the difference of speech. Outside of Lothian he does not mention the presence of English settlers. Instead he reiterates a remark of Isidore's to the effect that the Scottish people resemble the Irish in all things, in language, manners and character.

Hector Boece, writing a century later, also maintains a significant silence on the subject of the supposed Saxon descent of the lowlanders and the supposed expulsion of the Celt. He says instead that the Scots on the English border through much commercial intercourse and wars, had learned the Saxon speech, and had forsaken their own speech. (Saxonum linguam didicimus nostramque deseruimus.) The language was slightly pushed out, but not the men. Like Fordun, Boece adds that the people

[1] Book II, Ch. 9.

living on the higher ground still speak their own language. John Major, writing about 1520, says that one half of Scotland spoke Gaelic in his time and that many more did so a short time previously.[1] He adds that "we (i. e., the Scottish people) trace our descent from the Irish. This we learn from the English Bede. Their speech is another proof of this," and again, "I say then from whosoever the Irish traced their descent from the same source come the Scots tho at one remove, as with son and grandfather."

In the same century Bishop Leslie wrote his De Gestis Scotorum, which Father Dalrymple translated into English in 1596. The latter says that the "mair politick Scottis," by which phrase he translates the bishop's politiores Scoti, use the "Ingles toung," and that "the rest of the Scottis . . . . thay use thair alde Irishe tongue." About 1630 James Howell wrote that "the ancient language of Scotland is Irish, which the mountaineers and divers of the plain retain to this day."[2] Irish annalists, moreover, nowhere mention any racial difference between lowland Scots on the one hand and highland Scots and the Irish themselves on the other. To them Scotland is simply a kindred province or kingdom, and the frequent use of the phrase "Eire agus Alba" shows their recognition of the essential oneness of the people of both countries. Thus Armagh in the twelfth century was the national university for Ireland and Scotland. The decree that every lector in every church had to take there a degree applied to both countries and in 1169 the High King, Ruaidhri Ua Concobhair, gave the first annual grant to maintain a professor at Armagh "for all the Irish and the Scots."

1 Historie of Scotland, I, 85, 86.
2 Familiar Letters, Book II, Letter 55.

Even the phrases "highland" and "lowland" are unknown to the early writers. Gaelic knows nothing of these fictitious distinctions. Andrew of Wyntoun is the first writer to make mention of the former word. In his Orygynale Cronykil, written about 1420-4, he uses the phrase "Scottis hielande men." The word "lowland" does not make its appearance till another century had nearly passed away, when Dunbar employed it in his Flyting with Kennedie. Thus these terms, of which so much political use has since been made, are purely modern terms and the invention of English speakers. Philemon Holland, an Englishman, goes in 1610 a step further, when he says that "the Scots are divided into Hechtlandmen and Lawlandmen."[1] Tobias Smollett in 1771 was apparently the first writer to refer to lowland Scots as "Saxons" (Humphry Clinker), but Sir Walter Scott has also to be credited with the diffusion of the racial difference theory.

The Scottish lexicographer[2] sums up some points correctly when he says: "The difference between the Irish and the Scots is geographical only and not racial, as the records of both amply and abundantly prove. Both call themselves Gaidhail (Gael) in their own language, and fraternize instantly as soon as English, the language of disunion, is removed. Any difference between them is more imaginary than real and has been invented and assiduously accentuated for political reasons only, on the old and barbarous plan of 'divide and rule.' "[3]

[1] Camden, Britannia, I, 155.

[2] Dwelly, Faclair Gaidhlig (Gaelic Dictionary), Herne Bay, E. MacDonald & Co., 1902, Vol. I, Roimh-Radh (Preface), IV.

[3] For much of the testimony and evidence contained in the above Appendix I am indebted to two articles by H. C. MacNeacail in the Scottish Review (Autumn, Winter, 1918), written for the purpose of showing that the inhabitants of Scotland were Celts and not English or Teuton. I had already arrived at the conclusions given above and had set forth the evidence before meeting with Mr. MacNeacail's articles. I found much that was new among his well-arranged testimony and have made use of it here, though my line of argument is somewhat different from his.

APPENDIX C

THE HIGH MONARCHS OF IRELAND

THE following is a list of the Ard Righs or High Kings of Ireland from the beginning of the Christian era. The remarkable fact is to be noted that the descendants of King Niall I (379-405) occupied the throne of Ireland in unbroken succession till the usurpation of King Brian (1002-14), a period of nearly six hundred years. This list is distinct from the dynasties in the subsidiary kingdoms, some of which endured to the seventeenth century:

	A. D.		A. D.
Conari I	1	Caelbad	357
Lugaid I	65	Eochaid II	358
Conchubair I	73	Crimthann II	366
Crimthann I	74	Niall I (of the Nine	
Cairbre I	90	Hostages)	379
Feradach I	95	Dathi (Feradach II)	405
Fiatach	117	Laighaire	428
Fiacha I	119	Olioll	463
Elim	126	Lugaid III	483
Tuathal I	130	Muirchetach I	512
Mal	160	Tuathal II	533
Fedlimidh	164	Diarmuid I	544
Cathair	174	Domhnaill I joint }	
Conn Cedcathach (of the		Fergus II kings }	565
Hundred Battles)	177	Baitan I joint }	
Conari II	212	Eochaid III kings }	566
Art	220	Ainmire	568
Lugaid II	250	Baitan II	571
Fergus I	253	Aedh I	572
Cormac	254	Aedh (Slaine) II joint }	
Eochaid I	277	Colman kings }	598
Cairbre II	279	Aedh III	603
Fiacha II	297	Maelcoba	611
Colla	327	Suibne	614
Muiredach	331	Domhnaill II	627

334

Appendices

A succession of Irish provincial kings and princes, particularly among the O'Neills, laid claim to the throne of Ireland up to the seventeenth century.

APPENDIX D

IRISH KINGS OF SCOTLAND

THERE is a list of thirty-three Irish kings of the continually expanding kingdom of Dalriada in the west of Scotland beginning with the foundation of the Irish monarchy in Scotland by Fergus (c. 490-503) down to Alpin, the first Irish king of Scotland to be crowned at Scone. Beginning with Cainnech, or Kenneth, the son of Alpin, the Irish kings of united Scotland are as follows:

	A. D.		A. D.
Cainnech	844	Maelcolm II	1005
Domhnaill	860	Duncan I	1034
Constantin	863	Macbeth	1040
Aedh	877	Maelcolm III	1057
Eochaid	878	Domhnaill III	1093
Domhnaill II	889	(Duncan II	1094)
Constantin II	900	Edgar	1097
Maelcolm I	943	Alexander I	1106
Indulph	954	David I	1124
Duff (Dubh)	962	Maelcolm IV	1153
Cuilean	967	William I	1165
Cainnech II	971	Alexander II	1214
Constantin III	995	Alexander III	1249-1286
Cainnech III	997		

APPENDIX E

SOME WORKS OF REFERENCE

Migne: *Patrologiae Cursus Completus; Series Latina;* 217 Vols. including a large part of the poetic, epistolary, historical, philosophical and patristic Latin literature of the 1,000 years from Tertullian (d. 240) to Innocent III (d. 1216), Paris, 1844-55; with 4 Vols. of Indices, 1862-4.

Monumenta Germaniae Historica, folio series of *Scriptores,* etc., edited by Pertz and others (Hanover) 1826-91; continued in quarto series, Berlin, 1877- (in progress).

"Rolls Series"; Rerum Brittanicarum medii Aevi Scriptores, or *Chronicles and Memorials of Great Britain and Ireland during the Middle Ages,* published under the direction of the Master of the Rolls, 244 Vols., London, 1858-96.

Academy, Royal Irish, Proceedings and Trans.
Acta Sanctorum of the Bollandists ("Acta SS").
Adamnan, Life of St. Columba (edited Reeves).
Anecdota Oxoniensia, from MSS. in the Bodleian and other Oxford Libraries.
Anglia Sacra, 2 Vols.
Annals of the Four Masters, edited O'Donovan.
Bede, Historia Ecclesiastica, and other works.
Brehon Laws. Ancient Laws and Institutes of Ireland, Dublin, 1865-91, 6 Vols.
Bury, J. B., Life of St. Patrick.
Colgan: Acta Sanctorum.
Gildas: De Excidio Brit.
Giraldus Cambrensis: Opera (Rolls Series).
Gougaud, Dom L.: Les Chretientés Celtiques.
Haddan and Stubbs, Councils and Ecclesiastical Documents.
Healy, J.: Insula Sanctorum et Doctorum.
Hyde, D.: Literary History of Ireland.
Jonas, Vita S. Columbani.
Jones, Vestiges of the Gael in Gwynedd (N. Wales).
Joyce, P. W.: Social History of Ireland (2 Vols.).
Leabhar na g-Ceart, or Book of Rights.
Lanigan: Ecclesiastical History of Ireland.
Lynch, Cambrensis Eversus.
Montalembert, Les Moines d'Occident, Paris, 1863.
Nennius, Historia Britonum.

O'Hanlon: Lives of the Irish Saints, Dublin, 1875 et seq.

Skene: Celtic Scotland.

Schultze, W.: Die Bedeutung der Iroschottischen Monche, etc., (Centralblatt für Bibliothekswesen, 1889).

Stokes and Strachan: Thesaurus Palæohibernicus (2 Vols.).

Tain bo Chuailnge ("The Tain"), trs. Hutton.

Traube, L.: O Roma Nobilis (Abhandlungen d. K. Bayer. Akad. 1891); Perrona Scottorum (Abhandlungen, 1900).

Ulster Journal of Archæology, Old Series, 9 Vols. (Articles by Wm. Reeves, F. Keller, and Wattenbach).

Zimmer, The Irish Element in Mediæval Culture (translation of article in Preuss. Jahrbücher, 1887).

INDEX

A

Abban, work of, 253–255.

Abba's Hill, 254.

Aberbrothoc (Arbroath), monastery of, 325.

Aberdeen, 316, 326.

Abingdon, monastery of, 253–255.

Acca's Cross, 282.

Acha, 215.

Acts Parl. Scot., 324.

Adamnan, life of Columcille, 21, 95, 106, and note, 117, 119, 120–122, 126–156; "De Locis Sanctis," 54; "Historia Hibernorum," 78; career of Adamnan, 149–155; "Lex Adamnani," 152; "Vision of Adamnan," 154; Adamnan and the English, 200–202 and 215; relations with King Aldfrid, 214; Adamnan and Bede, 272.

Adda, 225–226.

Adrian at Canterbury, 264–268, 285–287.

Adrian IV, Pope, 191.

Aebba, 221.

Aedh, 106, 138.

Ædilhilda, 255.

Ædwine, 222.

Ælbert, 273.

Ængus the Culdee, on foreigners in Ireland, 53; his Felire, 112.

Æthelhun, 255.

Æthelwald, 257.

Æthelwine, work of, 255–256.

Æthelwulf, 274.

Agilbert the Frank, educated in Ireland, 56, 229, 241, 243.

Agricola, camp of, 103.

Aidan, King, 20–21, 66, 135, 139; defeats the English, 202.

Aidan, Bishop, real apostle of England, 195; among the English tribes, 201–202; influence against slavery, 210–211; school of 12

boys, 211; relations with Oswald, 211–213; as statesman, 213; King Oswin's veneration for, 216–219; death of, 217–218; Bede's eulogy of, 218–219; foundations in England, 219–224; date of death, 224; English churches dedicated to, 224; effects of his work, 231, 233, 243, 245, 248, 271, 273, 286.

Aileach, 158; king of, 308.

Ailech of the Kings, 281.

Airt, 91.

Aix-la-Chapelle, Irish in, 11.

Alba, explained, 46, 176.

Albeus, 53.

Albinus, 21.

Albiones, 176.

Alcuin, 3, 24, 55, 56, 75–76, 79, 96, 123, 154, 221, 265, 272, 273, 279, 285, 290.

Aldfrid, king of Northumbria, 58, 135, 151–152, 154, 214, 215, 228–229, 239, 272.

Aldhelm, 44, 56, 58, 61, 80, 184, 197, 250, 251, 252, 254; on English students in Ireland, 256–258; and Cellan, correspondence between, 258–261; teachers of, 260, 265–266; letter of to Eahfrid, 267–268.

Alduini, 255.

Aldwulf, 223.

Alemanni, impressed by Irish missionaries, 95–96, 165.

Alexander III, 115, 318; court of, 322.

Alfred, King, 95; Irish scholars and, 274–276, 291–292.

Alfred Jewell, 281.

Algeis, 247.

Alithir, Abbot, 139.

Allen, *Anglo-Saxon Britain*, cited, 277, 327–328.

Index

Alliaco, Cardinal, 191.
Alphabet, Roman practice of teaching, 124.
Altus, 148.
Amalgaidh, 182.
Amand, 16.
Ambrose, known to Irish, 39, 48.
Ammianus Marcellinus, quoted, 164–165.
Ampney Crusis, 281.
Amra Choluim Chilli, by Dallan Forgaill, 122.
Ancient Laws and Institutes of Ireland, 313.
Ancona, Pellegrinus in, 18.
Andelys, 223.
Andrew of Fiesole, 19.
Anecdota Oxoniensia, Stokes, 53, 124, 126, 136, 139, 140, 141, 158.
Anglesea, 178.
Anglesey, 170.
Anglia Sacra, Vita. S. Dustani, by Osbern, quoted, 289.
Anglia Sacra, 303, 305, 306, 309.
Anglo-Jute-Saxon conquest of Britain, 157–159.
Anglo-Saxon Chronicle, 95, 159, 202, 178, 214, 275, 294, 311, 325.
Anglo-Saxon civilization, mediocre imitation of Irish, 285–287.
Anglo-Saxon Cottoniana, map of the world, 278.
Anglo-Saxon students in Ireland, 55–57.
Angus (Augustin), treatise by 659, 18.
Angus, son of Erc, 114.
Anna, King, 246.
Annales Cambriae, 178.
Annals of the Four Masters, 43, 59, 154, 163.
Annals of Tighernach, 163, 272.
Annals of Ulster, 78, 272.
Annegray, 241.
"Anonymous History of the Abbots," 271.
Anselm, 309.
Apuleius known to Irish, 39.

Arbogast, 57.
Archpresbyter of the Gael, 116–118.
Archæological and Historical Collections of Ayr and Wigton, 316.
Archæological Journal, 81.
Architecture, schools of, in Ireland, 44.
Arculf, 54, 154.
Ardagh Chalice, 12, 74.
Ardrigh or High King, 115, 334.
Argyleshire, 114.
Aristotle, first translated by an Irishman from the Arabic into Latin, 25.
Aristotle, Irish familiar with, 38–39.
Arles, 199.
Armagh, founded before Bagdad, 3; importance of, 32–33; number of students in, 49; "metropolis of civilization," 52; schools and scholars, 55, 60, 112; university for Ireland and Scotland, 332; Synod at, decrees emancipation of English slaves, 310.
Armorica, 159.
Art, father of King Cormac, 163.
Art Mac Murrough, King of Leinster, 298.
Artchorp, 174.
Artuil, letter of, to Aldhelm, 261.
Asser, 276, 291.
Asterius, Bishop, 242.
Astronomy, taught by Irish, 21.
At the Wall, 226.
Athanasius, known to Irish, 39.
Attacotti, 165.
Aughrim, 299.
Augusta, 166.
Augustine (Ængus), work on miracles, 106, 190.
Augustine, known to Irish, 39, 48; of Canterbury, 196, 199, 200, 204, 204–205, 220, 232, 263–264.
Ausonius, 30.
Austria, Irish in, 12.
Avienus, 176.
Ayrshire, 316.
Azores, known to Irish, 11, 189.

Index

B

C

Index

Index

Columcille, 141; connection with Bangor in Wales, 182.
Comyn, D., *Intro. to Gaelic History*, quoted, 182.
Conaill Crimthann, 107.
Conaill Gulban, 107.
Conaire, 175, 176.
Conal Culban, descendants of, 234.
Conall, King, 130.
Conan, 255.
Conn of the Hundred Battles, 163.
Connaught, kingdom of, 107, 115, 161, 162.
Constans, 165.
Constantine, 169.
Constantinople, Irish in, 11, 18.
Corbican, 247.
Corbie, 211, 247, 276.
Corhampton, church of, 281.
Cork, Ogham inscriptions in, 171.
Cormac (of Cashel), quotes Irish authors, 30; Glossary of, 41, 173–174, 175–176, 183.
Cormac (King), university established by, 31–32; description of, at Tara, 91–92; "sovereign of Alba," 163.
Cormac, friend of Columcille, 126, 134, 141; indefatigable navigator, 142; approaches Arctic Circle, 143; visits Iceland, 143; among islands of the North, 189.
Corman, 211.
Cornwalch, 243.
Cornwall, 159, 170; Ogham inscriptions in, 171, 189.
Correspondence between Aldhelm and Cellan, 258–261.
Council of Bavaria establishes schools, 80.

Council of Constance, 190–192.
Craig, Sir Thomas, 315.
Craike, 221.
Cremona, 81.
Cricklade (Greeklade), 286.
Crimhthann, 176.
Crimthann Mor (Criffan the Great), 163–164.
Crith Gablach, Sequel of, 41.
Crowe, O'Beirne, 122.
Croyland Abbey, 198.
Cruachain, 158.
Cryptography, 187.
Cuchulain, 96–97; compared with Columcille, 119–121; valor of, 120.
Cuican, 274.
Cuimine, on Columcille, 122.
Culdreimhne, battle of, 108, 127–129.
Culinan, 174, 175.
Culture of Ireland living reality, 73–76.
Cumberland, 185, 186, 251.
Cummian, paschal epistle of, 106, 118; its remarkable erudition, 231, note; gave general Irish view, 262.
Cunceceastre, 221.
Cuthbert of Lindisfarne, 220, 271.
Cuthbert (of Canterbury) Boniface's letter to, on female pilgrimages to Rome, 287, 307.
Cynan (Caionain), 179.
Cynebil, 227, 248.
Cynefrid, 271.
Cynegils, 241, 243.
Cymri, 170, 176.
Cymric, 180.
Cymry (Comrades), 186.
Cynewulf, 265.
Cyssebui, 254.

D

Dagan, Bishop, 205, 267.
Dagobert, son, king of Austria, 57.
Daire (Derry) Columcille founds church and school at, 125–126.
Dairius, 177.

Dallan Forgaill, quoted, 64.
Dalriada, 102, 162.
Dalrymple, Father, 332.
D'Alton's History of Ireland, 297, note.

Index

E

F

Index

Index

H

Index

Homer, 100.

Honau, 10.

Honorius of Canterbury, 219, 241.

Horace, oldest manuscript in Irish hand, 75, 124.

Howell, James, *Familiar Letters,* quoted, 332.

Huber, cited, 275.

Howorth, *Golden Days of the English Church,* quoted, 206, 224, 264.

Hume, 320.

Hutton, *Finding of the Tain,* quoted, 33; *Writing of the Tain,* quoted, 35, 168.

Hy, island of, 130.

Hy Fiachrach, 66.

Hy Niall, 142.

Hyde, *Literary History of Ireland,* 42, 79, 126, 145, 162; *MacTernan Prize Essays,* cited, 65.

I

Iceland, discovered by Irish, 10; Irish in, 17, 18; Cormac in, 143, 189.

Ichtian Sea, 176.

Iliad, 119.

In Pisonem of Cicero, in Irish, 75.

In te Christe, 148.

Ina, dooms of, 304, 184, 188.

"Indarba mna n Dese," 174.

Inis Eoghain, king of, 308.

Inisboffin, 236, 237.

Iniscathy, 220.

Ingelborne, 250.

Ingethlingum, 226.

Iona, 3, 21, 54; Columcille at, 126; cause of Columcille's exile to, 127, 129; established, 130; Columcille and brethren at, 131–156; guests at, 134; almsgiving at, 134; ritual and ceremonial at, 134–136; authority of abbot at, 136; literary work and other occupations at, 136–140; drought at, note, 137; last scene at, 145–158; Adamnan at, 149–154; successors of Columcille at, 154; decline of, 154–155; burial place of kings of Scotland, 155, 182, 187; Saxons at, 201, 207, 209; Oswald at, 214; Easter in, 263.

Ir, descendants of, 161.

Ireland, home of Western learning, 1–4.

Ireland, schools of, 3–4; literary output in, 4; beginning of Christianity in, 7–8; claim to great past, 12; ark of safety for the old wisdom, 27–31; not included in ruin of Roman civilization, 28, ff; peace and prosperity in, 29, ff; beginning of Gaelic monarchy in, 29; Celtic invasions of, 29; Milesian dynasty in, 29–30; culture in, before St. Patrick, 30; Christians in, before St. Patrick, 31; educational proficiency of, 31–35; universities in, after introduction of Christianity, 32; intellectual leader of Christendom, 52–55; foreign students and visitors in, 53–55; Anglo-Saxon students in, 55–57; foreign students in, to twelfth century, 59–61; professional and lay education in, 62–65; secular schools in, proof of existence, 63–64; secular education in, reorganized, 66; cultivation of philosophy in, 69; English destruction in, 74–75; high culture of a living reality, 73–76; establishment of Gaelic kingdom in, 84; medieval, military strength and wealth of, 84–87; emigration of Norman French and Flemish to, 85–86; English slaves in, 87–88; not isolated from Europe, 88–90; Romans in, 89; luxurious civilization in, 90–91; abundance of gold in, 91–94; Danes in, 93–94; Christian, pagan spirit in, 96–98; home of liberal arts, 104; of the sixth century, 104–110; sense of freedom in, 109; always civilization in, 110; ancient pagan and medieval

Index

Index

Index

L

M

Index

Macbeth, quoted, 155, 275.
Mackinnon, Professor, cited, 316.
Macleane, *Pembroke College,* cited, 295.
Macrobius, known to Irish, 39.
Madelgisilus, 247.
Maelceadar, 16.
Maeldubh, 20, 58, 244.
Maelduf and other Irishmen in Wessex, 250–253, 260.
Maelinmain, 275.
Maelrubha of Skye, 155.
Maeve, Queen, 120.
Mageo, 237.
Magna Carta, 109; French influence in, 296.
Magnoald, 19.
Maidoc, 53.
Mair (Major), John, quoted, 315.
Major, *Historie of Scotland,* cited, 332.
Malcolm IV, 323.
Malcolm, 328.
Malmesbury, 10; derivation of name, 58, 183, 244, 250–251, 269.
Manuscripts, old, in Irish, 75–76.
Maolcalain, Abbot, 17.
Map of the world, Anglo-Saxon Cottoniana, 278.
Marcus, bishop of Soissons, 59–60, 81.
Marianus Scotus, 17; Irish foundations established by, 83, 279.
Marius Victorinus, known to Irish, 39.
Martianus Capella, known to Irish, 39.
Martyrology of Marianus Ua Gormain, 183.
Matthew of Paris, cited, 295.
Maximinanus Herudeus, 249.
Maximus, 169.
Maxwell, *Studies in the Topography of Galloway,* cited, 330.
Mayo of the Saxons, 58, 61; founded by Colman, 236–238.
Mayor's, *Bede,* cited, 259.
Meath, kingdom of, founded, 107; attack on, 151, 162.
Mellitus, 205, 226.

Melrose, 211, 221, 234, 271, 273.
Menevia, 276.
Menzies, Lucy, *St. Columba of Iona,* cited, 122.
Mercia, 195, 243, 270; Duima, Chad, and Ceallach in, 248–249.
Mercians, 218, 225.
Merioneth, 171.
Mermin, King, 187.
Meroving, ed. Krusch, 60.
Metz, Irish in, 11, 17.
Meyer, *Kultur der Gegenwart,* quoted, 11; *Ancient Irish Poetry,* quoted, 45; *Early Relations between the Gael and Brython,* cited, 145; *Otia Merseiana,* cited, 168; *Cymmrodor,* cited, 174.
Miathi, battle of, 202.
Michael Scotus, 25.
Micklewaite, *Archeological Journal,* quoted, 281, 282.
Midland England, won by Finan, 224–226.
Migne, *Patrologia,* Latina, cited, 24, 71, 88, 118, 154, 168, 169, 196, 197, 199, 221, 231, 256, 262, 268, 271, 272, 277, 279.
Milan, Irish in, 11, 187.
Milesian dynasty in Ireland, 29–30, 84–85; descendants, 161.
Milesius, descendants of, 161.
Military strength of medieval Ireland, 84–87.
Milman, *History of Latin Christianity,* cited, 295.
Milne, *Gaelic Place-Names in the Lothians,* cited, 330.
Mission of Augustine a failure, 204–205.
Mitchell, Rev. Anthony, quoted, 149.
Miurchartach, 164.
Mobhi, Columcille with, 125.
Mochona, quoted, 95.
Mochta, 179.
Modan in Stirling, 155.
Modesty of Irish pioneers, 22.
Moengal, 81, 82.
Molaisse, 140.
"Molossian hounds," 266.

P

Index

Q

R

S

Index

T

Tacitus on Ireland, cited, 89; *Life of Agricola,* quoted, 103.

Tadcaster, 222.

Tailtenn, 66, 112; synod at, 129.

Tain, cited, 89, 120.

Taine, *Hist. of Eng. Lit.,* cited or quoted, 288, 289, 290, 291–292.

Talorcan, 214.

Tara, 66, 102; cursing of, by Columcille, 108, 112; Parliament of, 128; Parliament of, Adamnan at, 152, 158.

Tara Brooch, 12, 74.

Taranto, Cathaldus in, 18.

Tatwine, Archbishop, 252.

Taylor, John, Pennyles Pilgrimage, quoted, 317.

Tenth century, work of Irish in England, 277.

Tertullian, 181.

Tewdor ap Rhain, 174.

Thanet, 200.

Theodore, 3, 224, 232, 258, 260; and "Molossian Hounds" at Canterbury, 264–268, 271, 285, 286, 304.

Theodosius (the elder), 165–166.

Theodulph of Orleans, 80.

Thesaurus Palaeohibernicus, referred to, 4.

Thomond, school of, 35.

Thomas, Bishop, 241.

Thorneyburn, 224.

"Three Fragments" of Irish Annals, quoted, 214–215.

Tigerneach, cited, 114, 154, 178, 202; quoted, 215, 272.

Tilbury, 227, 249.

Tir Conaill, wealth of literati in, 67.

Tirowen, 162.

Todd, ed. *War of the Gaels with the Galls,* cited, 145; *Proc. Roy. I. Acad.,* quoted, 266.

Torna-Eices, poem of, 168.

Tostig, 288–289.

Toul, Irish in, 11, 17.

Tours, Irish in, 11.

Traube, on Irish libraries, 76; cited, 188; *Perrona Scotorum, Abhandlungen der Bay. Akad.,* cited, 260.

Trias Thaum., cited, 142.

Tribes and Customs of Hy-Many, cited, 309.

Trivium, 37.

Tropic of Cancer, Irish at, 189.

Trouvères, 121.

Trumbert, Bishop, cross of, 282.

Trumhere, 226, 248, 271.

Trumwine's Cross, 282.

Tuda, 234.

Tunberht, 271.

Turin, 81.

Turner, *History of Philosophy,* quoted, 24; *Hist. of the Anglo-Saxons,* cited, 288, 289.

Tutilo (Tuthail) of St. Gall, 21–22.

Twelve Apostles of Erin, 105, 124.

Tyrconnell, founded, 107, 162.

Tyrone, founded, 107.

U

Ua Domnaill, 148.

Ua Dubhlaighe (O'Dooley), family of, 307.

Ua Ceallaigh (O'Kelly) family, 309–310.

Ua Clerigh, *Ireland to the Norman Conquest,* cited, 185.

Ui Liathain, 173.

Ui Maine, 309–310.

Ultan, 16, 21; modesty of, 23, 244, 247, 258, 274.

Ulster, kingdom of, formed, 107, 115; kings of, 161; Irishmen of, in North Britain and North Wales, 161.

Ulster J. of Arch., cited, 192.

Urbs Coludi, 221.

Ursicinus, at Mont Terrible, 15;

13/2'6